ON WAR

ON WAR

POLITICAL VIOLENCE
IN THE
INTERNATIONAL SYSTEM

by Manus I. Midlarsky

THE FREE PRESS
A Division of Macmillan Publishing Co., Inc.
NEW YORK

Collier Macmillan Publishers
LONDON

The Free Press
A Division of Macmillan Publishing Co., Inc.
866 Third Avenue, New York, N.Y. 10022

Collier–Macmillan Canada Ltd.

Library of Congress Catalog Card Number: 74–9195

Printed in the United States of America

printing number
1 2 3 4 5 6 7 8 9 10

Library of Congress Cataloging in Publication Data

Midlarsky, Manus I
  On war.

  Includes bibliographical references and index.
  1. War.   2. World politics.   3. International relations.   I. Title.
U21.2.M5   301.6′334   74–9195
ISBN 0–02–921200–6

Portions of the article appearing on pp. 16–27 and 48–77 from "Power, Uncertainty, and the Onset of International Violence," by Manus I. Midlarsky are reprinted from the *Journal of Conflict Resolution*, Vol. 18, No. 3 (Sept. 1974) pp. 395–431 © by permission of the publisher, Sage Publications, Inc.; the excerpt on pp. 147–163 from "Mathematical Models of Instability and a Theory of Diffusion," by Manus I. Midlarsky is reprinted from the *International Studies Quarterly*, Vol. 14, No. 1 (March 1970), pp. 60–84 by permission of the publisher, Sage Publications, Inc.

The extract appearing on pp. 166–179 is from Manus I. Midlarsky and Stafford T. Thomas, "Domestic Social Structure and International Warfare," in M. A. Nettleship, R. Dale Givens, and Anderson Nettleship, eds., *War: Its Causes and Correlates*, WORLD ANTHROPOLOGY, 1974. Reprinted by permission. Acknowledgments and thanks are extended to Stafford T. Thomas for his collaboration in performing the analysis.

For Liz, Susie, and Miriam

They shall lay hold on bow and spear; they are cruel, and have no mercy; their voice roareth like the sea; and they ride upon horses, set in array as men for war . . . .

(JEREMIAH, VI, 23)

. . . and they shall be consumed by the sword, and by famine; and their carcases shall be meat for the fowls of heaven, and for the beasts of the earth.

(JEREMIAH, XVI, 4)

Contents

List of Illustrations

List of Tables

xv

Preface

This volume is about war—that single collectively organized human effort which has taken more human lives than any other. It is not a historical recording of various wars, nor is it an exhortation to eliminate war, however desirable this may be as an end in itself. Rather, this volume is devoted to an analysis of the causes of war in the hope that, by discovering more about how wars begin and are protracted, we will be in a more knowledgeable position to institute the bases for a lasting peace.

We have known for some time now that World War I, with its nine million battle deaths, was not the "war to end wars" and World War II, with its millions of deliberately murdered civilians, added its own bitter specter to the more than fifteen million dead on the battlefield. As this volume was being written, wars occurred between Indians and Pakistanis, North Vietnamese and Americans, and between the Arabs and Israelis. The October War of 1973 also included a confrontation between the United States and the Soviet Union, with its implications for nuclear holocaust. For all of the destruction of the past, and the now even more deadly possibility of a future planetary decimation, it is clear that we have not yet grasped the essential features of the international system that make war so prevalent. Only when we can understand this complex system far more completely than we do now, will we be able to go about the business of adequately preventing the occurrence of wars.

A basic postulate of this work is that with adequate knowledge of the etiology of war and appropriate recommendations, a deadly institution created by human beings can be controlled by human beings. Although this appears to be a simple proposition, it differs substantially from the view that aggression is an instinctual biological trait of *Homo sapiens*, and it is this characteristic which is responsible for man's being a killer of his own species. To adopt such a position is virtually to accept the inevitability of political violence, or at least, to find justification for the most heinous crimes against humanity in a kind of biological determinism. Happily, we need not accept this view, for at least three reasons.

First, there is sufficient evidence that certain peoples have lived in peace for centuries without international war or civil strife. Primitive subnational units have enjoyed this experience, and developed countries such as Sweden also have known the recent absence of war, in this case, since the early nineteenth century. Even countries which have experienced war have varied widely, from say, one war entered into by Iran, to nine for France since the Congress of Vienna. There is considerable variation in the forms of sociopolitical organization, both nationally and internationally for these countries, which suggests this as a primary variable in the explanation of this differing war experience.

Second, even if one accepts the position that aggressive instincts are found in *Homo sapiens*, from the perspective of scientific explanation, all this means is that our relationships are affected by the same constant factor. There should be negligible change in the level of aggressive instinct among members of the same species as one moves from one to another, meaning that a citizen of one nation-state should have approximately the same level of instinctual aggression as one residing in another nation-state. This is especially the case for neighboring peoples such as the Swedes and Germans who would have experienced a similar evolutionary development over time, thus yielding a comparable level of instinctual aggression. Human beings would have built their ethical and organizational forms upon this constant instinctual base, and as we have already seen, there is wide variation in aggressive behavior among groups and nation-states. This variety in human experience could not be due to the operation of a constant factor, by definition, and therefore must be the result of differences in national and international sociopolitical structures, which in the last century and a half have resulted in peace, as in the instances of Sweden and Switzerland, or seven and eight wars, respectively, as in the cases of Germany (Prussia) and Russia. It is this variation in human behavior which is of social scientific interest and not the constant factors, which like rainfall, cloud cover, or a presumed instinct, are the "givens" of our planetary environment.

Third, even assuming a rampant instinctual urge to kill among human beings—instinct at a very high level of potential violence—the peaceful histories of various groups of human beings have shown that, at the very least, this urge can be controlled by certain modes of social organization. If we are to insure planetary survival in the nuclear era, then it is imperative that we control this instinct, assuming, of course, it indeed exists.

In contrast to the biological determinism implied by the concept of instinct, much of the analysis in this volume is based on the concept of probabilities. Between birth and death, which are the uniquely determined elements of our human environment, lies a vast range of possible behaviors, all of which can be assigned certain probability values. The concepts of power, social disorganization, national development, status, and the diffusion of political instability all receive some probabilistic interpretation in the subsequent explanations of war. Specifically, a conceptual framework is developed to treat the concepts of power gain, loss, constraints, and inversions, which characterize some of the basic phenomena of international politics related to war. The constraints on the capabilities of nations in the form of preventing a reduction of environmental uncertainty is suggested as a type of power loss associated with the onset of political violence, particularly in the international system.

These theoretical approaches are each tied to a given level of analysis, whether it be the international system, the boundary between it and the nation-state, or the nation-state itself. In the end, certain policy implications follow from the several analyses. Although it is difficult to suggest specific remedies for the problem of war, there are alternative possibilities which are derived in the concluding portions of this volume. Hopefully, one or more of these may contain within it the bases for decreasing substantially the future probabilities of war.

Portions of this volume were presented at several conferences, including meetings of the American Political Science Association, American Anthropological Association, the Western Political Science Association, Western Peace Research Society, and the Ninth International Congress of Anthropological and Ethnological Sciences. The *Journal of Conflict Resolution* agreed to have sections of Chapters II and III reprinted in this volume. The *International Studies Quarterly* and Mouton Publishers of The Hague, Netherlands, respectively agreed to have Chapters VII and VIII reprinted here in revised form. These publishers are to be thanked for their generosity in allowing portions of these papers to be reprinted.

Various councils and agencies have provided financial support for this work and to all of these, I am extremely grateful. The initial impetus came from a Research Fellowship of the Council for Intersocietal Studies of Northwestern University. Subsequent funding was provided by a Summer Research Initiation Fellowship of the Council for Research and Creative Work at the University of Colorado. A grant by the National Science Foundation, GS-40319, helped with the final stages of the project and has made it possible for these closing efforts to proceed smoothly and apace.

Several persons either read or commented on portions of the manuscript. Heartfelt and warm acknowledgments are extended to Stafford T. Thomas for his collaboration in performing analyses for Chapter VIII, and to Kenneth Boulding, J. David Singer, Raymond Tanter, Chadwick Alger, and Kenneth Janda for their help. All errors, of course, are strictly my own.

The environment in which one does research and writing is of great importance, and the Institute of Behavioral Science at the University of Colorado, directed by Gilbert White, provided exactly the type of atmosphere needed for this enterprise. My colleagues in the Department of Political Science gave the kind of friendly encouragement that can lessen the difficulties and frustrations of the writing task. Extremely competent research assistance was provided by Stafford T. Thomas and Walter Opello. The manuscript was typed in a most effective and painstaking manner by Ms. Georgia Borgens.

Finally, it is customary to thank one's wife and children for whatever assistance was rendered by them in the writing of a book. In this case, it is far more than that. My wife and colleague in research and publication, Dr. Elizabeth Midlarsky, gave invaluable help in both the generosity of time, spirit, and the incisive criticisms that can make the difference between success and failure in the execution of a given chapter. This she did freely, and for this, I most sincerely thank her. Because I love my two daughters, Susan and Miriam, very much, I hope that they may never see war again. For their graciousness in being, I thank them as well.

ON WAR

I

Introduction

"War," said Clausewitz, is "the continuation of political relations ... by other means."[1] Despite the apparent plausibility of this claim, we disagree. Political relations often, if not always, involve power relations, and politics in the international system may be no exception. The exercise of power entails the appearance of probabilities, for when a peaceful attempt at policy making or implementation has occurred, there is a probability less than one (certainty) that it has succeeded. The ordinary power of the state, for example, cannot prevent the occurrence of criminality or other forms of deviant behavior. There exists a probability value greater than zero that such behavior will be found within any non-vanishing time interval. The use of force, on the other hand, is an attempt at determining human relationships, for the coercion is most often aimed at the achieving of certainty in any given situation, as in extreme totalitarian rule. Thus, we accept the usual distinction between power and force whereby coercive processes are by definition found in the latter condition, but not in ordinary power relationships which involve some probability estimates.

War as political violence involving human injury and death is probably one of the most coercive and deterministic of conditions, and as a result, the ordinary power relations in politics may not apply. War, in this view, is not akin to politics as power relations, but is more like the coercion found in the application of force. We can understand war as a failure of normal power

---

[1] From Karl von Clausewitz, *Vom Kriege* (1832), quoted in John Bartlett, *Familiar Quotations*, centennial ed. (Boston: Little, Brown, 1955), p. 916.

(political) relations, such that force (coercion), in the form of political violence, results. War is, then, not "the continuation of political relations," but their termination in the onset of extreme coercion. Rather than a continuous political process, there occurs a discrete change from power to force, although the term *political violence* is still appropriate as a specification of the aggregate behaviors and goals of participants associated with the violence, in contrast, say, to random individualized homicides. The transition from the use of power to the use of force occurs; normal power relationships no longer can tolerate the existing strain and become untenable as a prelude to their rupture in the onset of war. To understand the onset of international violence, therefore, is to specify at the same time those conditions in the international system which may lead to the failure of ordinary political relationships.

To specify what is normal, however, is difficult under most circumstances and when dealing with the complexities of international politics can be problematic. Relationships which are treated as the ordinary occurrences of international politics and can operate peacefully for a time, may contain within them the bases of future strife. Alliances as ordinary international political behaviors, and boundaries among nations as standard, perhaps even essential, features of the international system, may be shown to have the property of probabilistically eventually being associated with violence.

Although the concept of power and power relationships themselves constitute a basic avenue to the understanding of the onset of war, there are other theoretical approaches which are appropriate for the particular level of analysis being considered. Indeed, a basic premise of this volume is that there should be a suitable correspondence between the particular theoretical framework chosen and its application at a given level of analysis.

Levels and Theories

In this treatment, we consider three levels of analysis for the study of internationally related political violence. The first is the international system itself, which requires for its existence interactions among two or more international actors. The term *system* here is used conceptually to categorize various kinds of organizations and processes which are linked together by the presence of an interaction effect. Thus, alliances, international organizations, processes of diplomatic representation, or interactions between national leaderships in two nation-state actors are all properties of the international system. (An example of the latter instance can be a diffusion of intervention behavior from one military leadership to another within the same region.) Our first concern, then, is the international system so defined analytically in terms of interaction effects. This concern with the system as a level of analysis derives from several considerations.

An important question in the international relations literature is the utility of various levels of analysis for the examination of research problems. Arnold Wolfers, for example, compares "the individual as actor" with "the state as actor" approaches to the analysis of international politics, and for most problem areas he prefers the latter alternative as more comprehensive and less susceptible to the reductionist and largely futile argument that human nature is corrupt and acquisitive.[2] Kenneth Waltz, in focusing attention on three "images" of international relations—the individual, the state, and the state system—also contrasts the arguments for each level as a preferred focus of analysis.[3] For the most part, Waltz perceives conditions within the state as responsible for the onset of international conflict, whereas the hope for future peace lies within the state system. Finally, J. David Singer, in an earlier work, did not opt for either the nation-state or the international system as a preferred level of analysis for the study of international conflict, but stressed the utility of each as suitable for the investigation of distinct theoretical problems.[4] More recently, Singer examines the relationship between alliance formation and international warfare, implying that the origins of war are to be found in the relations among nations, rather than in conditions internal to the nation-state.[5] The choice of a level of analysis apparently is dependent on a combination of the specific research problem and the researcher's preference. There may be no definitive choice among the various alternatives.

When we turn to empirical studies of war, however, we find that, with the exception of Singer's recent work, most of these studies have concentrated on the nation-state as the principal focus of analysis. Pitirim Sorokin, for example, cites internal changes such as a growing economy, a rapid rate of population increase, or territorial expansion as conditions leading to international warfare.[6] Lewis F. Richardson, in his emphasis on defense expenditures in the arms race, also implicitly subscribes to the notion that the

---

[2] Arnold Wolfers, "The Actors in International Politics," in W. T. R. Fox (ed.), *Theoretical Aspects of International Relations* (Notre Dame, Ind.: University of Notre Dame Press, 1959), pp. 83–106.

[3] See Waltz, *Man, the State and War* (New York: Columbia University Press, 1959), pp. 230–238.

[4] J. David Singer, "The Level-of-Analysis Problem in International Relations," *World Politics*, 14 (October 1961), pp. 77–92.

[5] J. David Singer and Melvin Small, "Alliance Aggregation and the Onset of War, 1815–1945," in J. D. Singer (ed.), *Quantitative International Politics: Insights and Evidence* (New York: The Free Press, 1968), pp. 247–286.

[6] See Sorokin, *Social and Cultural Dynamics*, vol. 3 (New York: Bedminster, 1937), p. 364.

"state as actor" is a preferred unit of analysis.[7] And Richard N. Rosecrance also concludes that conditions internal to the nation-state generally account for the onset of war. In particular, Rosecrance holds that the rise of secular ideologies, such as French egalitarianism and Soviet Communism, primarily are responsible for the origin of major conflicts. The dependence of revolutionary elites on mass support gives rise to an "elite insecurity," which, in turn, forces the elite to divert mass attention from internal problems by engaging in international conflict.[8]

This preoccupation with the "state as actor" leads to a number of analytic difficulties. First, intergroup conflict in general and international warfare in particular require the existence of at least two conflicting protagonists. A declaration of war is always against an adversary; it cannot exist without the presence of some antagonist. For this antagonism to exist, there must be some mutual interaction between the conflicting parties which eventually leads to the outbreak of war. The existence of this interaction implies that there is a political framework relevant to the origins of international warfare which exists apart from processes internal to the nation-state.[9] Second, it is known that a political framework of interstate interaction consists of diplomats, as well as international organizations. If war is a product of mutual antagonisms between states in an interactive setting, then can this political framework justifiably be omitted from an analysis of the origins of international warfare? It would seem that a comprehensive investigation of the onset of war would require an analysis of this framework, as well as those conditions internal to the nation-state which act as antecedents of war.

Our second level of analysis is the boundary between the system and the nation-state. This perhaps is a neglected area of international concern mainly because of the preoccupation with the nation-state itself and the more recent interest in the international system. This boundary delineates the interface between the nation-state and its environment; it is the point of contact

---

[7] In the differential equations which constitute his theory, Richardson introduced an interactive effect, whereby a nation reacts to an increase in a rival's armaments by increasing its own armaments expenditure. From this perspective, Richardson may be said to have employed the dyad as a unit of analysis. However, armaments expenditure is a property of the nation-state, and as such, his theory is centered on the "state as actor." See his *Arms and Insecurity* (Chicago: Quadrangle Books, 1960), pp. 12–23.

[8] Richard N. Rosecrance, *Action and Reaction in World Politics* (Boston: Little, Brown, 1963), pp. 304–306. Ernest B. Haas and Allen S. Whiting also argue that elite insecurity may result in external conflict, particularly during periods of rapid social change. See their *Dynamics of International Relations* (New York: McGraw-Hill, 1956), pp. 356–359.

[9] The extent to which such a framework exists may be dependent on the time period under investigation. For an analysis of the transformation of an internation system to an international system, see Paul Smoker, "Nation-State Escalation and International Integration," *Journal of Peace Research*, 4 (no. 1, 1967), pp. 61–75.

between national and international politics. As such, we can investigate several properties of the boundary, particularly those in which characteristics of each level interact with each other to result in international warfare. Inconsistencies between variables found in each level might contribute positively to the probability of war. The question of boundary permeability is also relevant here in two directions. We may investigate the impact of the nation-state upon the system in the form of international war, and also may consider the effect of the system upon the nation-state in relation to the occurrence of domestic instability.

The third level is the normal "state as actor" approach in which the various possible effects on war by domestic institutions are considered. Both internal socioeconomic change and the effects of social and political structure are treated in this approach.

Thus, there are three levels of analysis chosen here. They differ from certain prior treatments in that the boundary between the nation-state and international system is explicitly included as a separate level. Furthermore, the "individual as actor," indicated by Waltz and Wolfers, is omitted. Our concern here is with aggregate behaviors leading to war over a relatively long period of time and a large number of cases. Studies of the individual decision maker can be extremely useful in the analysis of crisis decision making, or why certain crises resulted in war and others did not.[10] However, the theoretical and methodological approaches often are in the form of psychological analyses of the individual and case studies and are, therefore, outside the scope of the present inquiry, which relies essentially on aggregate data and analyses appropriate for these data.

For each level of analysis chosen, there exist corresponding theoretical orientations for the explanation of international warfare. A framework is suggested first for the analysis of political violence within the international system, with power defined in terms of environmental uncertainty reduction. Basically, the variables indicated are the capabilities of nation-states and various constraints on these capabilities actually to reduce uncertainty. This prevention of uncertainty reduction may constitute a power loss to great powers. To be consistent with other approaches, the term *central powers* is used throughout this volume.

At the level of the international system, alliances exist as constraints on the

---

[10] For analyses of crisis decision making see, for example, Charles F. Hermann (ed.), *International Crises: Insights from Behavioral Research* (New York: The Free Press, 1972); Ole R. Holsti, "The 1914 Case," *American Political Science Review*, 59 (June 1965), pp. 365–378; and Dina A. Zinnes, Robert C. North, and Howard E. Koch, Jr., "Capability, Threat, and the Outbreak of War," in James N. Rosenau (ed.), *International Politics and Foreign Policy: A Reader in Research and Theory* (New York: The Free Press, 1961), pp. 469–482.

capabilities of nations and can serve as power losses for central powers. Alliances exist as important networks of interaction in the international system, perhaps not only for the purpose of providing protection for smaller powers, but also resulting in certain unintended consequences for central powers which ally primarily with smaller powers. If each country has some finite probability of becoming involved in war, then the greater the number of allies for the central power, the greater the uncertainty for that power.

Chapter II presents this conceptualization of power, along with the framework used to analyze types of power gain, loss, inversion, and constraint. Chapter III contains a detailed exposition of various kinds of losses and constraints in the form of alliances and boundaries between nations. The argument is extended to certain structural properties of the system and relationships between system polarity and the onset of war. Social disorganization of the system is treated in Chapter IV, with a somewhat different perspective being taken on the organizational properties of alliance formation resulting in war.

In Chapter V, the examination of the boundary between system and state begins in an analysis of the impact of boundary relations on war and continues through Chapter VII. First, the status inconsistency of nations is treated as an antecedent of war, whereby the inconsistency between the nation's ascribed status in the international system and its own achievement as the result of internal change is a condition found at the boundary between the actor and the system. This theory derives both from considerations of constraints on power exercise, to be developed in Chapter II, and from the application of status inconsistency concepts to the explanation of political violence. War here is seen as a form of political violence in the international system which may be, in part, a consequence of interactions between systemic and national status forms.

The second direction of boundary permeability is its impact on domestic instability. In Chapter VII, this process is understood as one of diffusion of domestic instability across international boundaries—a process which relies on small-group imitative phenomena for the onset of military intervention. The boundary of the nation-state is conceptualized as permeable to the effect of instability occurring in other countries, which can be analyzed initially by a mathematical probabilistic analysis. After this treatment, the process of diffusion is examined additionally by means of a social psychological theory of imitation. Small groups of decision makers may be affected by the behaviors of others in neighboring countries, and instability can result, in fact, as a consequence of national boundaries permeable to the behavior of other nation-states in the national environment.

Finally, we consider the nation-state as a level of analysis. In Chapter VI, the treatment of status inconsistency yields certain information regarding the effect of internal forms of achievement on international warfare. The rates of change of economic development, urbanization, transportation, population, and communication treated in this chapter reveal the effects of certain societal indicators on war experience. However, what is needed in addition is an even more explicit analysis of the effects on war of sociopolitical institutions, as is given in Chapter VIII. To achieve independence from the effects of correlates of industrialization treated in the earlier chapter, we consider the effects of social institutions in societies existing prior to the mid-nineteenth century.

The examination of the possible effects of domestic institutions on war is supplemented by an examination of the relationship of modernization processes to domestic instability. This latter analysis is undertaken to provide a validation of the assumption found in the treatment of diffusion: that systemic diffusion effects are more important as explanations of domestic instability, at least in Latin America, than are internal changes such as modernization processes. Thus, the relative importance of system and state as sources of instability is assessed and, in addition, the effects of modernization on instability are explicitly treated. The various levels of analysis and their associated theoretical approaches to the study of war are summarized in Figure 1.1.

The method of investigation in all cases is that of hypothesis-testing using aggregate data drawn from a wide variety of sources.[11] In virtually all cases, the conclusions are based on statistical analyses of the data. At times, due to problems of data availability or the unsuitability of analyzing a particular time period, these periods do not necessarily overlap. In some instances, this may be a disadvantage, as in the omission of the time period since World War II for the status inconsistency and alliance treatments—an exclusion dictated by the need for a manageable time period for the calculation of rates of change over time. In other cases, as in the analysis of the effects of domestic institutions on war, the use of an earlier time period allows for the

[11] For an analysis of the advantages and limitations of aggregate data analysis, see Michael Haas, "Aggregate Analysis," *World Politics*, 19 (October 1966), pp. 106–121. In regard to methodological approaches to the process of data gathering in international relations inquiry, probably the polar opposite to that used here is exemplified by simulation studies. In this latter approach, the possibilities for greater control of the data-generation process exist, in contrast to aggregate data which are "given." The simulation analyses are, by definition, attempting to be isomorphic to reality rather than representative of it, as in aggregate data studies. See, for example, Harold Guetzkow, Chadwick F. Alger, Richard A. Brody, Robert C. Noel, and Richard C. Snyder, *Simulation in International Relations: Developments for Research and Teaching* (Englewood Cliffs, N.J.: Prentice-Hall, 1963). Also see William D. Coplin (ed.), *Simulation in the Study of Politics* (Chicago: Markham, 1968).

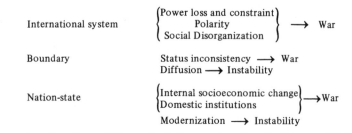

Figure 1.1 **Levels and Theoretical Approaches for the Study of Political Violence**

removal of any industrialization effects on these institutions, thus insuring a "controlled" examination of the impact of sociopolitical institutions.

At some points in the analysis, mathematical expressions and formulas are used to develop certain political relationships. Mathematical language provides the parsimony and clarity of communication necessary, at times, for the examination of these phenomena. It also allows for the development of mathematical models which can provide clear and concise abstract representations of reality. As such, essential features of sociopolitical relationships can emerge and can be highlighted in a manner that might not otherwise be possible using only verbal analyses. For example, the concept of power gain can be mathematically represented in the form of an environmental uncertainty reduction in Chapter III, whereas the cross-national diffusion of instability receives a similar kind of symbolic representation in Chapter VII. However, the mathematically disinclined reader may skip the formal presentations of these models without losing the thread of the analysis. The concepts themselves and the conclusions drawn from them are not rooted in the mathematics per se, but in the analytical presentations of this volume.

Varieties of Political Violence

Prior to any of these analyses, however, we must look more closely at the phenomenon of war. Clearly, violence is not a homogeneous phenomenon and so we should consider various kinds of political violence that can help us understand international warfare itself.

Concepts that have appeared in connection with theories of political development may be useful in the comparison of types of political violence. Conflict between two or more actors presupposes their mutual desire for some valued entity. The focus of conflict may be concrete, as in the case of territory or political office, or it may be abstract, as in the form of status or prestige. Given a sufficiently long time period, an interactive system may develop in which each protagonist reacts to activity by the others pertaining to the valued entity. An interdependency develops over time, and in this sense of interdependent parts of a whole, one may speak of a conflict system.[12] The notion of development is appropriate here, for once the concept of a conflict system is understood, in the form of interacting components which are therefore interdependent, then greater or lesser degrees of systemic development can be specified. Political violence is treated as one form of conflict behavior; it can occur within a conflict system at some point in time after the conflict has begun, although it does not necessarily have to occur.[13]

Consider five forms of political violence: riot, rebellion, revolution, civil war, and international war.[14] If we seek to compare them on some common dimensions, we may use concepts suggested by Samuel Huntington for the analysis of developing systems. Here, a conflict system exists in the form of two or more protagonists interacting with one another in a clearly interdependent fashion (later, unopposed invasions are omitted from consideration as wars because of this lack of interdependence) and can, therefore, as systems, experience development over time. Huntington has suggested structural differentiation and participation as criteria, where the former refers to organizational components which can be found in the conflict system and the extent to which they are differentiable from one another, whereas participation concerns the number of individual protagonists and the extent of their involvement in the conflict.[15]

If we accept the riot as a relatively spontaneous expression of activity in which there is little organized violence, and the international war as a violent event based on a large degree of military, economic, and social organization, we may understand the two forms as opposite ends of the structural

[12] The concept of conflict systems with strong interactions among components is developed in Kenneth Boulding, *Conflict and Defence* (New York: Harper Torchbooks, 1962), especially pp. 1–40. The dynamics of international conflict within interactive settings is treated in Lewis F. Richardson, *op. cit.*

[13] An act of political violence is defined here as an attempted or actual injury (ordinarily not sanctioned by law or custom) perpetrated on persons or property with the actual or intended consequences of effecting transformations either within structures of political authority or within economic and/or social systems. The definition is said to apply at the levels of local, national, or international politics.

[14] A treatment of internal war which approximates this type of rank ordering but, by definition, omits consideration of international war, is found in Harry Eckstein, "On the Etiology of Internal Wars," *History and Theory*, 4 (no. 2, 1965), pp. 133–163.

[15] Samuel P. Huntington, *Political Order in Changing Societies* (New Haven: Yale University Press, 1968), pp. 12–39. The concept of structural differentiation is treated by Huntington primarily as institutionalization, and increased participation is associated with the process of modernization.

differentiation continuum. Similarly, from the perspective of the number of persons actively involved in the conflict, the riot and the major international war can be placed at the extreme ends of participation, where this latter variable refers to the number of individual persons as combatants or civilian casualties.

Similar reasoning can be applied to the three intermediate cases of the set. The rebellion can be ranked above the riot on the two measures, followed by the revolution and civil war in increasing rank order. As indicated by writers such as Hannah Arendt and Chalmers Johnson, the rebellion often is a localized phenomenon which occurs in a given region of a country and generally is not supported by a complex organization.[16] The extent of participation often exceeds that of the riot, but is less than that found in major revolutions. Pugachev's peasant rebellion of 1773–1775 is a case in point, as is the Tibetan revolt of 1958–1960. A major revolution such as the French or Russian, in contrast to the rebellion, often is supported by a complex organizational hierarchy even prior to its success in ousting the incumbents, and at some point in the revolutionary process virtually all groups and regions of the country are actively involved.

Turning now to the civil war, the degree of structural differentiation is clearly evident in the form of at least two governments actively in a state of violent conflict, and the degree of participation is high. A correlate of participation, as will be seen, may be the number of persons killed in the violence: the American Civil War and Nigerian Civil War are examples of conflicts in which the numbers of deaths exceeded those which occurred in any other dyadic instances of violence within their respective time periods. International wars such as the Thirty Years' War, the Napoleonic Wars, and World Wars I and II exhibit the greatest degrees of structural differentiation and participation. The presence of large numbers of nation-states organized both at the levels of conflicting alliance systems and internal military organizations, as well as the great sizes of armies in violent conflict, place this form of political violence in the highest rank.

But each of these types in itself may be variegated and as a result, given the existence of international war itself as a rather complex phenomenon, the two variables—structural complexity and participation—may be used to differentiate among several types. Indeed, several categorizations of war have been constructed on the basis of variables similar to the ones suggested here. Quincy Wright has developed a typology of war which distinguishes among four categories (1) the civil war, which takes place within the boundaries of a

---

[16] See Hannah Arendt, *On Revolution* (New York: Viking Press, 1963), pp. 40–41; and Chalmers Johnson, *Revolutionary Change* (Boston: Little, Brown, 1966), pp. 135–144.

sovereign nation; (2) the balance of power war, in which members of a state system are at war among themselves; (3) the defensive war, which acts to guard a civilization against the intrusions of an alien culture; and (4) the imperial war, in which one civilization attempts to expand at the expense of another.[17] In this set of distinctions, the boundary conditions of the conflict appear to be the primary criteria of classification. Whether a war is categorized as an imperial or civil war apparently depends upon the extent to which the conflict is contained within, or extended beyond, certain boundaries, implying the presence of both structural differentiation and participation. J. David Singer, Melvin Small, and George L. Kraft, Jr., follow Wright's classification in distinguishing among civil, colonial, and international wars, but with a more focused emphasis in that wars between civilizations are not explicitly introduced.[18]

Evan Luard introduces a somewhat different perspective in his treatment of war; he places greater emphasis on the motives of nation-states in their initiation of war, although implicit in these reasons for expansion are the notions of complexity and participation. Luard divides "Wars of Aggression" into four categories. Expansive wars are defined as those concerned with the "conquest of foreign territories not previously controlled. . . ."[19] The Japanese invasions of Manchuria and China are examples of this type, as are the German and Soviet invasions of various European countries in the interwar period. Irredentist wars are, according to Luard, "directed against territories inhabited mainly by people of the same race as the conquerors . . . ."[20] The Nazi occupations of Austria and the Sudetenland belong in this category. Strategic wars, as a third category, may be motivated by a desire on the part of a nation to enhance its logistic and military position vis-à-vis some real or imagined threat. The Soviet invasion of Finland in 1939 may have been induced by such a perceived threat, and the Israeli participation in the Suez campaign might have been similarly motivated. Finally, Luard speaks of coercive wars as those which entail the placing of constraints on the operations of a sovereign government. Examples of this type provided by Luard are the Arab invasion of Israel in 1948 and the Soviet repression of the Hungarian uprising in 1956.

Apparently, Wright developed his categories by means of a rank order

[17] Quincy Wright, *A Study of War* (Chicago: The University of Chicago Press, 1942), pp. 639–640.

[18] J. David Singer, Melvin Small, and George L. Kraft, Jr., "The Frequency, Magnitude and Severity of International War, 1815–1945" (Ann Arbor: Mental Health Research Institute reprint 159, University of Michigan, July 1965).

[19] Evan Luard, *Conflict and Peace in the Modern International System* (Boston: Little, Brown, 1968), p. 68.

[20] *Ibid.*

ranging from major violence internal to the nation-state (civil war) to violent confrontations between civilizations in the form of the imperial war. The scope of the conflict, in effect, serves as the principal criterion for ranking the categories. In Luard's typology on the other hand, a rank order classification is not developed; rather, discrete motivations are the primary means for the construction of his set of categories.

The classification to be developed in this treatment of political violence is based on a combination of these premises of rank order and scope, along with the explicit use of the variables *structural differentiation* and *participation*. In addition, two variables specific to political violence are included. These are the intensity of violence in the form of the number killed, and duration, as a temporal indicator. Finally, the motivation of actors is taken into account and later in the volume is analyzed in the form of escalations and deescalations of conflict systems. The variables and the categories of war are found in Table 1.1.

Following the ordering principle of structural differentiation or complexity, the simplest unit in international warfare is chosen as the basis for the lowest level of warfare, the territorial war. This form of conflict concerns the authoritative administration of a given territory. The contested territory acts as the primary focus of conflict, and seldom do other issues intrude into the principal focus of attention. Conceptually, this is the simplest and most primitive of

TABLE 1.1. **Varieties of War**

Type of war	Structural differentiation[a]	Participation[b]	War duration	No. killed	Motivation of at least one set of protagonists
Normative	High	High	Long	Very high	Fundamental change in the policy framework within nations and within the international system
Coercive	Moderate	Generally moderate	Moderate	High	Fundamental change in the policy framework within nations and within a particular region
Regional	Low to moderate	Generally moderate	Moderate	Low to moderate	Moderate changes within a regional policy framework
Territorial	Very low	Limited to two	Short to moderate	Low to moderate	Territorial change

[a] Alliances and/or military-industrial organization.
[b] Protagonists and size of armies.

wars since the protagonists are in conflict over one of the most tangible, visible, and necessary of human commodities. In addition, the protagonists do not exceed two in number and, therefore, participation is at a minimum. Examples of this type are the Chaco War between Bolivia and Paraguay, as well as the Italo-Turkish War of 1911–1912. In the former conflict, the Chaco Boreal, lying between Bolivia and Paraguay, was the territory at issue, and in the second, the political control of Libya was the primary source of conflict.

A second category, the regional war, also has as a point of issue the administration of a given territorial entity. However, the policy framework and power relations of an entire region may be involved, and the protagonists generally exceed two in number. The presence of additional participants and their policy goals increases both the participation and complexity of this type of war. The War of the Pacific between Bolivia and Peru on the one hand, and Chile on the other, may be illustrative of this category, as are the First and Second Balkan Wars. In each of these instances, the crucial issues not only involved the authoritative administration of given territories, but also concerned the specific policy framework governing a given region. Chilean dominance of the Pacific coastal region following the War of the Pacific replaced prior Bolivian and Peruvian control of trade and economic development in that area. The consequences of the two Balkan Wars included a reduction of Turkish and Bulgarian importance in the determination of policies and international relations for that region.

The coercive war as a third category depends somewhat on the number of participants, but more so on the extent of transformation of policy both internal to a nation-state and in its regional environment. Thus, the complexity of policy issues, as well as additional participation, are present here. Whereas the regional war may alter a policy framework, the coercive war transforms it. The intention of at least one of the protagonists is to reshape drastically the existing state of relationships among a small number of nations. As in the territorial and regional wars, the authoritative administration of certain geographical entities is also at issue. Examples of coercive wars are the Franco-Prussian War of 1870–1871 and the Sino-Japanese War of 1937–1941. In the former, the objective of German and French diplomacy was not simply the control of certain territories such as Alsace-Lorraine, but the future of the policy framework for Western Europe. Moreover, as a result of this war, the structure of diplomatic relationships in the region was drastically altered by the attendant unification of Germany. Indeed, the emergence of a unipolar diplomatic system centered at Berlin has been observed to be a consequence of this war.[21] The Sino-Japanese War of the

---

[21] See Rosecrance, *op. cit.*, pp. 250–254.

late 1930's was, in its essentials, a conflict for the control of the Chinese heartland and all of East Asia. Japanese hegemony within the region was the goal of that country's policy makers.

Finally, the normative war includes the coercive aspects of the previous category, and in addition, includes elements of rebellion against an international normative framework. As such, the number of participants is larger than for any of the other categories, and the intensity and scope of desired change on the part of one set of protagonists also are greater. As before, the element of territoriality also is germane to the conflict. The Thirty Years' War, ending only in the Peace of Westphalia in 1648, and the Napoleonic Wars are earlier examples of this type. In both World Wars I and II, the norms governing international discourse were challenged by a group of nations, and in the second of these wars in particular, the explicit rejection by the Axis Powers of the Treaty of Versailles and League Covenant constituted a challenge to the dominant norms of the international system.

Perhaps it is only when human beings clash over important abstractions and modes of civilization that the most widespread and intense wars occur, just as the bloodiest civil wars are fought over the "appropriate" forms of domestic sociopolitical relationships. In any event, four categories are posited for the occurrence of international warfare.[22] These form a rank-ordered set in which each element in a lower rank also is found at all levels above it. This ordered set will prove to be useful in explaining certain anomalous results to be found in succeeding analyses. The explanation of these international wars begins with the analysis of power in international relations, as presented in Chapter II.

---

[22] There are certain similarities between this categorization and those developed for internal violence. See, for example, James N. Rosenau, "Internal War as an International Event," in J. N. Rosenau (ed.), *International Aspects of Civil Strife* (Princeton, N.J.: Princeton University Press, 1964), pp. 45–91; Samuel P. Huntington, "Patterns of Violence in World Politics," in S. P. Huntington (ed.), *Changing Patterns of Military Politics* (New York: The Free Press, 1962), pp. 17–50; and Raymond Tanter and Manus Midlarsky, "A Theory of Revolution," *Journal of Conflict Resolution*, 11 (September 1967), pp. 264–280.

II

Power, Uncertainty, and the Onset of Political Violence

In order to reflect properly on the role of power in relation to political violence—an approach that may have been neglected by Clausewitz and others—it is necessary to consider its prior conceptual development and empirical applications. Indeed, the concept of power traditionally has been a primary concern in the study of politics; yet for a time it seemed as if this concept had fallen into disuse as a specific focus of inquiry. Its contemporary revival has been primarily at the hands of those whose purpose would be its quantification and systematic application.[1]

Perhaps certain of the difficulties with the use of this concept derive from the many contexts which can be found for its application. On the one hand,

---

[1] See, for example, Robert A. Dahl, "The Concept of Power," *Behavioral Science*, 2 (July 1957), pp. 201–215; James G. March, "Measurement Concepts in the Theory of Influence," *Journal of Politics*, 19 (May 1957), pp. 202–226; William H. Riker, "A Test of the Adequacy of the Power Index," *Behavioral Science*, 4 (April 1959), pp. 120–131; Dorwin Cartwright, "Influence, Leadership, Control," in James G. March (ed.), *Handbook of Organizations* (Chicago: Rand McNally, 1965), pp. 1–47; Steven J. Brams, "Measuring the Concentration of Power in Political Systems," *American Political Science Review*, 62 (June 1968), pp. 461–475; and Bruce M. Russett, "Probabilism and the Number of Units Affected: Measuring Influence Concentration," *APSR*, 62 (June 1968), pp. 476–480.

AUTHOR'S NOTE: Portions of this chapter from "Power, Uncertainty, and the Onset of International Violence," by Manus I. Midlarsky are reprinted from the *Journal of Conflict Resolution*, Vol. 18, No. 3 (Sept. 1974) © by permission of the Publisher, Sage Publications, Inc.

power is of particular importance in normative political theory. Even theories concerned mainly with institutional frameworks, or the supremacy of a single institution within a wider framework, must refer somehow to the "separation of powers." On the other hand, the "quantum of power" has been thought to be an appropriate unit of measurement in the systematic study of politics, for with the choice of power as a focus of analysis, and the precise construction of a measure of power, then possibilities for a mathematical treatment of politics may follow.

At the outset we will indicate that our intention is not to treat explicitly the differentiations among the various notions of influence, power, and authority. Following Harold Lasswell and Abraham Kaplan, we can understand influence as a generalized and variable form of impact, power as a form of influence related to policy, and authority as legitimized power.[2] The emphasis on power in this study derives from our primary concern with political violence as behavior directed ultimately at the transformation of public policy in various political settings, with special emphasis on the international system. Political violence is contrasted with other forms of violence at a later point in this chapter. One may distinguish, however, among various usages of the power concept and then trace the development of current systematic conceptualizations of power. Specifically, it can be shown that an important analytic strain in contemporary studies of power leads to the definition of power as the ability to effect a reduction of environmental uncertainty, and the exercise of power as the actual reduction of that uncertainty.

The analysis in this chapter is divided essentially into three parts, with the first indicating trends in the literature leading to the formulation of power in terms of uncertainty. Certain properties of the definition and varieties of power conditions are then indicated. A third section addresses itself to the theoretical "power of power" in this conceptualization, by means of a reconsideration of theories concerning the onset of political violence.

Power and Uncertainty

A distinction that is important for subsequent analyses is that between power as an attribute, and the exercise of power as a behavior. In the former perspective, we find a generalized view of the power concept, where, for example, power may be perceived as originating in a divine right, a historic necessity, a collective decision, or in the capacity of a national system. The work of Hannah Arendt is typical in this regard. In her analysis of the American

[2] Harold D. Lasswell and Abraham Kaplan, *Power and Society: A Framework for Political Inquiry* (New Haven: Yale University Press, 1950), pp. 55–102.

Revolution, the power of the people to influence their future resided in collective decisions by which certain institutions and representatives within those institutions were endowed with legitimacy.[3] Power as an attribute of a system also is found in various treatments of international politics. In the works of A. F. K. Organski and Klaus Knorr, for instance, power often is treated as equivalent to the capabilities of nations as measured by population, gross national product, and the size of the armed forces.[4]

The behavioral aspect of power as a relational concept is found in the work of Lasswell and Kaplan. In their focus on public policy, they interpret power over decision-making "relationally, not as a simple property."[5] Power should be analyzed primarily as it is exercised, rather than as an attribute. Among those who systematically measure power, there also is a tendency to emphasize the behavioral or relational aspect. Questions often asked are: who has control; who is being controlled; or how is control established in coalitions. It is in this concern with relations that we see the beginnings of the analytic strain which leads directly to the interpretation of power in terms of uncertainty. By *relation* is meant here the verbal or mathematical specification of a degree of association between a unit and its environment, either in the form of probabilities for the occurrence of certain behaviors or in the actual frequency of occurrence. Thus, the probability that A can exert some influence over B is an example of such a relation, whereas national characteristics such as GNP or population are illustrations of attributes which in themselves do not specify associations with aspects of their environment.

Within a non-probabilistic frame of reference, Dorwin Cartwright has formally defined power as the maximum strength that A can employ in attempting to force B to comply with A's request. Cartwright's measure explicitly accounts for B's resistance to this request.[6] If one interprets *force* as a capacity to influence the giving of rewards, then there exists a similarity between this formalization and that of Georg Karlsson.[7] His definition of power is the difference between the maximum and minimum reward needed by A to influence B successfully.

Using a probabilistic frame of reference, which has become a fundamental basis for later research in this area, Robert A. Dahl has formulated an

[3] Hannah Arendt, *On Revolution* (New York: Viking Press, 1963), pp. 165–178.

[4] See A. F. K. Organski, *World Politics*, 2nd ed. (New York: Knopf, 1968), pp. 207–220; Klaus Knorr, *Military Power and Potential* (Lexington, Mass.: D. C. Heath, 1970).

[5] Lasswell and Kaplan, *op, cit.*, p. 75.

[6] Dorwin Cartwright, "A Field Theoretical Conception of Power," in Dorwin Cartwright (ed.), *Studies in Social Power* (Ann Arbor: University of Michigan Press, 1959), pp. 183–220.

[7] Georg Karlsson, "Some Aspects of Power in Small Groups," in Joan H. Criswell, Herbert Solomon, and Patrick Suppes (eds.), *Mathematical Methods in Small Group Processes* (Stanford: Stanford University Press, 1962), pp. 193–202.

analytically similar expression for A's power over B. As Dahl puts it, "My intuitive idea of power, then, is something like this: A has power over B to the extent that he can get B to do something that B would not otherwise do."[8] The introduction of probabilistic concepts into the measurement of the power also brings with it the concept of uncertainty. For if A can affect B's behavior such that a particular outcome becomes more probable, then by Dahl's definition, A's power is increased, and at the same time uncertainty with regard to B's behavior has been reduced.

The formulation by James G. March is in some respects even closer to the concept of uncertainty reduction. According to March one can "identify one role (R_1) as more influential than another (R_2) *with respect to a given behavior* (sic) if when R_1 does that behavior the possible outcomes are more constrained than they are when R_2 does the same behavior."[9] The constraint on possible outcomes by the more powerful role position implies a reduction of uncertainty, since the probabilities for the occurrence of certain events are now greater after the intervention by R_1. This formalization also is generalizable to a set of behaviors.

Finally, Karl W. Deutsch has proposed that "The weight of the power or influence of an actor over some process is the extent to which he can change the probability of its outcome."[10] If one applies the criterion that the sum of the probabilities for the outcomes must be equal to unity (normalization), then the increase in the probability of one outcome implies the reduction in the probabilities of one or more of the other outcomes. Uncertainty concerning the results of the various alternatives therefore is reduced to the extent of the changes in probabilities. Deutsch's definition of power implies uncertainty reduction perhaps more clearly than any of the other formulations, because only the normalization criterion must be added to arrive at the definition proposed here; namely, the exercise of power as uncertainty reduction.

It should be noted that other systematic measurements of power tend to be consistent with this interpretation. In the area of coalition formation, a measure devised by Lloyd Shapley and Martin Shubik and employed by William Riker implies that the uncertainty about a decisional outcome has been reduced when the last needed actor joins the winning coalition.[11] The matrices of internation influence situations proposed by J. David Singer

[8] Dahl, *op. cit.*, pp. 202–203.

[9] March, *op. cit.*, p. 210.

[10] Karl W. Deutsch, *The Analysis of International Relations* (Englewood Cliffs, N.J.: Prentice-Hall, 1968), p. 24.

[11] See L. S. Shapley and Martin Shubik, "A Method for Evaluating the Distribution of Power in a Committee System," *American Political Science Review*, 48 (September 1954), pp. 787–792; Riker, *op. cit.*

depend both on the preference orderings of alternatives and on their estimated likelihoods, so that the outcomes of influence attempts are governed
by probabilistic calculations of actors.[12] A measure of influence constructed
by Steven J. Brams assumes large values when influence is concentrated in the
hands of a relatively small number of decision makers, and Bruce M. Russett
employs a similar construct in his measurement of influence.[13] One may be
able to establish a monotonic relationship between these indicators of influence
or power and the range of probable outcomes. In this fashion, the higher the
values of these power measures the greater the probabilities of various
outcomes desired by the group of decision makers.

As a consequence of the distinction between power as an attribute and the
exercise of power as a behavior, and of the prior probabilistic interpretations,
one can conceptualize power as the ability to reduce environmental uncertainty, and the exercise of power gain for the benefit of an actor as the
actual reduction of the uncertainty. A state of uncertainty is defined as one
in which there exists a set of alternate possible events, and the probability of
occurrence for any one element of the set is not appreciably greater than that
for any other element. Although the values of the probabilities for the mathematical measure of uncertainty to be introduced vary from 0 to 1, this definition deliberately excludes those instances when an event is virtually certain
to occur as the result of certain behaviors. Thus, for example, we do not
consider settings such as concentration camps, slave camps, or forms of
extreme totalitarian rule. In these instances, threat systems or force are the
primary means of insuring compliance, and we are faced more with *deterministic* behavioral systems, than with the *probabilistic* ones found in
the great majority of political systems. The determinism of the use of force
is then excluded from the domain of the exercise of power by the preceding
definitions.

There are several properties of this conceptualization which can be identified.
The first is the distinction between power as an attribute and the exercise of
power as a behavior. Power as the ability to reduce uncertainty is defined as
a capacity or capability. As such, it is an attribute of a system which may be
present even when it is not being exercised. The extent of a nation's economic
development, energy production, armed forces, or other indicators of its
capacity or capability often are employed as measures of national power.
They are the static "givens" of a system at any point in time, and only upon
their use in a particular fashion can we say that power has been exercised.
The power of the presidency also is an attribute of a system which is defined

---

[12] J. David Singer, "Inter-Nation Influence: A Formal Model," *American Political
Science Review*, 57 (June 1963), pp. 420–430.
[13] Brams, *op. cit.*; Russett, *op. cit.*

according to a legal role position and certain discretionary powers emanating both from precedent and a personal role definition. Presidential power is exercised only when certain behaviors occur that are consistent with legal and personal role definitions.[14] The attribute of power as an ability to reduce uncertainty also is the property of a monarchy legitimated by a doctrine of divine right, or of a population which has a sovereign mandate. When the monarch or the population utilizes its ability to reduce uncertainty, as in a decision regarding matters of public policy, it can be said that power has been exercised.

Power is said to be exercised when certain processes or events occur such that uncertainty is reduced. Given a set of alternative probabilities for a behavior with the normalization criterion of the sum of the probabilities equal to unity, then the increase in the probability of occurrence for one possible outcome simultaneously implies a reduction in the probability of occurrence for one or more of the other possible outcomes. When this process has taken place, a reduction in uncertainty has been effected. The exercise of power as suggested by Machiavelli consists of a rather severe set of directives for the reduction of uncertainty, especially when the elimination of opponents is suggested. And, as Tocqueville commented on the tyranny of the majority, it would be difficult to find a more effective exercise of the reduction of uncertainty than by reference to either a real or fictitious generalized sentiment as a justification for repressive action.

A second property of this formulation is that it refers directly to the behavior of power exercise. In certain of the formal approaches, such as those of Cartwright and of Karlsson, the measure of power is dependent both on the intentions of the power user and on those of the object of power exercise. Cartwright refers to a "need for g as a motive base" where "g" refers to a desire for power, and Karlsson defines utility functions for both the user and object of power exercise which are dependent on the subjective evaluation of outcomes.[15]

Although the problem of motivation may be of extreme importance in studying the psychology of individuals, in questions of political behavior, particularly at the level of international systems, it may be less important, and more difficult to examine empirically. Interview methods would constitute a possible means of determining intentions, but often those whose exercise of power is of greatest interest (e.g., national leaders) do not reveal their motives for a very long time after leaving their positions, if at all. Few leaders of

[14] For a discussion of presidential power which emphasizes the role definition of the presidency, as well as certain organizational constraints on the power of the presidency, see Richard E. Neustadt, *Presidential Power* (New York: Wiley, 1960).

[15] Cartwright, "A Field Theoretical Conception"; Karlsson, *op. cit.*

prominence would admit to exercising their power in certain situations or to having power exercised upon them. In certain cases, the most powerful individual within a political setting assumes an official position of relatively minor importance, as in certain instances of military coups.[16]

The problem of the non-observable also appears in studies of community power. Reputation has been taken as a measure of influence or power since the power over decision making often is a process or event which is difficult to observe empirically. Quite conceivably, the controversy among the elitist, pluralist, and "non-decision-making" interpretations of community politics can be traced directly to the problems encountered in observing the variable which is most central to the argument.[17] The difficulties in determining intentions, motives, or "resistance" (in Cartwright's terms) to the power user, argue for a conceptualization of power with the behavior of units as the primary referent. Indeed, this is the purpose of one of March's treatments of power. By focusing on the outcomes of various role interactions, March attempts to obviate the necessity for dealing directly with intentions.[18]

A third and corollary property of the definition is a level of generality which does not specifically indicate the agents of power exercise, although it can be used in this fashion. Often, the question of who exercised power over whom becomes the focus of research, to the exclusion of questions concerning the mechanisms for the exercise of power. We may note that the exercise of power is a behavior and our analysis is confined to the behavior itself. This emphasis on behavior does not exclude from consideration the relational aspects of power exercise. If a behavior is observed which is consistent with our definition

[16] The primary agent in the initiation of a coup often may not appear until some time after it has taken place, as in the instance of Nasser's replacement of Naguib in Egypt. Thus, the precise determination of who exercises power may be extremely difficult, if not impossible, until such an event has taken place. For an analysis of a process leading to the initiation of coups, see Martin C. Needler, "Political Development and Military Intervention in Latin America," *American Political Science Review*, 60 (September 1966), pp. 616–626.

[17] Among the primary advocates of the ruling elite model are C. Wright Mills, *The Power Elite* (New York: Oxford University Press, 1956); and Floyd Hunter, *Community Power Structure* (Chapel Hill: University of North Carolina Press, 1953). For criticisms of this model, see Robert A. Dahl, "A Critique of the Ruling Elite Model," *American Political Science Review*, 52 (June 1958), pp. 463–469; Nelson W. Polsby, "Three Problems in the Analysis of Community Power," *American Sociological Review*, 24 (December 1959), pp. 796–803; and Raymond E. Wolfinger, "Reputation and Reality in the Study of 'Community Power'," *American Sociological Review*, 25 (December 1960), pp. 636–644. For studies which emphasize certain normative aspects of the elitist and pluralist models, see Jack L. Walker, "A Critique of the Elitist Theory of Democracy," *American Political Science Review*, 60 (June 1966), pp. 285–295; Robert A. Dahl, "Further Reflections on 'The Elitist Theory of Democracy'," *APSR*, 60 (June 1966), pp. 296–305; and Richard M. Merelman, "On the Neo-Elitist Critique of Community Power," *American Political Science Review*, 62 (June 1968), pp. 451–460.

[18] March, *op. cit.*

then we know that some unit had, in fact, operated on its environment to affect the behavior.

This level of generality lends itself readily to the concepts of power loss, power constraints, or a "power vacuum." In many interpretations of power, particularly the quantitative, the concept of power itself is defined with reference to specific parties A or B. Thus, A can exercise power over B, but the reduction in A's power over B or the concept of no one having any power over B is seldom introduced. This lack of emphasis on the reduction or absence of power may result partly from the preoccupation with who is exercising power, instead of the actual power exercise.

In any event, we know that there are many situations in which power is more conspicuous by its absence than by its presence. This is particularly the case in international politics, where there occurs a wide variety of situations in which the pattern of events exhibits the lack of influence or control by any single actor. In situations of this type, it can be said that an *increase* in uncertainty has occurred, and if the increase is great enough, as Charles A. McClelland has noted, then there may exist a state of international crisis.[19] Thus, the interpretation presented here is oriented not only to an increase or decrease in the power exercised by an actor, but also to the virtual absence of power exercise as defined by a very high degree of uncertainty as to eventual outcomes.

A final property of the definition refers to what March has called the problem of "the power of power."[20] After an exhaustive analysis of approaches to the conceptualization and measurement of power, March has concluded that the concept of power may be inadequate as an organizing focus for the analysis of the political process. Alternative perspectives, according to March, may have greater utility in explaining political events and processes. Although the concept itself and its mathematical or operational referent cannot be expected to provide explanation in and of itself, still the property of theoretical utility should exist. This argument highlights a nexus between the traditional considerations of power treated primarily as an attribute in normative political theory, and the contemporary approaches which emphasize behavior or relations.

Theoretical uses of power and the mathematical conceptualizations which

[19] McClelland employs a measure of relative uncertainty as an indicator of an international crisis; see his "Access to Berlin: The Quantity and Variety of Events," in J. David Singer (ed.), *Quantitative International Politics: Insights and Evidence* (New York: The Free Press, 1968), pp. 159–186. John D. Sullivan uses a similar form of analysis in his "Quemoy and Matsu: A Systematic Analysis," mimeographed (Los Angeles: May 1964).

[20] James G. March, "The Power of Power," in David Easton (ed.), *Varieties of Political Theory* (Englewood Cliffs, N.J.: Prentice-Hall, 1966), pp. 39–70.

emphasize power relations among units are not, of course, mutually exclusive. Indeed, one can argue that the two should be mutually supportive and that an important, if not a primary, criterion for the evaluation of a mathematical conceptualization of power is its theoretical utility. That is, can one readily use this concept in the construction or adaptation of political theory, and what is the degree of explanatory power achieved by such theory? Thus, we would ask of any approach to the formulation and measurement of power that it be usable within a theoretical context for the explanation of political phenomena, and that it enhance our understanding of the process of the exercise of power. Theoretical explanation, in a formal sense, demands only the statement and empirical validation of relationships among variables. However, this aspect of social scientific inquiry often appears to be emphasized to the exclusion of explanation or understanding in the *verstehen* sense. Criteria for the evaluation of a particular conceptualization should include not only the extent to which it lends itself to theoretical explanation, but also the degree to which it increases our understanding of the nature of a given phenomenon. It is suggested that the present conceptualization of power has some theoretical utility, and this aspect of the definition will be taken up in the subsequent sections on varieties of power conditions and theories of political violence. Chapter III will deal further with this issue in the treatments of power loss in alliance systems and power constraints as the result of geographical frontiers. At this point let us consider the different types of power conditions which can emerge from this particular conceptualization.

Varieties of Power Conditions

There are several possible variations on this conceptualization of power as uncertainty reduction. First, for the sake of illustration, we consider the actor A alone in a given environment. Three possible outcomes can be isolated with regard to uncertainty reduction; they will be amplified more fully in the dyadic and n-adic cases, but for now serve to illustrate simply the concept of uncertainty reduction for actor A.

One possible variation refers to the obvious case of an increase in the probability of an outcome desired by A and the simultaneous reduction in the probabilities of the remaining alternatives. This would accord with our intuitive notion of the exercise of power. A desired outcome has been made more likely and undesired ones made less likely, and as a result we can call this activity one of power gain. As an illustration, suppose the initial probability of winning a poker hand is approximately equal to .50 (and the possibility of losing and someone else winning is, therefore, .50) when the cards have been dealt, but by a judicious observation of the other players and an effective betting strategy, as well as card selection as in "draw poker," this probability is increased to .70, and the probability of losing is equal to .30. This second set of probabilities clearly represents a certain amount of uncertainty reduction in the direction desired by A.

A second possibility is the converse of the first in which the actor by his own actions reduces the probability of an outcome favorable to himself. This can occur in situations in which self-defeating behaviors occur accidentally or with some mistaken purpose, and a power loss is incurred as a result. If, in our poker example, the player accidentally reveals his hand, or by injudicious betting or bad card selection reduces his chances of winning, say from .70 (.30 of losing) to .50 (.50), then such a power loss has been incurred.

There is a null case, or that of power constraint, in which the probability of a favorable outcome, never very high to begin with, remains substantially the same even after some intervention by A. The probability of winning a poker hand (.50 initially), remains the same even after the betting and card selection. Thus, with regard to actor A, we can identify three types of uncertainty condition depending on the direction of change or the lack of changes in the probabilities of desired outcomes.

These three conditions illustrate the concept of uncertainty change or constancy with regard to a single actor. These instances, however, are illustrative and have considered only the effect on A for purposes of explication, without direct reference to other actors in the system. In the dyadic and n-adic conditions, the effect on other actors is introduced. We begin with the actors A and B. In the dyadic condition our concern is only for the two principals, whereas in the n-adic state the actor B is not a single agent but a generalized "other" consisting of actors $\beta, \gamma, \ldots$, who are the participants in this n-adic environment. This latter condition is probably more realistic for problems of international politics.

Let us now consider a more formal exposition of the various possibilities inherent in the definition of changes in uncertainty which are to be found in Table 2.1. There exists a set of probabilities prior to any increase or decrease in uncertainty. These are the a priori probabilities in contrast to the set of a posteriori probabilities which incorporate the effects of behaviors generated by one or more actors in the system. With the exception of the bottom two rows in Table 2.1, the dyadic and n-adic conditions are the same, since it is immaterial whether B is a single actor or generalized "other" for these cases, so long as we are emphasizing the effects on A. The last two rows, however, illustrate conditions which no longer emphasize A, and the dyadic and n-adic conditions are therefore separated.

TABLE 2.1. **Power Relations of Actor A in Dyadic and N-adic Conditions**

	A priori probabilities		A posteriori probabilities	
	Dyadic	*N-adic*	*Dyadic*	*N-adic*
Power of A	A/B	A/$\beta, \gamma, \ldots$	A/B	A/$\beta, \gamma, \ldots$
Control	.99/.01	.99/.01	.99/.01	.99/.01
Subservience	.01/.99	.01/.99	.01/.99	.01/.99
Constraint	.50/.50	.50/.50	.50/.50	.50/.50
Gain	.50/.50	.50/.50	.70/.30	.70/.30
Loss	.70/.30	.70/.30	.50/.50	.50/.50
Reversal (loss by B or $\beta, \gamma, \ldots$ gain by A)	.30/.70	.30/.70	.70/.30	.70/.30
Inverse gain (loss by B or $\beta, \ldots$)	.30/.70	.30/.60, .05, $\ldots$	.50/.50	.30/.50, .15, $\ldots$
Inverse loss (gain by B or $\beta, \ldots$)	.70/.30	.70/.10, .15, $\ldots$	.50/.50	.70/.24, .01, $\ldots$

Consider first, with regard to A, three possible static conditions: control, subservience, and constraint. In the first, A is dominant with respect to outcomes desired by him. Specifically, the probability of an outcome desired by A is equal to .99, whereas that for B is .01. An intuitive notion of control suggests that no intervention in the system would appreciably alter these probabilities. To use our poker example, if A has four aces, then it is highly unlikely that any efforts by B, through judicious betting, card selection, or otherwise, will alter the control properties of A's hand. Similarly, given the four aces held by A, none of the actors $\beta, \gamma, \ldots$, in the n-adic condition will have a likelihood of winning much above the .01 level. Conversely, our actor A will have a very low probability of winning if some other player B in the dyadic or $\beta, \gamma, \ldots$, in the n-adic state had four aces. This is the subservient condition detailed in the second row of Table 2.1.

As indicated in the previous single actor illustration, the constraint condition arises when the probabilities of favorable outcomes for all parties remain at the same equal level even after some attempt to alter them. If player A receives only a random selection of cards, then even the most judicious betting and card selection honestly accomplished will not substantially alter the probabilities of winning. This condition is illustrated in the third row of Table 2.1.

These three categories are static in the sense that the initial conditions obtain even after intervention. In contrast, the dynamic cases of changes in uncertainty interest us in the case of gain, loss, and reversal found in the next three rows of the table. Here the absence of constraining factors in the form of a playable hand allows A to intervene successfully in the form of "smart" poker playing designed to maximize his own advantage. By reducing uncertainty in his own direction, A has gained some power over the game vis-à-vis B or the collection of players $\beta, \gamma, \ldots$.

The concept of loss is structurally identical, and opposite in direction, but because of the directionality implied by the notion of loss, separate inclusion in the table is required. Here, an initial advantage is given up in the form of an uncertainty increase. This may be done by the poor poker player who accidentally reveals the state of his hand or by injudicious betting reduces the probability of winning.

Power reversal in A's favor can be understood as a combination of a power loss by B combined with a simultaneous or subsequent power gain by A. Each of the probabilities would have to pass either discretely or continuously from the low–high levels to the high–low levels, and these changes can be described by the combination of loss and gain. Again using our poker example, a reversal will take place if a player with a superior hand initially who plays badly (B), combines with a good player who receives inferior cards initially (A), but plays them into a winning hand. The concept of reversal to A's detriment could also be included here in the form of a shift say from .70/.30 to .30/.70; however, this process is formally the same as that included in Table 2.1 and does not add anything new to the concept of reversal which, of course, does not imply directionality of change.

It should be noted here that increases and decreases in uncertainty are the primary building blocks of changes in power relationships. Thus, in the case of a simple power gain by A, there is a single decrease in uncertainty in the direction favored by A. Also the changes in probabilities occur within a relatively narrow range of values. In the case of reversal there are two changes in uncertainty values. The uncertainty increases initially as the probabilities shift toward equal values while B loses power, and then the uncertainty decreases again as A gains power. An increase in uncertainty is followed by a decrease along lines suggested by the sixth row of Table 2.1. At time t_1 the probabilities are .30/.70, at t_2 .50/.50 and at t_3 .70/.30. In this instance, the changes in uncertainty traverse almost the entire range of probability values.

Finally, we consider two variations that differ somewhat from the previous set in that separate reference must be made to the n-adic condition. This is because certain effects on A derive solely from the gains and concomitant losses of other actors in the system. The first of these variants is the concept of an inverse gain, which is a gain by A solely as the result of B's loss. In this instance, it cannot be said that A did anything to direct the probabilities in his favor but, nevertheless, A gains as the result of B's mistake or some other loss pattern. This process is shown in the next to last row of Table 2.1. In the dyadic case, B loses to the extent of a .20 change in the probability of his winning, and this loss is automatically gained by A despite the absence of any efforts on his own behalf. In the n-adic condition, however, A does not have to be the direct recipient of β's loss. The actor γ can gain and does to the extent of a .10 change in probability as the result of a loss by β, thus leaving A in the same position as he was at the outset.

The reason that the term *inverse gain* is applicable despite the absence of a change in probability for A in the n-adic case may be understood as follows. If β is an opponent of A, then although no immediate benefit accrues to A, still the weakening of an opponent would redound to A's benefit. In the poker setting, if β happens to be a business opponent of A, then any large losses by β, even if not won by A, would still be desirable to him. Similar arguments hold for the concept of inverse loss.[21] Here the opponent β gains, but not at A's expense in the n-adic condition. The power increase of an opponent, of course, would not be desired by A.

Power relations in Table 2.1 were expressed as numerical illustrations for convenience and ease of explication. These numbers are, however, specific cases of general conditions which can be stated in terms of the inequalities— greater than ($>$), less than ($<$), much greater than ($\gg$), much less than ($\ll$)— and equality ($=$). Thus, the control condition in the first row would have the representation $\gg$ with regard to A in all four columns, the constraint condition $=$ in the columns, whereas power gain would be represented as $=$ in the first column and $>$ in the third. The two cases of inversion for the n-adic conditions mechanically require somewhat more complex symbolic representations, but conceptually present little problem.

The latter two examples of n-adic relations are perhaps more indicative of real-world instances of power relationships particularly in international politics. Seldom does a great power gain directly as the result of a loss by a competitive power, except perhaps in the tightest of bipolar zero–sum confrontations. Rather, other countries can benefit or lose from the changes in fortune of a great power and not necessarily an opponent.

Having specified the usages of this concept of power in a variety of possible dyadic and n-adic settings, let us now turn to further examinations of utility in connection with approaches to the understanding of political violence.

---

[21] Although the probability values here in the dyadic condition are the same as in the case of simple power loss, the processes differ. In the case of power loss, A loses through some mechanism initiated by himself, while in inverse loss, it is B who actively gains at A's expense.

Theories of Political Violence

The theoretical utility of a treatment of power may be assessed both with regard to its usage in connection with conceptual categories, such as control or subservience, and in relation to more formal theoretical frameworks. Our concern with the latter centers on the explanation of political violence. In a departure from certain previous definitions, we define an act of political violence as an attempted or actual injury (ordinarily not sanctioned by law or custom) perpetrated on persons or property with the actual or intended consequences of effecting transformations either within structures of political authority or within economic and/or social systems. This definition is said to apply at the levels of local, national, or international political systems. The term *transformation* refers to a fundamental change, however narrow in scope, and should be contrasted with the concept of *translation*, which concerns some movement along an established and legitimate dimension.[22]

[22] Previous definitions either have included all forms of civil strife or have been more narrowly restricted to the process of revolution or internal war. As an illustration of the first type, Ted Gurr defines civil strife as "all collective, non-governmental attacks on persons or property, resulting in intentional damage to them, that occur within the boundaries of an autonomous or colonial political unit [p. 247n]." Harry Eckstein confines his domain primarily to the polity in his definition of internal war as "any resort to violence within a political order to change its constitution, rulers, or policies [p. 133]." See Ted Gurr, "Psychological Factors in Civil Violence," *World Politics*, 20 (January 1968), pp. 245–278; and Harry Eckstein, "On the Etiology of Internal Wars," *History and Theory*, 4 (no. 2, 1965), pp. 133–163.

With regard to the scope of domestic violence, the definition proposed in this volume may be viewed as midway between the definitions of Gurr and Eckstein. The exclusion of attempted or actual translations of the political, economic, or social systems restricts the definition somewhat when compared to Gurr's, but the inclusion of violence directly related to the economic and social systems is more inclusive than the definition proposed by Eckstein. In contrast to both definitions, however, the one I present is constructed to apply also at the level of international politics and to this extent is more inclusive than either. For purposes of application to international violence, the term *structures of political authority* may be interpreted to mean certain structures of the international system which specify norms governing international behavior. General purpose international organizations, treaties, or alliance systems are considered to be structures of this type.

In a subsequent work, Gurr explicitly distinguishes between collective and political violence and defines the latter concept as "all collective attacks within a political community against the political regime, its actors—including competing political groups as well as incumbents—or its policies." See Ted Gurr, *Why Men Rebel* (Princeton, N.J.: Princeton University Press, 1970), pp. 3–4. This definition, however, is said to apply to all forms of riots, which would include attempted translations such as contested area (neighborhood) riots or certain rural food riots.

The coup, as an illegal replacement of personnel within the structure of political authority, is a transformation resulting in a small but fundamental change within that structure. On the other hand, the election of personnel with an ideology differing from that of the incumbent leadership may be understood as a translation, or movement, of the system along a legitimized dimension. A strike leading to violence that was called for purposes of establishing union legitimacy and the right to collective bargaining is an attempted transformation of an economic system. Yet a strike for purposes of increased wages, which was accompanied by violence, would be termed an attempt at the translation of an economic system. Similarly, the recent commodity riots in American cities can be seen as attempted transformations of economic and social systems; whereas the contested area (neighborhood) riots in American cities during the past generation, or certain food riots in rural areas of developing countries, would be seen as attempted translations.[23] Thus, we exclude from consideration those instances of violence which often have been treated as "political," but have neither actual nor intended consequences for the transformation of political, economic, or social systems.[24]

Recent studies of political violence have employed variants of frustration–aggression theory as a basis for the explanation of this phenomenon. For example, relative deprivation as a perceived disparity between value expectations and value capabilities, or the lack of a need satisfaction defined as a gap between aspirations and achievement, in its relationship to political violence generally relies on the psychological state of frustration, and aggressive attitudes emanating from it. The basis for this theory is found in the works of psychologists such as John Dollard and his associates in their pioneering work on frustration and aggression, and in the later research of Leonard Berkowitz.

Political scientists who have employed this approach as a general basis for the explanation of political violence are, among others, James C. Davies, Ted Gurr, Ivo and Rosalind Feierabend, and Douglas Bwy.[25] And these

[23] For the distinction between commodity and contested area riots, see Morris Janowitz, "Patterns of Collective Racial Violence," in Hugh D. Graham and Ted R. Gurr (eds.), *Violence in America: Historical and Comparative Perspectives* (New York: Bantam Books, 1969), pp. 412–444.

[24] This definition effectively excludes many instances of strikes, riots, or protests which would be included in the "turmoil" dimension specified by Rudolph J. Rummel and Raymond Tanter. See Rudolph J. Rummel, "Dimensions of Conflict Behavior Within and Between Nations," *Yearbook of the Society for General Systems Research*, 8 (1963), pp. 1–50; and Raymond Tanter, "Dimensions of Conflict Behavior Within and Between Nations, 1958–1960," *Journal of Conflict Resolution*, 10 (March 1966), pp. 41–64.

[25] See John Dollard, Leonard W. Doob, Neal E. Miller, O. H. Mowrer, and Robert R. Sears, *Frustration and Aggression* (New Haven: Yale University Press, 1939); and

studies already have provided considerable empirical evidence that in certain cases justifies the use of propositions deriving from this theoretical framework. However, there may exist other instances in which objective (exclusive of attitudinal referents) societal attributes and behaviors assume precedence, and in these cases, the present conceptualization of power may be used to derive a theoretical framework which may supplement or replace the frustration–aggression approach. In particular, the *occurrence* of political violence, or frequency as a variable in contrast to intensity and duration, may be better explained by the framework to be introduced. Furthermore, evidence pertaining to Latin American and Sub-Saharan African urban settings challenges the theoretical importance of the "revolution of rising expectations." Competition for jobs and other scarce resources may be of greater importance in explaining political violence in these regions.[26] In addition, there exist difficulties in the use of attitudinal concepts drawn from frustration–aggression theory, such as aspirations or expectations, in the explanation of political violence as behavior.

Leonard Berkowitz, *Aggression: A Social Psychological Analysis* (New York: McGraw-Hill, 1962). The theory of need satisfaction, or the *J*-curve, was originally suggested by James C. Davies in his "Toward a Theory of Revolution," *American Sociological Review*, 27 (February 1962), pp. 5–19. A utilization and test of the theory is found in Raymond Tanter and Manus Midlarsky, "A Theory of Revolution," *Journal of Conflict Resolution*, 11 (September 1967), pp. 264–280. The theory of relative deprivation as applied to civil violence is presented in Ted Gurr, "Psychological Factors"; and a test of the theory is found in Gurr, "A Causal Model of Civil Strife: A Comparative Analysis Using New Indices," *American Political Science Review*, 62 (December 1968), pp. 1104–1124. Both the theory and results of the empirical tests can be seen in Gurr, *Why Men Rebel*.

Ivo K. and Rosalind L. Feierabend systematically employ the concept of societal frustration, which can be seen as a general statement of both the concepts of need satisfaction and relative deprivation. See, for example, their "Aggressive Behaviors Within Polities, 1948–1962: A Cross-National Study," *Journal of Conflict Resolution*, 10 (September 1966), pp. 249–271. The basic theories of these writers also can be found in Graham and Gurr (eds.), *op. cit.*, ch. 17–19.

A somewhat different psychological perspective on the study of political violence is found in David C. Schwartz, "A Theory of Revolutionary Behavior," in James C. Davies (ed.), *When Men Revolt and Why: A Reader in Political Violence and Revolution* (New York: The Free Press, 1971), pp. 109–132. For cross-national studies of political violence with particular importance for Latin American politics, see Douglas P. Bwy, "Dimensions of Social Conflict in Latin America," in Louis H. Masotti and Don R. Bowen (eds.), *Riots and Rebellion: Civil Violence in the Urban Community* (Beverly Hills, Cal.: Sage Publications, 1968), pp. 201–236; and Bruce M. Russett, "Inequality and Instability: The Relation of Land Tenure to Politics," *World Politics*, 16 (April 1964), pp. 442–454.

[26] See Anthony R. Oberschall, "Rising Expectations and Political Turmoil," *Journal of Developmental Studies*, 6 (October 1969), pp. 5–22; and Joan M. Nelson, *Migrants, Urban Poverty and Instability in Developing Nations, Occasional Papers in International Affairs*, no. 22 (Cambridge, Mass: Harvard University Center for International Affairs, 1969).

Perhaps the primary difficulty in the current usage of frustration–aggression theory or its variant, relative deprivation, in political science applications is that it is perceived to be of sufficient generality to provide a basis for the explanation of virtually all forms of aggressive behavior, including political violence. We would not concur with the statement that "there is a certain inevitability about the association between such [relative] deprivation and strife,"[27] or that "the basic relationship is as fundamental to understanding civil strife as the law of gravity is to atmospheric physics."[28] This interpretation of a general applicability has led to a number of difficulties; however, as we shall see later, the theory may have valid specific applications within a probabilistic framework which itself includes certain theoretical constraints.

Problems in the Use of Frustration–Aggression Theory

One can isolate four problem areas in the use of the frustration–aggression approach as a general theory. These are (1) the underlying rationale of the approach, (2) the relationship between attitude and behavior, (3) ambiguous operationalization, and (4) specificity of explanation. Certain of the following limitations of the theory are recognized by political scientists who have used the frustration–aggression approach.[29] However, the qualifications which perhaps should be imposed on its utility for the explanation of political violence generally have not appeared in the empirical applications of the theory, and so for the sake of clarity and completeness, these limitations should be stated. In addition, the following comments are suggested specifically for the application of the theory to political violence and not necessarily to other forms of aggression.

The social-psychological rationale underlying the use of frustration–aggression theory and its variants for the explanation of political violence is not altogether clear. Psychological studies have shown that the occurrence of an aggressive response to frustration may be dependent upon an individual's response hierarchy. If the aggressive response occupies a low position on this

---

[27] Gurr, "A Causal Model of Civil Strife," p. 1120.

[28] Gurr, "A Comparative Study of Civil Strife," in Graham and Gurr (eds.), *op. cit.*, p. 596. In a later work, Berkowitz differentiates between deprivation and frustration, in that the removal of a customary reward is not seen by him to be equivalent to the thwarting of goal-directed behavior. In addition, Berkowitz employs the concept of an "anticipatory goal response." The likelihood of aggression in response to frustration is said to be greatest when the attainment of the goal is anticipated and then thwarted. See Leonard Berkowitz, "The Frustration–Aggression Hypothesis Revisited," in L. Berkowitz (ed.), *Roots of Aggression: A Re-Examination of the Frustration–Aggression Hypothesis* (New York: Atherton, 1969), pp. 1–28.

[29] Probably the best literature review of frustration–aggression theory for its application to the study of political violence, including certain qualifications of the theory, is found in Gurr, *Why Men Rebel*, ch. 2.

hierarchy, then it would have a low probability of appearing as a consequence of frustration. According to Albert Bandura and Richard H. Walters, "Frustration may produce a temporary increase in motivation and thus lead to more vigorous responding."[30] However, a vigorous response need not take the form of aggression, but may instead consist of "dependency, withdrawal, somatization, regression, apathy, autism, or constructive task-oriented behavior."[31] Even cooperative responses have been shown to result from frustration. In a child behavior study, strong friends showed an increased cooperation when frustrated, whereas the same experience led to little change in behavior among weak friends.[32] Other studies failed to demonstrate any significant differences in aggression between frustrated and non-frustrated children.[33] The relief of frustration-induced anxiety, or the correction of a frustration-related dissonance, thus may take many forms, only one of which is the perpetration of violence. Other emotional states such as apathy, can be outcomes of systematic frustration, instead of anger which has been suggested as an intervening variable between frustration and aggression.

The results of the various experimental studies accord with certain elementary observations. There are few persons indeed whose expectations are fulfilled to the extent that they experience no discrepancies between what they have (or expect to have) and what they aspire to have. The great and small frustrations of everyday life are such that if all frustrations, even only large ones, were greeted by violence, then no society could continue to exist as a viable political unit. One can turn the proposition around, as did John Dollard and his associates, and state that although frustration may not always lead to aggression, still "aggression is always a consequence of frustration."[34] However, the proposition in this form is difficult to falsify directly since it depends first on observation of the dependent variable and second on an ex post facto analysis to determine the presence and extent of frustration. Given the broad definition of frustration as the thwarting of goal-directed behavior, then in virtually any context it may be possible to discover some event or process that can be interpreted as frustrating. To restate the problem

[30] Albert Bandura and Richard H. Walters, *Social Learning and Personality Development* (New York: Holt, Rinehart, 1963), p. 135.

[31] *Ibid.*, p. 67.

[32] See M. Erik Wright, "The Influence of Frustration upon the Social Relations of Young Children," *Character and Personality*, 12 (December 1943), pp. 111–122.

[33] See, for example, Suzanne F. Jegard and Richard H. Walters, "A Study of Some Determinants of Aggression in Young Children," *Child Development*, 31 (December 1960), pp. 739–747; and Paul Mussen and Eldred Rutherford, "Effects of Aggressive Cartoons on Children's Aggressive Play," *Journal of Abnormal and Social Psychology*, 62 (March 1961), pp. 461–464.

[34] Dollard et al., *op. cit.*, p. 27.

in terms of social learning theory, we may want to discover the *conditions* under which the aggressive response to frustration is *learned*,[35] and by implication those conditions under which it is not learned, rather than employ the relationship between frustration and aggression as a general theory.

To be sure, intervening variables often are introduced between the frustration variable (relative deprivation) and political violence. Gurr, for example, employs institutionalization, legitimacy, coercive potential, and facilitation as intervening variables.[36] The first three refer to characteristics of the political authority whether in the form of developed institutions, extent of acceptance of these institutions, or the extent to which the government can mobilize forces to quell an insurgent opposition. Facilitation essentially refers to support for the present violence whether in the form of past strife, or the existence and extent of facilitating structures such as a Communist Party. Thus, the intervening variables examined are institutionally or structurally derived, or refer to the past history of violent behavior. This is in marked contrast to relative deprivation defined as a psychological state. Gurr does continually refer to the psychological effect of these variables on the general population. However, the measures chosen (e.g., extent of foreign or domestic origin of institutions and their durability as measures of legitimacy) in themselves generally do not directly reflect the psychological state of the population.[37]

Two questions are relevant here. The first asks whether this approach is a direct explanation of political violence. Essentially, the choice of the intervening variables implies a "funneling" process whereby a general societal frustration finds a narrower focus for action in the form of violence directed at the polity. However, given the presence of variables concerned with political institutions needed to make frustration–aggression theory applicable, might we not choose a more parsimonious approach which directly refers to the political process? The study of access to the political system in the form of political power might be an obvious alternative.

---

[35] For a discussion of social learning in relation to certain political science concerns see Richard M. Merelman, "Learning and Legitimacy," *American Political Science Review*, 60 (September 1966), pp. 548–561. A relationship between social learning and political instability is treated in Manus Midlarsky, "Mathematical Models of Instability and a Theory of Diffusion," *International Studies Quarterly*, 14 (March 1970), pp. 60–84. Other studies that have opted for theoretical approaches which diverge from relative deprivation as a general explanation of political violence are Donald G. Morrison and Hugh Michael Stevenson, "Integration and Instability: Patterns of African Political Development," *American Political Science Review*, 66 (September 1972), pp. 902–927; and Edward N. Muller, "A Test of a Partial Theory of Potential for Political Violence," *APSR*, 66 (September 1972), pp. 928–959.

[36] Gurr, "A Causal Model of Civil Strife," pp. 1104–1106.

[37] *Ibid.*, p. 1115.

In the final analysis, Gurr finds that aside from social-structural facilitation, his combined measure of persisting relative deprivation bears the strongest controlled relationship to political violence.[38] And the indicators upon which the measure of persisting deprivation is based (and do not directly measure it) can be used within other frameworks. Economic discrimination, political discrimination, separatist tendencies, or dependence on foreign capital are such indicators which can be interpreted readily within a framework for the analysis of political power. Finally, even if one accepts the relationship between frustration and aggression as a behavioral regularity, there still exists the inferential leap from frustration to violence, and especially to political violence. The perpetration of injury is only one form of aggressive behavior, albeit an important one, and political violence is an even more narrowly restricted form of aggression. Given the various possibilities for aggressive responses to frustration, the specific choice of political violence must be better understood.

In political science applications of the general theory, the relationship of frustration to aggression often is not tested directly. The use of frustration–aggression theory assumes that the behavior of political violence derives from the attitudinal state of frustrated aspirations or expectations when compared to achievements or perceived capabilities. Yet, the linkage between attitude and behavior frequently is not established. Most often, variables pertaining to the economy and polity are used as measures of attitudinal states. Economic discrimination, political discrimination, separatist tendencies, or dependence on private foreign capital as societal attributes or behaviors are illustrations of measures used to operationalize relative deprivation as a psychological state from which certain attitudes derive.[39] As a result, there exists a discernible slippage between concept and measurement and the validation of theory takes place inferentially.

The basic problem may be one of the adaptation of psychological theories originally suggested for purposes of explaining individual differences to problems of political behavior in the aggregate. As a result, aggregate societal data have been used in statistical tests of hypotheses appropriate to the problem of explaining the aggregate behaviors of political violence, but perhaps inappropriate as measures of the psychological states of individuals.

This problem is not simply one of the "correct" choice of empirical indicators, for if one seeks to explain specific aggregate behaviors such as violence directed at the polity, then a theory based on the perceptions of individuals and one formulated for explaining the behavior of aggression (not political violence specifically) may be less appropriate than other approaches.

[38] *Ibid.*, p. 1121.
[39] *Ibid.*, pp. 1109–1112.

Perceptions and attitudes clearly are of importance in the understanding of certain aspects of political behavior. However, the fact that certain types of aggregate measures have been used almost uniformly in the applications of frustration–aggression theory to the study of political violence indicates not only the practical problems of measurement, but also perhaps the greater statistical explanatory power of these measures.[40] We shall see later that certain of the same measures used for empirical tests of varieties of frustration–aggression theory at the same time could be employed as operationalizations of concepts in the tests of hypotheses emanating from the present conceptualization of power.

Potential ambiguity in the operationalization of concepts may be inherent in the use of frustration–aggression theory and its variants as a general explanation of political violence. Relative deprivation as an example of a frustrating condition is defined as a difference between two perceptions, those of value capabilities and value expectations. We may ask, for example, whether the level of education is to be considered a measure of the perception of capability or expectation. Clearly, greater education represents a form of increased personal capability, but at the same time may inform the individual that given his new educational level, he should expect more than he already has. Or consider a variable such as communications or transportation. When a country increases its communications and transportation networks, it has advanced a societal capability.[41] Yet, increased contacts via communications and transportation to different parts of a country, or to other countries, may have an effect on the expectations of groups in society. No longer can an elite easily maintain its distance from the mass, as well as its high standard of living, when these privileges become visible to the mass of the population. And even without the existence of a privileged group whose affluence could suddenly become visible, communications and transportation could raise expectations simply by virtue of a diffusion effect whereby a population realizes that there are other persons somewhere, perhaps in other countries, whose quality of life is significantly better than their own.

An ambiguity may, in fact, derive from the postulated difference between two perceptions—value capabilities and value expectations—which may allow

[40] The vast majority of applications of frustration–aggression theory to political violence including those by Gurr, the Feierabends, and Bwy, have employed aggregate measures of frustration or relative deprivation.

[41] For an illustration of the use of communications and transportation variables as measures of societal achievement, see Manus I. Midlarsky, *Status Inconsistency and the Onset of International Warfare* (Evanston, Ill.: Ph.D. diss., Northwestern University, 1969); and *idem*, "Measurement and Modeling in the Study of Political Violence" (Paper presented at the 1968 Annual Meeting of the American Political Science Association, Washington, D.C., September 2–7).

for overlap in both conceptual and operational meanings. Indeed, it can be argued that one's expectations concerning future justifiable rewards cannot be entirely divorced from perceptions of present capabilities. Just as time series for continuous monotonic functions often exhibit significant correlations between successive points in the series (autocorrelation), so, too, expectations of what one should have in the future may be dependent on perceptions of current capabilities, as illustrated by a variable such as the level of education. Although the extent of difference between the two perceptions is to be measured, the fact that these are perceptions by the same individual implies some dependence between the two. If, analytically, we were to expect some overlap of the two perceptions, then societal indicators chosen for each would, a priori, be expected to have some dual meaning.

The use of the concept of relative deprivation requires the specification and consistent usage of a referent, but the referent sometime shifts when the theory is put to the empirical test. The theoretical statement of relative deprivation, for example, proposes that deprivation exists in the form of a disparity between the expectations of a group and its perceived capabilities, the referent being its own perceptions of capability. However, the use of economic or political discrimination as measures of relative deprivation implies that the group is deprived relative to other groups in society. One can assume that all groups have equal expectations of the goods and conditions to which they are justifiably entitled and, in addition, the types of perceptions concerning capabilities are the same. Given the adequacy of these assumptions, then if one group perceives itself as having a lower capability of securing its justifiable goods and conditions, the actual deprivation of this group relative to other groups would be equivalent to the disparity between expectations and perceived capabilities. Yet, if over time, a group (slaves, concentration camp inmates, systematically persecuted minorities) is conditioned to believe that it justifiably should expect to receive less than others, its actual deprivation relative to others in society is not equal to its own disparity between expectations and perceived capabilities.

The previous argument suggests that the use of the concept of relative deprivation defined in the form of a disparity between expectations and perceived capabilities should be specific to the group which experiences the deprivation. The use of the national population as a group or unit to explain political violence *within* the nation-state would appear to be unsatisfactory because acts of political violence often are committed by specific smaller groups within the nation. Only certain groups within national societies may experience a relative deprivation, and it is these groups which should be subject to analysis, not the entire population. For example, the American black population may experience a relative deprivation which can serve as an explanation for political violence in that community. However, acts of political violence committed by various white groups may not be subject to the same explanation. One can, of course, abandon societal indicators in tests of frustration–aggression theory and in this way obviate part of the problem. However, the strong empirical relationships established between various of these indicators and the measures of political violence argue that they be retained, but perhaps subjected to some reinterpretation.

The last of our considerations refers to the lack of a differentiation between the specific aspects of political violence for which frustration–aggression theory is suggested as an explanation. A theory or theories for the explanation of the *occurrence* of political violence may differ from those which pertain to the characteristics of the conflict, such as intensity measured by the number of persons killed or duration as a temporal measure. Only those events which occur temporally prior to the onset of the conflict may have any bearing on its initiation in a causal sense, for the variable itself refers only to that moment when the conflict is begun. On the other hand, variables such as the number of deaths during a conflict, or the duration of the conflict, can be dependent upon processes which originate after the conflict has begun. Once under way, the conflict can be governed by processes of escalation, deescalation, attrition, or other interactions which may depend more on strategic options than on sociopolitical variables which indeed may have led to the onset of the conflict. Thus, one would seek to differentiate *theoretically* between the frequency of political violence, on the one hand, and intensity or duration, on the other. Anger as the intervening variable between frustration and aggression indeed may be related to intensity and duration in that the greater the anger, the greater the propensity to continue the violence at whatever cost. But in order to suggest a relationship between frustration or anger and the *onset* of political violence, one must specify the point at which a transition occurs from attempts to effect translations of the system, to attempts at transformation, indicated by the occurrence of political violence.

A Theoretical Framework

Certain of these difficulties may be resolved, not by rejecting frustration–aggression theory, but by modifying it to account for these and other possible criticisms. There exists sufficient empirical evidence confirming the theory in certain instances to suggest its retention and application to political science concerns in a somewhat different form. The following framework is proposed as such a modification. Political violence may occur when a unit (group, national region, or nation-state) has the capability to reduce uncertainty in its environment, but is constrained from doing so, and the uncertainty persists or increases.[42] The unit must be analyzed with regard to its capabilities, and the exercise of these capabilities within its own political context. Thus, for the study of political violence within the nation-state, the group itself must be chosen as the unit of analysis, not the entire nation. Similarly, for the analysis of international warfare, the nation-state can be a unit of analysis. It will be recognized that this framework is based on the definition of power as the ability to reduce uncertainty and the exercise of power as the actual reduction of this uncertainty. Accordingly, if power exists but cannot be exercised for the benefit of a particular unit, force in the form of political violence may result. It should be noted that the preceding constitutes a theoretical framework for the analysis of political violence, not a broad or middle-range theory in the sense of linked propositions and detailed specifications of variables. Rather, certain parameters or boundaries are established by the framework, within which the analysis of political violence may take place. In addition, the concept of *constraint* is not equivalent to *frustration* since the constraint on the exercise of abilities can be the result of voluntary agreements, as will be seen in Chapter III, which concerns alliance-related uncertainty and the onset of war.

A similarity between the present framework and the variants of frustration–aggression theory is the concept of a disparity between two conditions. However, uncertainty here does not generally refer to a psychological state or attitude, but to a societal condition pertaining to a given unit. In contrast to variants of frustration–aggression theory which suggest differences between perceptions, the present approach suggests differences between attributes and behaviors. Given the relatively clear understanding of a behavior as observable action, and an attribute as a determinate property, the possibilities for ambiguous operationalization are lessened.

The capability of a group, national region, or nation-state is viewed here as an objective attribute, and the extent to which it controls its environment also is objective and independent of any attitudinal referent. The framework also is specific to a given unit since it refers only to that group's ability to

----

[42] As a disparity between two conditions, and as a statement which refers only to societal behaviors, the present framework exhibits certain similarities to the proposition that the likelihood of revolution is greatest when political modernization has not proceeded at the same rate as social and economic modernization. See Samuel P. Huntington, *Political Order in Changing Societies* (New Haven: Yale University Press, 1968), p. 265. The concept of dissynchronized development in relation to the onset of revolution can be found in Chalmers Johnson, *Revolutionary Change* (Boston: Little, Brown, 1966), ch. 4–6. In contrast to revolutions, coups d'etat under certain circumstances may occur as the product of a diffusion effect whereby the occurrence of a coup in one country may affect the occurrence of a coup in a neighboring country at a later point in time; see Midlarsky, "Mathematical Models of Instability."

exercise control over its environment and to its actual exercise of control. Rather than allowing a slippage between theory and measurement, one can specify within the framework the kinds of uncertainty which may be related to the onset of political violence. Economic or political discrimination which have been used as measures of societal frustration (relative deprivation) then can be seen as indicators and maintainers of economic and political uncertainty, which next can be compared to the ability of the group experiencing the discrimination actually to reduce this uncertainty. Furthermore, rather than combining the two forms of discrimination with other variables into a single measure of frustration, as has been done in certain cases, one can quantitatively compare the two with regard to the impact of each on the onset of political violence. One can also indicate forms of psychological uncertainty which may be related to the condition of frustration, such that one can *specifically* test the relationship between frustration and political violence. This would seem to be a preferred alternative to frustration as a general (untested) category wherein a single psychological state or attitude becomes a progenitor of all political violence. Thus, we would argue for a framework which explicitly allows for certain inductive procedures, rather than the implicit use of induction in the various operational measures of societal frustration.

The present framework specifies that only those with ability to reduce uncertainty yet are prevented from doing so will initiate violent acts with political intent. As a parametric constraint indicated by the framework, this leads us to exclude from the universe of those who would initiate political violence, groups rendered incapable of controlling their own environment. For example, given this framework, one would not ask why there was a relative absence of slave rebellions in the antebellum South, or why there were few revolts in the Nazi concentration camps, despite the existence of intense frustrations and relative deprivations (even within the slave settings and concentration camps). Whatever capabilities had existed prior to internment were systematically rooted out by a process of atomization and an effective depoliticization, until a state of extreme social disorganization was achieved.

As an obverse statement, one would indeed expect a considerable degree of political violence in developing countries, particularly those with populations experiencing a rapid increase in their capabilities. The greater number of persons with increased education and training skills may not be matched by the number of job openings or other avenues of expression commensurate with these abilities. As such, in many of the countries of Asia, Africa, and Latin America, the revolution of rising *capabilities* may be a more appropriate characterization of a mobilization process with implications for political instability, rather than the revolution of rising *expectations*. The Paretian circulation of elites then may be relevant as a direct explanation of the illegal replacement of personnel within the structure of political authority.

When a particular group has attained sufficient capability to be able to exercise control over its environment, but is continually prevented from doing so, then force in the form of political violence may result. If all non-violent avenues for the control of the environment have been exhausted and there is a constant or increasing discrepancy between ability to control and the actual exercise of control, the group may resort to political violence. If we treat political violence as one type of force exerted in national or inter-national societies, then the present framework specifies a condition under which the transition from the exercise of power to the use of force takes place.[43] The previous efforts to alter the probabilities of events such that there occur concrete or ascriptive recognitions of abilities, are replaced by efforts to determine outcomes in a clear and unambiguous fashion. Thus, a new form of conflict comes into existence in which systems previously ruled by the probabilities for the occurrence of events now are exposed to attempts to make these systems deterministic.

The concept of attributes of the actor in the form of capabilities and that of the availability of choice are central to the present framework. Depending on the specific application, the capability of a group can be defined in the form of specific competencies, achievements, self-esteem, lack of a sense of fatalism, past history of capability, knowledge and information, or simply the capability to bear arms and the availability of such armaments. The concept of choice among various alternative possibilities for the actualization of a goal is indicated by the concept of uncertainty. There exists a variety of possible outcomes, none of which prior to the intervention of the actor in re-ducing uncertainty is substantially more probable than any of the others. Furthermore, there must exist an awareness of the alternate possibilities. When the preceding conditions are met and there exists a prevention of the exercise of ability, even as a result of a voluntary agreement, political violence may be an outcome of this constraint. The preceding description is diagram-med in Figure 2.1. The alternative of political violence is not placed in the same direction as the nonviolent goal, and in fact is orthogonal to it, since the ultimate consequences of political violence often are quite different from the original goal-orientation. An example would be an attempt to reform the

---

[43] The distinction between power and force is found in Hannah Arendt, "Reflections on Violence," *Journal of International Affairs*, 23 (no. 1, 1969), pp. 1–35; and in H. L. Nieburg, *Political Violence: The Behavioral Process* (New York: St. Martin's Press, 1969), pp. 10–11. Certain relationships between power and violence, particularly those found in classical political thought, are suggested by E. V. Walter, "Power and Violence," *American Political Science Review*, 58 (June 1964), pp. 350–360.

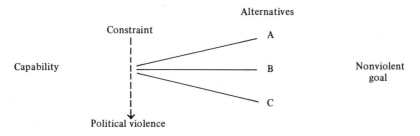

Figure 2.1 **The Prevention of Uncertainty Reduction**

political authority to make it more democratic, which leads ultimately to mass revolution and the possibility of an authoritarian form of government.

Comparisons with Other Frameworks

Whereas the present framework emphasizes the capabilities of actors and the prevention of uncertainty reduction (maximization of the chosen alternative, either A, B, or C), frustration–aggression theory stresses the process of frustration. Since the concept of frustration often is defined as the thwarting of goal-directed behavior, it generally implies the analysis of a "negative" range of behaviors. There exists some process or entity which impedes the goal-directedness of an actor. The emphasis often is (although it does not have to be) placed on the experience of frustration or the frustrating mechanism (e.g., relative deprivation) rather than on the attributes of the actors in the form of capabilities or the available alternatives for action. Although this emphasis is of importance in certain instances, it does not allow for the examination of those cases where the absence of attributes such as an actor's abilities in certain areas is of importance. Frustration–aggression theory would be directly applicable when an alternative was chosen but was then thwarted by some external agency, or if an alternative were forced upon the actor. The thwarting of alternative C is illustrated in Figure 2.2. It should be noted that if capabilities in the form of competencies for social action are absent or removed from the actor and the alternatives for action not available, then frustration–aggression theory may no longer apply. The earlier reference to concentration camps and slave camps, or the atomization and persecution of minorities, could be illustrative of a systematic removal of abilities to organize for effective action and the severe reduction of alternative possibilities for action. Despite the existence of extreme frustration, the relative absence of *political* violence (directed against authority structures) would tend to argue against the applicability of frustration–aggression theory as a general explanation of the absence of political violence in this context.

A further distinction between frustration–aggression theory as it has been understood and the present approach is that this framework allows for the occurrence of violent consequences as the result of certain voluntary agreements. The term *constraint* is not equivalent to frustration, but may include a prevention of the exercise of capabilities with the consent and active support of the actor. This, of course, stands in major contrast to the concept of frustration as the blocking of goal attainment, with the clear implication that the frustrating mechanism is involuntarily applied. The subsequent analysis of power loss in alliance systems illustrates the relationship between the uncertainty associated with alliances as voluntary instruments of national policy, and international war as a form of political violence. As will be argued in the case of major powers, alliances lead to the prevention of the exercise of power as the reduction of uncertainty in times of international crises. Moreover, as will be seen, uncertainties associated with geographical frontiers which are neither voluntary nor involuntary also can result in international violence.

The theory of status inconsistency would appear to be better subsumed within the present framework than in the frustration–aggression approach. Status inconsistency defined as a gap between achieved and ascribed status emphasizes first the capabilities or achievements of actors and then the importance of these actors attributed to them by others. The attribution or ascription of importance, although susceptible to influence by the actor, often is independent of any of his actions and, virtually by definition, he is prevented from directly choosing among available alternatives to maximize his ascription.

In prior research on international warfare, and more recent analyses found in Chapters V and VI, measures of achievement employed are a nation's economic development, population growth, rate of urbanization, and the development of communications and transportation systems. Despite a rapid rate and level of development of these aspects of national achievement, the nation cannot directly and overtly employ them to increase its ascribed importance as measured, for example, by the number and rank of diplomats received by that nation from all other nations.[44] Frustration–aggression theory would indeed account for the feeling of frustration or relative deprivation experienced by decision makers in a nation of high status inconsistency, but would not emphasize the critical attribute of achievement as a form of national capability. Furthermore, the concept of frustration itself as the thwarting of goal-directed behavior would appear to be less applicable

---

[44] See Midlarsky, *Status Inconsistency and the Onset of International Warfare.*

because the concept of a goal in relation to national ascription would seem to be diffuse, and the overt behaviors of nations are not ordinarily directed specifically to the goal of higher ascription.

If we look to the concept of relative deprivation itself as a type of frustration, then the emphasis would be on ascription, to the virtual exclusion of achievement. The perceived discrepancy between value expectations ("the goods and conditions of the life to which they believe they are justifiably entitled") and value capabilities ("the amounts of those goods and conditions that they think they are able to get and keep")[45] can, in this context, refer directly only to a discrepancy in the ascribed condition whereby the justifiable expectation of high ascribed status and the predicted actuality of this status diverge.

This is not to say, however, that frustration–aggression theory in its classic form may not be applicable to forms of aggression other than political violence or to certain types of political violence. Where the aggressive response to frustration occupies a high position in a response hierarchy, and where various competencies are present, frustration–aggression theory may be appropriate to the study of political violence. In addition, the framework proposed here is suggested primarily for the explanation of a specific variable —the onset of violence—because of the probabilistic nature of the framework and the dependent variable (frequency) for which it is suggested as explanation.

The frustration–aggression approach as one type of explanation of political violence is incorporated with others presented in Figure 2.2. For the sake of completeness, certain "direct" approaches to aggression which do not rely on the concept of social choice are indicated. The extent to which these approaches rely on deterministic explanations of aggression is indicated by the darkness of the arrow. The instinctual theory of aggression—that it is innate in man—as proposed by Konrad Lorenz and popularized by Robert Ardrey is represented by the boldfaced arrow.[46] An evolutionary-adaptive approach to the study of aggression has emphasized the need for various species, including man to adapt continually to a changing environment. Aggression and violence can be outcomes of the adaptation process. This approach has been suggested by David N. Daniels and his associates, and in a somewhat different form, by Peter A. Corning.[47] Given a lesser degree of determinism, this perspective is represented by a lighter arrow. Finally, the social learning of

[45] Gurr, "A Causal Model of Civil Strife," p. 1104.

[46] Konrad Lorenz, *On Aggression* (New York: Harcourt, Brace, 1966); and Robert Ardrey, *The Territorial Imperative* (New York: Atheneum, 1967).

[47] David N. Daniels, Marshall F. Gilula, and Frank M. Ochberg (eds.), *Violence and the Struggle for Existence* (Boston: Little, Brown, 1970); and Peter A. Corning, "The Biological Bases of Behavior and Some Implications for Political Science," *World Politics*, 23 (April 1971), pp. 321–370.

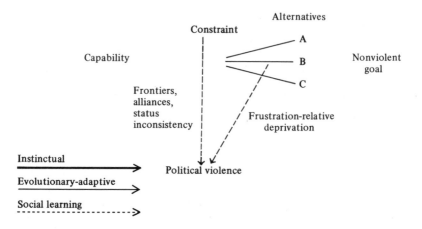

Figure 2.2 **Illustration of Five Approaches to the Study of Political Violence**

violence as the result of prototypical violent behaviors which are observed and imitated would be the least deterministic of this group of theories. The learning of violence, in contrast to environmental effects and instincts for violence, is subject to conscious control and social choice, but once chosen and initiated would lead directly to a form of self-generating violence. The work of Bandura and Walters is representative of this orientation and is indicated by the dotted arrow.[48]

If the preceding analysis is valid, then we should adopt an explicitly relativistic or probabilistic interpretation of the applicability of the frustration–aggression approach or relative deprivation as an explanation of political violence. Frustration is one specific type of constraint, and the *extent* to which frustration can be used to explain political violence may depend on the capabilities of actors. Put another way, the probability that frustrating experiences may lead to political violence could be dependent on specific competencies such as self-esteem or information level.

A Test of the Role of Capabilities

This proposition can be empirically tested in at least one context. In Gurr's analysis of collective violence he finds, using the frustration–aggression approach, thirteen countries which have actual scores on the total magnitude

[48] Bandura and Walters, *op. cit.* For a more recent presentation of this approach, see Albert Bandura, *Aggression: A Social Learning Analysis* (Englewood Cliffs, N.J.: Prentice-Hall, 1973).

of civil strife (TMCS, a composite measure consisting of pervasiveness, duration, and intensity) which differ from the predicted scores by approximately one standard deviation or greater. The extent of collective violence in these countries is least explained by the frustration–aggression approach. Gurr comments, "The lack of apparent substantive similarities among the thirteen poorly-predicted polities suggests that the analysis has included measures of most if not all the general determinants of magnitudes of civil strife."[49]

However, in light of the preceding analysis, one would indeed expect that an association exists between certain attributes of these countries and the extent of explanation provided by Gurr's treatment. As suggested in the analysis of this chapter and in Figure 2.2, the greater the capability or competency with the constraints (as frustrations) held constant, the greater the applicability of frustration–aggression theory. Rather than treating this set of countries as a group of apparently unrelated entities, we would rather now view the residual degrees of explanation (actual minus predicted) as a variable which itself is subject to explanation. Specifically, it is suggested that one ability or competency of populations is educational level, and that this varies directly with the suitability of the frustration–aggression approach. The greater the educational level, the lower the absolute value of the difference between the actual and predicted totals of civil strife, implying the greater applicability of frustration–aggression theory.

The measure of the level of education employed here is a percentage ratio based on the total enrollment at the primary and secondary levels related to the estimated population 5–19 years old, published by UNESCO.[50] The absolute value of the residual prediction is used since we are concerned primarily with the general applicability of the frustration–aggression framework. The number of cases is too small to deal effectively with the question of overprediction or underprediction. A rank order test of the relationship is employed because much of the original data in Gurr's analysis were in coded form, and as a conservative estimate, the absolute value of the residual prediction really should not be viewed as anything but an approximate measure of the extent of explanation. Similar reasoning applies to the rank order use of the enrollment ratio as an approximate measure of the level

[49] Gurr, "A Causal Model of Civil Strife," p. 1118.

[50] The enrollment ratio was used by Gurr as one of his measures of persisting deprivation. However, this prior usage would appear to have little effect on the residuals because the ratio is combined with five other measures as an index of persisting relative deprivation. This variable is then related to other variables which also are composites of five or six measures. Thus, the residual degree of explanation should be little affected by any single indicator upon which the aggregate variables (e.g., deprivation, legitimacy) are based.

TABLE 2.2.   **Residual Prediction and Level of Education for Countries with Least Predicted Civil Strife**

Country	Absolute value of residual prediction[a]	Rank	Enrollment ratio[b]	Rank
Congo (Kinshasa)	17.1	1	40	8
Rwanda	15.5	2	38	10
Yemen	14.2	3	6	13
Paraguay	12.2	4	52	5
Indonesia	9.9	5	35	11
Dominican Republic	9.8	6	48	6
Upper Volta	9.3	7	7	12
Italy	9.2	8	54	4
Ecuador	8.5	9	46	7
Belgium	8.1	10	91	1
Zambia	7.4	11	39	9
Argentina	7.3	12	59	3
Israel	7.1	13	67	2

[a] These values are found in Gurr, "A Causal Model of Civil Strife," p. 1120.

[b] With two exceptions, the values are for the year 1963, which is the midpoint of the 1961–1965 period of Gurr's analysis. The exceptions are Indonesia (1961) and the Dominican Republic (1962), which are the closest years to the midpoint reported in the data source, the *UNESCO Statistical Yearbook, 1965*, pp. 117–137.

of education. In addition, the distributions of the two original sets of data diverge sufficiently to warrant the use of a nonparametric statistic.[51] The data in both original and ranked form are presented in Table 2.2.

A value of the Spearman rank correlation coefficient, $r_s = -.60$, was calculated between the ranks of the two variables. This value is significant at $p < .025$.[52] Thus, there exists an inverse relationship between the level of

[51] The relationship between the enrollment ratio and the residual prediction variable is curvilinear, so that a nonparametric measure of association would give higher absolute values than its linear parametric analogue. The data for residual prediction are found in Gurr, "A Causal Model of Civil Strife," p. 1120; the enrollment ratio values are in the *UNESCO Statistical Yearbook, 1965* (United Nations Educational, Scientific, and Cultural Organization, 1966), pp. 117–137.

[52] This level of significance is stated for a one-tailed test, appropriate for the directional hypothesis of the relationship between capabilities and the applicability of frustration–aggression theory. The table values can be seen in Sidney Siegel, *Nonparametric Statistics for the Behavioral Sciences* (New York: McGraw-Hill, 1956), p. 284. A value of the Kendall Tau $\tau = -.41$ was calculated and also is significant at $p < .025$. To a limited extent we can deal with the question of the direction of explanation by examining only those cases with higher magnitudes of civil strife than predicted by frustration–aggression theory. A value of $r_s = -.60$ was calculated for the ten cases with positive residuals (actual minus predicted), and this value is significant at $p < .05$.

The use of significance tests for populations of countries, or other sets which are generated without regard to sampling considerations, is treated in David Gold, "Statistical Tests and Substantive Significance," *The American Sociologist*, 4 (February 1969), pp. 42–46. Other treatments of the use of significance tests in social science research are found in Denton E. Morrison and Ramon E. Henkel (eds.), *The Significance Test Controversy* (Chicago: Aldine, 1970).

education and the unexplained strife, using the frustration–aggression approach. Put another way, the greater the capability of populations in the form of education level, the greater the applicability of frustration–aggression theory (smaller residual prediction). The extent of explanation provided by this theory appears to depend upon a capability of actors, and when one such ability is employed, a regularity is found among a set of seemingly disparate countries.

The framework proposed in this chapter is in some respects more general than frustration–aggression theory and in others, more specific. The concept of the constraint on the exercise of capabilities can refer to voluntary agreements which lead to violence and can include frustration—the thwarting of goal-directed behaviors—as a specific type of prevention. Capabilities of individuals or populations can refer to various types of competence; however, when one variable is chosen it can be quite specific. The educational level of a population can serve as one measure of the capability to reduce uncertainty, whereas the extent to which this level of education is utilized for the benefit of that population can be a measure of the actual reduction of uncertainty. Within the present framework, education clearly is a capability or attribute. Similarly, the use of education for personal or collective reward is a behavior. Although perhaps other operational problems may be introduced by the choice of this variable, the interpretive difficulties (within the relative deprivation framework) of whether the level of education is an increased capability or expectation tend to be avoided.

The concept of uncertainty itself, which is central to the definition of power, is of very great generality, yet if we choose a probabilistic isomorph of the concept, it has a specific mathematical definition. With the use of this definition, the framework is specific to the *occurrence* (or frequency as a variable) of political violence. The probabilistic uncertainty measures, at least initially, should be related only to other probabilistic measures such as frequency. Once the conflict is under way, whether in the form of riot, revolution, or international warfare, processes other than the sociopolitical may govern the mechanics of the conflict. Note, however, that there could be positive relationships between variables suggested by the framework and the intensity and duration of a conflict if only because actors who engage in a greater frequency of violence also may experience larger values of intensity and duration. Finally, it should be noted that the present formulation places the study of political violence within the realm of explanation of political power. The definition of power itself and its theoretical usage incorporate the state of the polity and society which render those who are able to reduce uncertainty incapable of controlling their environment.

III

Power Loss, Power Constraint, and International Stability

Given the importance of the concepts of capabilities and constraints, as indicated in the formulations of Chapter II, we shall examine both in relation to the onset of one form of political violence—international warfare. When certain capabilities exist, but constraints appear which either voluntarily or involuntarily limit uncertainty reduction, then by these previous arguments, political violence may result. The same outcome of violence may be reached if the constraints are not suddenly imposed, but exist in a relatively constant state over a period of time. It will be recognized that the former instance of the appearance of constraining conditions is an illustration of power loss in Table 2.1, while the constant condition of power constraint is identified as such in that table.

Power Loss and Power Constraint

In the following analysis, alliance formation is considered as an instance of power loss, whereas geographical frontiers serve as power constraints which can lead to violence. Quantitative measures appropriate for each are indicated in the subsequent section, and an alternate approach stemming from theories of international stability suggested by Deutsch and Singer and by

Rosecrance is introduced.[1] Based on these analyses, a logarithmic relationship emerges theoretically between polarity and international conflict behavior, which is then subjected to an empirical examination.

The term *power loss* is used for alliances because of the contrast between the ability to exercise options prior to alliance formation and the relative inability thereafter. The term *power constraint* is employed for the geographical frontiers as relatively constant environmental factors which are much less subject to decision-making options. Alliance-related uncertainty is treated first, followed by the analysis of uncertainties associated with national frontiers.

Alliances bear strong implications for power relationships in international politics and therefore may provide a useful context for the examination of the present conceptualization of power.[2] It is suggested that smaller powers will ally with larger ones to attain a sense of security which they are unable to achieve alone. With regard to the larger power, however, the number of alliances it has entered into and the time spent in alliance represent a degree of uncertainty which may render it incapable of controlling certain events. Once allied with the smaller power, the larger one is committed to protect it in case of war.[3] Yet events within the smaller country often are not subject to control by the larger power, and many of the international interactions of the smaller country cannot be regulated by the larger one. Certain of these events

[1] See Karl W. Deutsch and J. David Singer, "Multipolar Power Systems and International Stability," *World Politics*, 16 (April 1964), pp. 390–406; and Richard N. Rosecrance, "Bipolarity, Multipolarity, and the Future," *Journal of Conflict Resolution*, 10 (September 1966), pp. 314–327.

[2] For relationships established between alliances and war, see J. David Singer and Melvin Small, "National Alliance Commitments and War Involvement, 1818–1945," in James N. Rosenau (ed.), *International Politics and Foreign Policy: A Reader in Research and Theory*, rev. ed. (New York: The Free Press, 1969), pp. 513–542. The formation of alliances is treated in Bruce M. Russett, "Components of an Operational Theory of International Alliance Formation," *Journal of Conflict Resolution*, 12 (September 1968), pp. 285–301; George Liska, *Nations in Alliance* (Baltimore: Johns Hopkins University Press, 1962); and in the various analyses found in Julian R. Friedman, Christopher Bladen, and Steven Rosen (eds.), *Alliance in International Politics* (Boston: Allyn and Bacon, 1970). The classic examination of alliances in relation to the balance of power is found in Hans J. Morgenthau, *Politics Among Nations: The Struggle for Power and Peace*, 4th ed. (New York: Knopf, 1967); whereas the phenomenon of international warfare itself is treated comprehensively in Quincy Wright, *A Study of War* (Chicago: University of Chicago Press, 1942); and in Lewis F. Richardson, *Arms and Insecurity* (Chicago: Quadrangle Books, 1960).

[3] Three categories of alliance commitment may be identified. These are (1) the defense pact, which requires military intervention in the event of an attack on an alliance partner; (2) the neutrality or non-aggression pact, which stipulates neutrality for the other signatories in the case of an attack on one partner; and (3) the entente, which simply requires consultation and/or cooperation when an ally is involved in international military operations. See J. David Singer and Melvin Small, "Formal Alliances, 1815–1939: A Quantitative Description," *Journal of Peace Research*, 3 (no. 1, 1966), pp. 1–32.

or interactions may involve the smaller country in war which then, via the alliance commitment, may include the larger power as well.

In its initial state, prior to alliance formation, each larger country has power in the form of an ability to maintain direct control over its foreign policy decision making and its involvement with other countries. It is relatively free to choose a policy orientation which may maximize its interests short of a war involvement. After alliance formation, however, the uncertainty of the alliance partner's behavior becomes the responsibility of the larger country.

In the case of power loss in alliance systems, there exists prior to alliance formation a relatively high probability that decisions will be made largely at the decision maker's discretion; e.g., .70 in the fifth row of Table 2.1. The probability of external factors affecting the decision is, say, .30. After alliance formation, however, the probability of maintaining direct control could be .50, whereas the probability of an external input from an ally seeking protection in time of war might also be .50. The availability of alternative courses of action is seriously circumscribed in a crisis situation.

To the extent of this increase of uncertainty in its environment, an increased number of alliances constitutes a power loss to the larger country. The relationship of this power loss to war is specified by the following sequence. The power loss is incurred at the moment that the uncertainty of the alliance partner's behavior becomes the responsibility of the great power. An international crisis may be induced by the smaller country, and because of the alliance commitment, the larger power cannot freely choose among alternative courses of action. War may then result for the great power which did not itself initiate the crisis. The interactions between Austria–Hungary and Germany prior to World War I, Poland and Great Britain before World War II, and the involvement of the United States in Indochina may be illustrations of this relationship.[4]

It is hypothesized for a group of nations called the *central powers* that the number of wars they experience should be related to the uncertainty represented by the number of alliances each has experienced and the time spent in alliance. These powers will indeed by the only ones which could incur such a loss because of their initial status as countries with some power capability. Countries such as the United States, the Soviet Union, and Great Britain are included in this category.[5] These countries also have experienced the major

---

[4] Whereas the alliance between Austria–Hungary and Germany prior to World War I is an example of a formal alliance commitment, that between the United States and South Vietnam is not of the same formal variety. Nevertheless, because of the interpretation which U.S. decision makers placed on this country's international obligations, both alliances may have had similar effects with regard to war involvement.

[5] The countries included in this category are: Austria (Austria–Hungary) (until 1919), England, France, Germany (Prussia), Italy (from 1860), Japan (from 1895), Russia,

proportion of alliances and wars found in the international system during this time period. The theory would not be applicable to smaller powers, since within the alliance framework, they are not generally seen as protectors of the larger country's behavior.

Listing of Nations and Wars

Having presented the basic hypothesis, we turn now to a listing of the nations, wars, and alliances included in our statistical universe. Singer and Small, in their analysis of the composition of the international system, list various criteria by which they place countries in the international (total) system and subcategory, the central system.[6] Since the subsequent analysis in this study is dependent upon their precedent, it would do well to review their criteria of compilation.

In order for a nation to be included in the international system, it must have had a population of at least one-half million persons. Such a population threshold excludes politically insignificant countries such as Monaco or Andorra, yet not nations such as nineteenth-century Guatemala or El Salvador. If the population criterion were raised to, say, one million, these latter two countries would be excluded.

The second criterion is that of diplomatic recognition by the two most prestigious nations of this time period—Britain and France. These countries came closest to being legitimizers of the international system; and if a nation met the other criterion, and, in addition, received from the legitimizers a permanent mission headed by an officer at or above the level of chargé d'affaires, then the nation was classified as a member of the system. Beyond 1920, however, this mode of legitimation was no longer employed as a criterion. Between 1920 and 1940, according to Singer and Small, "a state was considered an independent member of the system if it (a) was considered independent according to historical consensus, and (b) either had a population over 500,000 or was, however briefly, a member of the League of Nations."[7]

The distinction between total and central systems is more intuitive and pertains to the extent of a country's participation in European-centered diplomacy. If a country participated in the major alliance systems emanating

---

Spain (until 1914), Turkey (Ottoman Empire), United States (from 1899). These countries were chosen on the basis of their having been centers of international activity in the nineteenth and early part of the twentieth century.

[6] J. David Singer and Melvin Small, "The Composition and Status Ordering of the International System, 1815–1940," *World Politics*, 18 (January 1966), pp. 236–282.

[7] *Ibid.*, p. 247.

from Europe, it was classified as a member of the central system. This criterion also includes countries such as Japan as of 1895 and the United States from 1899. More detailed information on the classification procedure is found in Singer and Small.[8] In addition, a group of countries called the central powers is treated as a subset of the central system. These are the most active countries, both diplomatically and militarily, in the time period under consideration. Table 3.1 presents the countries included in this analysis with dates of entry into the total and central systems, as well as the attainment of central power status.

Our criteria for the listing of wars depend on the characteristics of the participant nations, as well as on the properties of the wars themselves. In order for an international war to have existed, at least one of the protagonists on either side had to be a member of the international system, thus satisfying the requirements that at the time of the conflict it had a population in excess of half a million, and de facto recognition from Britain and France, the legitimizers of the international community. Civil wars are excluded by the requirement of a legal declaration of war between the participants, and colonial wars are omitted by an additional prerequisite that at least one of the sides in the conflict consist of completely sovereign entities.

According to Singer and Small, however, the declaration of war, in itself, is not sufficient.[9] For a nation to be included as a participant, it had to send its forces into the combat zone and must have suffered casualties. Thus, despite the fact that virtually all of the Latin American nations declared war on the Axis Powers during World War II, only Brazil and Mexico sent troops to the combat zone; therefore, of the Latin American countries, only these two are classified as having participated in World War II. Small isolated incidents are also excluded from the listing of wars, as are relatively unopposed occupations. The German occupation of Denmark and the Italian take-over of Albania are cases in point.

Finally, the total number of battle-connected deaths had to exceed 1,000 and be attributable to at least two causes: (1) deaths of military personnel due to combat-related causes such as wounds, gas, or starvation under siege; and (2) deaths of military personnel due to accident, disease, or exposure.

---

[8] Singer and Small differentiate between the total and central system only through the year 1919. In the present study, the central system is carried through 1940 in order to differentiate between nations on the periphery of major international events and those which have been more closely involved; see *ibid.*, pp. 245–248.

[9] J. David Singer and Melvin Small, "The Frequency, Magnitude and Severity of International War, 1845–1940" (Ann Arbor: Mental Health Research Institute, The University of Michigan, August 1965), pp. 10–11. Also see the more recent compilation by these same authors in *The Wages of War, 1816–1945: A Statistical Handbook* (New York: Wiley, 1972).

TABLE 3.1. **Composition of Total and Central Systems, and Central Powers**

	Qualifies as nation-member of total system	Loses membership in total system	Qualifies as nation-member of central system	Qualifies as central power
Afghanistan	1920			
Albania	1914[b]	1939	1914	
Argentina	1841[b]			
Australia	1920			
Austria (Austria-Hungary)	1815	1938	1815	1815–1919
Baden	1815	1870		
Bavaria	1815	1870		
Belgium	1830[b]		1830	
Bolivia	1848[b]			
Brazil	1826[b]			
Bulgaria	1908[b]		1908	
Canada	1920			
Chile	1839[b]			
China	1860[b]		1895	
Colombia	1831[b]			
Costa Rica	1920			
Cuba	1934[c]			
Czechoslovakia	1919[b]		1919	
Denmark	1815		1815	
Dominican Republic	1887[a]			
Ecuador	1854[b]			
Egypt	1936[c]			
England	1815		1815	1815
Estonia	1920			
Ethiopia	1898[b]	1936		
Finland	1919[b]		1918	
France	1815		1815	1815
Germany (Prussia)	1815		1815	1815
Greece	1828[b]		1828	
Guatemala	1849[b]			
Haiti	1859[b]			
Hanover	1838[a]	1866		
Hesse Electoral	1815	1866		
Hesse Grand Ducal	1815	1867		
Holland	1815		1815	
Honduras	1899[a]			
Hungary	1920			
Iran (Persia)	1855[b]			
Iraq	1932[c]			
Ireland	1921[c]			
Italy (Sardinia)	1815		1815	1860
Japan	1860[b]		1895	1895
Korea	1888[b]	1905		
Latvia	1920			
Liberia	1920			

TABLE 3.1 (*continued*)

	Qualifies as nation-member of total system	Loses membership in total system	Qualifies as nation-member of central system	Qualifies as central power
Lithuania	1920			
Luxembourg	1920			
Mecklenburg-Schwerin	1843[a]	1867		
Mexico	1831[b]			
Modena	1847[a]	1860		
Mongolia	1920			
Morocco	1847[b]	1911		
Nepal	1920			
New Zealand	1920			
Nicaragua	1900[a]			
Norway	1905[b]		1905	
Panama	1920			
Papal States	1815	1860		
Paraguay	1896[a]			
Parma	1851[a]	1860		
Peru	1838[b]			
Poland	1919[b]		1919	
Portugal	1815		1815	
Rumania	1878[b]		1878	
Russia	1815		1815	1815
El Salvador	1875[a]			
Saudi Arabia	1927[b]			
Saxony	1815			
South Africa	1920			
Spain	1815		1815	1815–1914
Sweden	1815		1815	
Switzerland	1815		1815	
Thailand (Siam)	1887[b]			
Two Sicilies	1815	1860		
Turkey	1815		1815	1815
Tuscany	1815	1860		
United States	1815		1899	1899
Uruguay	1882[a]			
Venezuela	1841[b]			
Württemberg	1815	1870		
Yemen	1934[b]			
Yugoslavia (Serbia)	1878		1878	

[a] Crossed population threshold.
[b] Recognized by legitimizers.
[c] Released from de facto dependence. (Note that all others had qualified at, or prior to, the 1815 or 1920 dates.)
SOURCE: Reprinted from *The Composition and Status Ordering of the International System: 1815–1940*, by J. David Singer and Melvin Small, WORLD POLITICS, vol. XVIII, No. 2 (copyright © 1966 by Princeton University Press), p. 249. Reprinted in revised form by permission of Princeton University Press.

Military personnel who were wounded or diseased are generally counted as casualties by the belligerents, but are not included in the subsequent tabulations. Table 3.2 presents the listing of wars between 1815 and 1945, using the previously enumerated criteria.

Quantitative Measures

In order to test the hypothesis of power loss in alliance systems and other hypotheses put forward in this chapter, we must have measures of power gain, loss, and constraints, all of which involve the concept of uncertainty. Indeed, the concept of change in uncertainty values is of central importance and, as such, the primary operationalizations are for this concept and its derivatives. A mathematical isomorph $U(X)$, is given in the discrete case by

$$U(X) = - \sum_{i=1}^{N} p(x_i) \log_b p(x_i) \tag{1}$$

where $p(x_i)$ is the probability of occurrence of the ith event x_i, and there are N number of such events. The logarithm is taken to an arbitrary base b. If the probabilities for three alternative outcomes are, respectively, $\frac{1}{4}$, $\frac{1}{4}$, $\frac{1}{2}$, then the uncertainty is, by equation (1)

$$U(X) = -[\tfrac{1}{4} \log_b \tfrac{1}{4} + \tfrac{1}{4} \log_b \tfrac{1}{4} + \tfrac{1}{2} \log_b \tfrac{1}{2}]. \tag{2}$$

For the continuous case, the measure of uncertainty $U(x)$, is

$$U(x) = - \int_{-\infty}^{+\infty} f(x) \log_b f(x) \, dx, \tag{3}$$

where $F(x)$ is a continuous probability density function defined on x. One can prove mathematically that a function of this form is the only one that will satisfy certain criteria of consistency for a mathematical measure of uncertainty.[10]

[10] See E. T. Jaynes, "Information Theory and Statistical Mechanics," *Physical Review*, 106 (May 1957), pp. 620–630. The concept of uncertainty originally was associated with that of entropy in physics. Recently, it has been interpreted, with some notable success, as a measure of information. The first such usage is found in Claude E. Shannon and Warren Weaver, *The Mathematical Theory of Communication* (Urbana, Ill.: University of Illinois Press, 1964). This work incorporates articles first published by Shannon in the *Bell System Technical Journal* (July and October 1948). Norbert Wiener also employs this concept in his analysis of cybernetics, *Cybernetics: Or Control of Communication in the Animal and Machine*, 2nd ed. (Cambridge, Mass.: The M.I.T. Press, 1961). Other treatments are found in Ronald Ash, *Information Theory* (New York: Wiley, 1965); Amiel Feinstein, *Foundations of Information Theory* (New York: McGraw-Hill, 1958); and John B. Thomas, *An Introduction to Statistical Communication Theory* (New York: Wiley, 1969). For relationships between physics and information theory, see Leon Brillouin, *Science and Information Theory*, 2nd ed. (New York: Academic Press, 1962); and *idem*, *Scientific Uncertainty and Information* (New York: Academic Press, 1964).

TABLE 3.2.   **List of Wars and Dates of Occurrence, 1815–1945**

Wars	Dates of occurrence
Franco-Spanish	1823
Russo-Turkish	1828–1829
Mexican	1846–1848
Austro-Sardinian	1848–1849
Danish	1848–1849
Roman	1849
La Plata	1851–1852
Crimean	1853–1856
Persian	1856–1857
Italian	1859
Moroccan	1859–1860
Roman	1860
Sicilian	1860–1861
Mexican Expedition	1862–1867
Colombian	1863
Schleswig-Holstein	1864
Spanish	1865–1866
Austro-Prussian	1866
Franco-Prussian[a]	1870–1871
Russo-Turkish	1877–1878
Pacific	1879–1883
Central American	1885
Sino-Japanese	1894–1895
Greco-Turkish	1897
Spanish-American	1898
Boxer	1900
Russo-Japanese	1904–1905
Central American	1906
Central American	1907
Moroccan	1909–1910
Italo-Turkish	1911–1912
First Balkan	1912–1913
Second Balkan	1913
World War I	1914–1918
Greco-Turkish	1919–1922
Chaco	1928–1933, 1934–1935
Sino-Japanese	1931–1933
Italo-Ethiopian	1935–1936
Sino-Japanese	1937–1941
Russo-Finnish	1939–1940
World War II	1939–1945

[a] From this point on, the wars are included in the status inconsistency analysis.

SOURCE: Reprinted in revised form with permission of the Macmillan Publishing Co., Inc. from "Alliance Aggregation and the Onset of War, 1815–1945," by J. David Singer and Melvin Small in *Quantitative International Politics: Insights and Evidence*, ed. by J. D. Singer. Copyright © 1968 by The Free Press, A Division of Macmillan Publishing Co., Inc. (New York: The Free Press, 1968), pp. 262–266.

For the measurement of the exercise of power gain as a reduction in uncertainty values, we introduce the concept of a difference between two states of a system. Let us define $U_{kt}(X)$ as the uncertainty facing actor k at time t with regard to outcomes X. Temporally or longitudinally we can state that a reduction in uncertainty has occurred when the uncertainty at one point in time t_i is greater than the uncertainty at a later time t_{i+1}. In terms of the uncertainty measures, we can write

$$U(X)_{kt_i} > U(X)_{kt_{i+1}}, \tag{4}$$

where $t_{i+1} > t_i$, or that

$$U(X)_{kt_{i+1}} - U(X)_{kt_i} < 0. \tag{5}$$

The difference between the uncertainty measures over time should be some negative value indicating reduction. Similarly, in the continuous case we require for a reduction in uncertainty that

$$U(x)_{kt_i} > U(x)_{kt_{i+1}}, \tag{6}$$

where $t_{i+1} > t_i$, or that

$$U(x)_{kt_{i+1}} - U(x)_{kt_i} < 0. \tag{7}$$

More formally, we can understand the probability function $f_k(x|t)$ as the distribution of outcomes x facing actor k over the range of the temporal variable t, such that a reduction in uncertainty is effected when the time derivative of the uncertainty measure is less than zero, or that

$$\frac{d}{dt}\left[-\int_{-\infty}^{+\infty} f_k(x|t) \log_b f_k(x|t)\, dx \right] < 0. \tag{8}$$

Let us now consider the concept of maximum uncertainty for both the discrete and continuous cases since they will assume particular importance in the following analyses. When all of the alternative outcomes are equal to one another, say, $\frac{1}{3}$, $\frac{1}{3}$, $\frac{1}{3}$, then the uncertainty is

$$U(X) = -[\tfrac{1}{3}\log_b \tfrac{1}{3} + \tfrac{1}{3}\log_b \tfrac{1}{3} + \tfrac{1}{3}\log_b \tfrac{1}{3}] \tag{9}$$

and, by calculation for any logarithmic base, can be verified to be a larger value than that for the previous illustration (2) with unequal alternative outcomes. Formally, this can be seen as an example of any case involving equally possible outcomes. Only when all of the $p(x_i)$ are equal to each other will the expression (1) attain its maximum value, for if one probability value is only slightly higher than others (one event is somewhat more likely than others), then a slight reduction in uncertainty has been effected. Thus, when all of the $p(x_i)$ are equal to one another, or $p(x_i) = 1/N$, then

$$- \sum_{i=1}^{N} p(x_i) \log_b p(x_i) = - \sum_{i=1}^{N} \frac{1}{N} \log_b \frac{1}{N}$$

and

$$- \left[\frac{1}{N} \log_b \frac{1}{N} + \frac{1}{N} \log_b \frac{1}{N} + \cdots + \frac{1}{N} \log_b \frac{1}{N} \right] = \log_b N$$

or

$$U(X)_{\max} = \log_b N. \tag{10}$$

For the calculation of maximum uncertainty in the continuous case, we refer only to the temporal dimension, since this form of analysis will be applied in the later test of a theory employing these concepts (e.g., years in alliance). When a peak value of the variable is specified ($t = t_M$) and only positive values of t are allowed ($0 < t \le t_M$), then

$$U(t_M) = \log_b t_M. \tag{11}$$

Appendix A includes two separate calculations of this value, the second of which illustrates the concept of a maximum uncertainty upon the transformation of coordinates. For purposes of illustration, equation (11) is graphed in Figure 3.1, for the base e in the natural logarithmic form, $U(x) = \log_e x$ for $x \ge 1$. The most general variables $U(x)$ and x are used because of later reference to this figure in different contexts. It will prove to be useful in examining the consequences of alliance formation and the emergence of multipolar systems with many actors.

Maximum uncertainty has an additional property in the continuous case which is extremely useful for our purposes. We are interested in the change in uncertainty as indicated by the inequality (8) or its simple analogue (7). Put another way, this is the same as asking what happens to an actor upon taking on additional responsibilities which have uncertainty values with regard to eventual outcomes.

Suppose that a given nation-state actor finds itself represented within a coordinate system which at time t defines its set of responsibilities with regard to other nation-states. Let us define this as a linear single axis coordinate system represented, for example, by alliance aggregation or some other representation of international responsibilities linking certain nation-states with one another. Now suppose, in addition, that this linear single axis, called x, is expanded by a given amount to become the linear y coordinate defined by

$$y = ax, \tag{12}$$

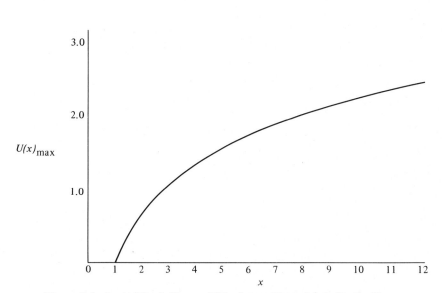

Figure 3.1 **Logarithmic Form of Maximum Uncertainty for the Base** *e*

where the value of *a* is a measure of the change from the *x* to the *y* coordinate. Such a change could be effected by the taking on of new alliance commitments or some other set of responsibilities with uncertain outcomes. The greater the value of *a*, represented, say, by the time spent in alliance, the greater the transformation of the linear coordinate. In the language of mapping, equation (12) states that values of *x* are mapped into the values of the *y* coordinate.[11] Intuitively, this process may be conceived of as a deformation, whereby the *x* coordinate is "stretched" continuously until it reaches the limits of the *y* coordinate axis specified by (12). This process is diagrammed below for the transformation $y = 2x$.

——————   ——————————

x y

The question now is what change in uncertainty has occurred upon this transformation, or given the quantities $U(x)$ and $U(y)$ for the two coordinates, what relationship exists between them. The second part of Appendix A shows

[11] For a clear introductory discussion of transformations and mapping, see Angus E. Taylor, *Advanced Calculus* (Boston: Ginn and Co., 1955), pp. 259–278.

that the difference between the two uncertainty values, $\Delta U(x:y)$, is given by the logarithm of the absolute value of a, or

$$\Delta U(x:y) = \log |a|. \qquad (13)$$

This value, $\log |a|$, is equal to the maximum uncertainty for M, where M is some positive number greater than unity—e.g., equation (11). For values of $|a|$ or M less than unity, the coordinate axis would experience a contraction rather than an expansion. Thus, the notion of maximum uncertainty upon the transformation of coordinates and the straightforward calculation of this value yield the same results. Intuitively, the increase in uncertainty equal to its maximum value can be understood in the following manner. When the coordinate is deformed positively, new points are added to the coordinate line, and no point on the line has a greater probability density value than any other. Equiprobability for all points exists and specifies the use of the maximum uncertainty measure.

The two approaches for calculating maximum uncertainty in the continuous case also are consistent with the concept and measurement of uncertainty in the discrete case. For continuous variables, no point on the line coordinate x or y has a greater probability of occurring than any other, whereas in the discrete case, no particular one of the N outcomes has any greater probability of occurring than all of the others. The two cases are compared below:

Continuous	Discrete
——————	· · · · · · · · · ·
(a)	(b)

In (a) we have the equiprobability of occurrence for all points on the line; in (b) there exists equiprobability of occurrence for all discrete points in the figure.

Test of Power Loss in Alliance Systems

The maximum uncertainty measure is used in both the discrete case of frequency of alliance and the continuous case of time spent in alliance. For the discrete case, the inequality (5) is used. When there is no a priori reason to expect that any particular alliance gave rise to any single war, then among, say, the twenty-two alliances and seven wars experienced by Germany, there is no definite association between specific data points of each of the two variables. As a result, when the data are aggregated in this fashion over the 130-year period (1815–1945), each alliance is as likely to result in war as any other. For this equiprobable case, the measure of maximum uncertainty is appropriate. In addition, plausibility for the use of this measure comes from an original derivation of the mathematical expression for uncertainty. This derivation requires that if there are two separate comparable conditions, such as two alliances or two frontiers, then a final state of uncertainty associated with them must be the sum of the two. The only mathematical function that will satisfy this requirement is the logarithm.[12] Given each alliance as a separate policy condition, we would expect that a total uncertainty value for each country would be the sum of the separate values and that each of the total uncertainties would be associated with the total number of wars. This is precisely what is being tested in the subsequent analysis.

With regard to continuous measures of alliance formation, the concept of maximum uncertainty is applicable according to the same arguments used for the discrete case. In addition, we can apply the argument of the transformation of coordinates in continuous uncertainty space. Using time as a variable, for example, the longer the time spent in alliance by a given country, the greater the linear uncertainty space of the central power engaged in the several alliance organizations, as diagrammed previously for the transformation of one line coordinate into another which is double the original size.

In terms of the inequality (5) for discrete measures of uncertainty, the value

---

[12] This requirement is found in Shannon and Weaver, *op. cit.*, pp. 48–51, 116–118; as well as in Jaynes, *op. cit.*, pp. 629–630. Given a set of equally likely outcomes, then a final state of uncertainty based on q choices must be decomposable into a series of such choices. If we have two separate events 1 and 2, and a third event is said to be a product of the first two, then the final state of uncertainty must be the sum of the two preceding uncertainties, or

$$U(3) = U(1) + U(2).$$

In a set of q choices from u equal possibilities, this implies that

$$f(u^q) = qf(u). \tag{1n}$$

In order to derive an expression for $f(u)$ that will satisfy the requirement (1n), we first differentiate this equation with respect to u and obtain

$$f'(u^q)u^{q-1} = f'(u).$$

A second differentiation of (1n) with respect to q gives us

$$f'(u^q)u^q \log_e u = f(u).$$

Eliminating $f'(u^q)$ from both equations, we can write

$$f'(u)u \log_e u = f(u)$$

or that

$$\frac{df(u)}{f(u)} = \frac{du}{u \log_e u}.$$

Integrating both sides of this equation yields

$$\log_e f(u) = \log_e (\log_e u) + \text{Constant}$$

or that

$$f(u) = K \log_e u.$$

of $U(X)$ at the beginning of the time period can be set equal to zero for convenience. This is justified in light of no alliances existing in 1815 at the end of the Napoleonic Wars, and the alliance-related uncertainty, therefore, also is equal to zero.[13] Thus, setting $U(X)_{kt_i} = 0$, we have from (5)

$$U(X)_{kt_{i+1}} < 0 \qquad\qquad (14)$$

in the case of a decrease in uncertainty, but for the hypothesis of a power loss carrying with it an increase in uncertainty, we have

$$U(X)_{kt_{i+1}} > 0. \qquad\qquad (15)$$

The uncertainty over the time period examined here, 1815–1945, should have some positive value. By equation (10), and the previous arguments, this positive value is hypothesized to be

$$U(X)_{max} = \log_b N.$$

An entirely analogous set of expressions exists for the continuous case, beginning with the inequality (7).

The alliance indicators and the uncertainty measures based on them are each three in number. These are the number of alliances, number of defensive alliances, and years in alliance. Defensive alliances represent a stronger commitment than do other forms of alliance agreement and should be differentiated from the total number. The variable years in alliance introduces a continuous temporal dimension which should be compared to frequency. These variables, as well as the frequency of war, are listed in Table 3.3.

The procedure for the test of the hypothesis is as follows. The alliance variables and the uncertainty measures based on each are correlated with the frequency of war for the central power nations. Variables such as the intensity and duration of war are not treated here because they pertain to characteristics of the conflict itself. Once under way, the conflict can be governed by processes of escalation, deescalation, attrition, or other interactions which may depend more upon strategic options than upon sociopolitical variables which may have led to the onset of the conflict.

If the hypothesis has validity, then the uncertainty measures as logarithms of the alliance indicators for the central powers should demonstrate a higher correlation with the frequency of war than the indicators themselves. In addition, the results of a partial correlation analysis should support the independent effect of the uncertainty measures on the frequency of war.

The results are presented in the form of a correlation matrix to indicate the relationships among the alliance indicators and uncertainty measures, as

---

[13] The logarithm of zero is undefined, and so a convention must be adopted for those instances when no alliances exist. Thus, for values of alliance formation less than unity $(0 < z < 1)$, the function $z \log z$ is defined equal to zero in the limit as z approaches zero through positive values.

TABLE 3.3.   **Alliance Variables and the Frequency of War, 1815–1945**

	No. alliances[a]	No. defensive alliances	Years in alliance	No. wars
Afghanistan	4	1	19	0
Albania	1	1	14	0
Argentina	2	0	7	1
Australia	0	0	0	1
Austria (Austria-Hungary)	17	8	106	7
Baden	2	2	55	2
Bavaria	2	2	55	2
Belgium	1	1	17	2
Bolivia	2	1	15	2
Brazil	2	0	7	2
Bulgaria	4	2	13	4
Canada	0	0	0	1
Chile	2	0	7	2
China	2	1	10	5
Colombia	3	1	8	1
Costa Rica	1	0	4	0
Cuba	1	0	4	0
Czechoslovakia	7	5	20	0
Denmark	1	0	1	2
Dominican Republic	1	0	4	0
Ecuador	3	2	8	1
Egypt	1	1	4	0
England	16	8	71	5
Estonia	4	1	17	0
Ethiopia	0	0	0	2
Finland	2	0	8	2
France	20	9	69	9
Germany (Prussia)	22	10	111	7
Greece	7	3	15	6
Guatemala	1	0	4	2
Haiti	1	0	4	0
Hanover	1	1	28	1
Hesse Electoral	1	1	51	1
Hesse Grand Ducal	1	1	51	1
Holland	0	0	0	1
Honduras	1	0	4	2
Hungary	3	0	13	1
Iran (Persia)	4	0	14	1
Iraq	2	1	8	0
Ireland	0	0	0	0
Italy (Sardinia)	21	5	50	11
Japan	6	1	30	7
Korea	0	0	0	0
Latvia	4	1	17	0

SOURCE: Reprinted in revised form with permission of the Macmillan Publishing Co., Inc. from " Alliance Aggregation and the Onset of War, 1815–1945," by J. David Singer and Melvin Small in *Quantitative International Politics: Insights and Evidence*, ed. by J. D. Singer. Copyright © 1968 by The Free Press, A Division of Macmillan Publishing Co., Inc. (New York: The Free Press, 1968), pp. 262–266, 268–271.

TABLE 3.3 (*continued*)

	No. alliances[a]	No. defensive alliances	Years in alliance	No. wars
Liberia	0	0	0	0
Lithuania	2	0	14	0
Luxembourg	0	0	0	0
Mecklenburg-Schwerin	1	1	23	1
Mexico	2	0	7	3
Modena	2	2	14	0
Mongolia	1	1	4	0
Morocco	0	0	0	2
Nepal	0	0	0	0
New Zealand	0	0	0	1
Nicaragua	1	0	4	1
Norway	0	0	0	1
Panama	2	0	4	0
Papal States	0	0	0	2
Paraguay	2	0	7	1
Parma	2	2	10	0
Peru	3	2	17	2
Poland	4	2	19	1
Portugal	3	2	29	1
Rumania	11	6	51	3
Russia	32	9	91	8
El Salvador	1	0	4	3
Saudi Arabia	1	1	3	0
Saxony	1	1	51	1
South Africa	0	0	0	1
Spain	6	1	35	5
Sweden	0	0	0	0
Switzerland	0	0	0	0
Thailand (Siam)	0	0	0	1
Two Sicilies	0	0	0	2
Turkey	16	6	30	9
Tuscany	1	1	2	0
United States	2	0	6	5
Uruguay	2	0	7	0
Venezuela	1	0	4	0
Württemberg	2	2	55	2
Yemen	1	1	3	0
Yugoslavia (Serbia)	12	7	38	4

[a] For the analysis of the central powers, the variables are adjusted to account for the time a given nation enjoyed that status.

NOTE: The alliance variables are based on the number of alliance organizations to which the country belonged, rather than the number of country allies.

well as between these variables and the frequency of war. Table 3.4 presents the correlation matrix for the period 1815–1945. It can be seen that the values for the uncertainty measures are greater than those for the alliance indicators themselves.

As a means of visually ascertaining the goodness of fit of at least one of the

TABLE 3.4. **Product-Moment Correlation Coefficients among Alliance Indicators, Uncertainty Measures, and the Frequency of War for the Central Powers, 1815–1945**

	No. alliances	$U(X)_{max}$, No.	No. defensive alliances	$U(X)_{max}$ Def.	Years in alliances	$U(t_M)$	Frequency of war
No. alliances	1.00						
$U(X)_{max}$, No.	.95	1.00					
No. defensive alliances	.84	.88	1.00				
$U(X)_{max}$, Def.	.85	.94	.97	1.00			
Years in alliance	.72	.76	.88	.84	1.00		
$U(t_M)$	.75	.87	.84	.88	.92	1.00	
Frequency of war	.72	.81	.59	.71	.40	.58	1.00

variables, the uncertainty measure for the number of alliances is graphed versus the number of wars. The plot is quite linear. Despite the regularity of the plot, however, we must consider the possibility of a spurious relationship arising from the dominance of a linear component. That is, alliances themselves may contribute directly to the onset of war, as is found in the work of Singer and Small, and this linear association may make a major contribution to the values found in Table 3.4. (The plot in Figure 3.2 is linear with respect to the uncertainty measures but not, of course, with regard to the number of alliances.) Thus, the variable alliance formation itself must be controlled, and as a result, we use partial correlations in which the values for the number of alliances or time spent in alliance are held constant while assessing the relationships between the uncertainty measures and war.

For the three uncertainty measures, the values of the partial correlation coefficients are .58, .70, and .59, respectively, for the relationships among the logarithms of the number of alliances, number of defensive alliances, and years in alliance, on the one hand, and the frequency of war, on the other. These values are significant at $p \leq .05$ for those who would be interested in significance levels as a criterion of acceptability for populations of countries.[14]

The interpretation of our findings now must be made within the framework of the three variables, alliances, uncertainty, and the frequency of war. Until now, the hypothesis has been in the form of alliances resulting in uncertainty,

[14] One-tailed tests are employed in accordance with the directional hypotheses of the theory. The tabled values for correlation coefficients at the .05 and .01 significance levels are found in Helen M. Walker and Joseph Lev, *Statistical Inference* (New York: Holt, Rinehart, 1953), p. 470. The reader is also referred to the various treatments of this question in Denton E. Morrison and Ramon E. Henkel (eds.), *The Significance Test Controversy* (Chicago: Aldine, 1970).

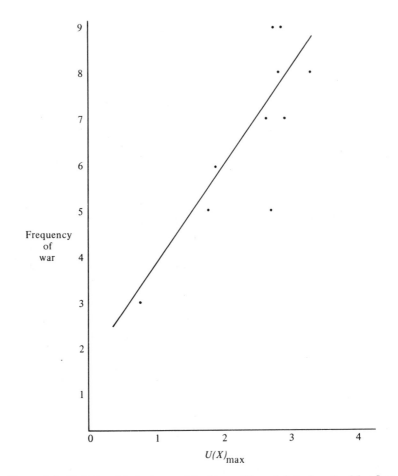

Figure 3.2　**Relationship between Maximum Uncertainty for the Number of Alliances and the Frequency of War, 1815–1945**

which then leads to war. The power loss is incurred at the moment that the alliance is formed, for it is at this time that the uncertainties of the alliance partner's behavior may begin to affect the central power.

However, the relationship between the uncertainty measures and the frequency of war is subject to a different interpretation. The formation of alliances prior to a war may be indicative of an uncertainty experienced by the potential alliance partners. The coming of a war may be sensed by policy makers, and an atmosphere of uncertainty may develop which leads to a quest for security by means of an increased number of alliances. Thus, in this second interpretation, the uncertainty exists prior to the formation of alliance systems, in contrast to the previous model, which suggests that uncertainty follows alliance formation.

There is a method, causal inference analysis, by which we may investigate which of the two models has greater empirical validity. Although the partial correlations indicate that the uncertainty measures bear significant relationships to the frequency of war, they do not specifically indicate which of the two models is preferable. Table 3.5 presents a causal inference analysis of both models.[15] For the analysis of the first model, the uncertainty measures are the intervening variables between alliance formation and the frequency of war; whereas in the second, the alliance indicators are the intervening variables. The last column presents the differences between observed and predicted values. These differences, which are consistent across the indicators, suggest that the first model—uncertainty following alliance formation—has greater empirical validity.

These results add support to our conclusion that there is an alliance-related uncertainty which comes into existence after the alliance is formed and, in turn, is positively associated with the frequency of war. Alliances may be formed as a result of certain intentions of decision makers (e.g., ideological, or reactions to perceived threat), and then a degree of uncertainty is added to the environment of the central power which has accepted the new ally. In

TABLE 3.5.   **A Causal Inference Comparison of Two Models**

I.
Alliances $(X_1) \rightarrow$ Uncertainty $(X_2) \rightarrow$ War (X_3)

Prediction	Deduction		Results	Differences
		No. alliances	.72 vs. (.95)(.81) = .77	.05
$r_{13.2} = 0$	$r_{13} = r_{12}r_{23}$	No. defensive	.59 vs. (.97)(.71) = .69	.10
		Years	.40 vs. (.92)(.58) = .53	.13

II.
Uncertainty $(X_2) \rightarrow$ Alliances $(X_1) \rightarrow$ War (X_3)

Prediction	Deduction		Results	Differences
		No. alliances	.81 vs. (.95)(.72) = .68	.13
$r_{23.1} = 0$	$r_{23} = r_{12}r_{13}$	No. defensive	.71 vs. (.97)(.59) = .57	.14
		Years	.58 vs. (.92)(.40) = .37	.21

[15] Prior applications of causal inference analysis to the study of political violence are found in Ted Gurr, "A Causal Model of Civil Strife: A Comparative Analysis Using New Indices," *American Political Science Review*, 62 (December 1968), pp. 1104–1124; and in Manus Midlarsky and Raymond Tanter, "Toward a Theory of Political Instability in Latin America," *Journal of Peace Research*, 4 (no. 3, 1967), pp. 209–227. For general treatments of this method, see Hubert M. Blalock, Jr., *Causal Inferences in Nonexperimental Research* (Chapel Hill: University of North Carolina Press, 1964); and Herbert A. Simon, *Models of Man* (New York: Wiley, 1957).

the following analysis of uncertainty associated with geographical frontiers, there will be much less need to distinguish between two rival explanations for the findings.

Test of Power Constraints in Geographical Frontiers

Whereas alliances constitute policy commitments which carry with them uncertainties for central powers, there may exist geographical constraints in the form of boundaries with other nations which also lead to environmental uncertainties. On the one hand, alliances via their uncertainties may result in a power loss, while on the other, the number of borders a nation has with surrounding countries may serve as power constraints in the form of continual uncertainties associated with them.

The sequence of events in this instance is comparable to that found in the case of alliances. A central power shares a common border with another, generally smaller, country, and events within that country are not under the direct control of the larger country. Over a period of time, there is a probability greater than zero that there will occur an event such as the emergence of a regime hostile to the larger country or the alliance of one neighboring country with a competitor major power. International violence may be a consequence of this activity. Clearly, this finite probability would be equal to zero if no such frontiers existed. Thus, the probability of international violence resulting from these behaviors would also be equal to zero. These probabilities, in turn, translate into a given uncertainty value for each major power with a number of land borders greater than zero and, as in the treatment of alliances, should be associated with the number of wars experienced by central power nations. Examples of the relationships suggested here would be the long period of conflict of both Russia and Germany with surrounding countries on all sides of their respective frontiers.

In Table 2.1 (Chapter II) the condition of power constraint is represented by a constant uncertainty. This condition is formally indicated by the inequality

$$U(X)_{kt_{i+1}} > 0. \tag{16}$$

Operationally, this test is identical to the one used in the analysis of power loss in alliance systems. In contrast to the case of alliance formation, however, the expression (16) is indicated directly by the constraint condition. The difference between the two empirical tests resides in the assumptions required. In the case of alliance-related uncertainty we assumed, based on the historical evidence in 1815, that $U(X)_{kt_i} = 0$. Here, in the test of the effects of power constraints, no such assumption, however valid, is needed, and by equation

(10), along with the previous arguments, the value of this uncertainty in relation to war is hypothetically,

$$U(X)_{\max} = \log_b N.$$

The variables here are the number of borders for each central power and the associated uncertainty values. Data for the frontiers are found in Richardson,[16] and the values for the number of wars are the same data used in the previous analysis of alliance-related uncertainty.

A product-moment correlation coefficient was calculated for the central powers and is equal to $r = .84$ for the relationship between the uncertainty associated with the number of borders and the frequency of war.[17] This relationship is plotted in Figure 3.3 and is regular, as is the plot in Figure 3.2.

When a control is incorporated for the relationship between the number of frontiers themselves and the number of wars, the value of the partial correlation between the uncertainty and war is equal to .69. This value is significant at $p \leq .05$, again, for those who would be interested in significance levels for populations of countries.

We note the similarity in value between this partial correlation and that for the relationship with defensive alliances and the onset of war (partial $r = .70$). Both values lie at the upper end of magnitudes for the controlled relationships obtained in this study. Apparently, the stronger the commitment between the source of uncertainty and the central power, either in the form of fixed (defensive as the strongest) policy commitments or fixed geographical constraints, the stronger the relationship between the uncertainty values and the onset of war.

This similarity serves as one type of validation for the entire analysis. For only in the case of virtually inescapable commitments or adjacencies do we find the highest magnitudes of relationships between the uncertainty values and war, as suggested by the initial theory. Additionally, in the present analysis there is much less need to differentiate between the two cases of uncertainty preceding or following the geographical condition. National borders are relatively constant over time, and whatever uncertainty is associated with the geographical condition is far more likely to have been a consequence of the frontiers than their antecedent.

[16] See Lewis F. Richardson, *Statistics of Deadly Quarrels* (Chicago: Quadrangle Books, 1960), p. 177.

[17] The island nations of Great Britain and Japan were omitted from this analysis. The effect of frontiers as power constraints would operate differently for sea powers than for countries with at least one land border. In the former instance, decision makers would have certain options open as to whether to seek contact with other countries. These alternatives would not be available to countries which have neighbors immediately adjacent to themselves.

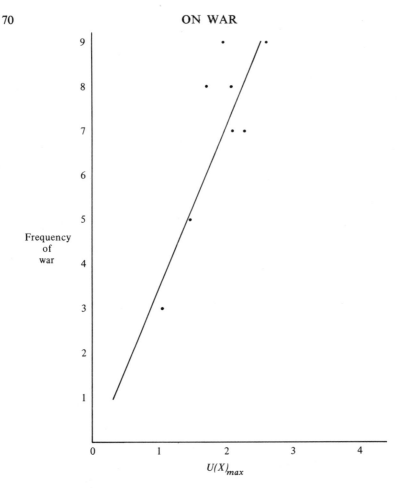

Figure 3.3 **Relationship between Maximum Uncertainty for the Number of Borders and the Frequency of War, 1815–1945**

An additional observation of this type comes from inspection of the vertical intercepts in Figures 3.2 and 3.3, in the manner of Richardson.[18] When the two plots are extrapolated to zero values of uncertainty or $U(X)_{max} = 0$, then in the case of alliance-related uncertainty, the value for the number of wars is approximately equal to two, whereas that for the frontiers is about equal to zero. This finding is consistent with the observation that a certain number of wars can result from origins other than alliance formation; the zero number of wars associated with zero uncertainty in the analysis of

[18] See Lewis F. Richardson, *Arms and Insecurity, op. cit.*, p. 33.

frontiers suggests that war will occur for land-bordered nations only when the uncertainty associated with common frontiers is greater than zero. The existence of common borders, therefore, may verge on being a necessary condition for international warfare, yet alliances may be more remote from this concept of necessity.

The historical evidence indicates that with the exception of a small number of wars between countries sharing a common sea border (e.g., Sino-Japanese, 1895), or overtly colonial ventures, such as the Mexican Expedition by France in 1862, virtually all wars have begun across a land border between two countries, or their colonial extensions. Indeed, even World Wars I and II as global conflicts began with disputes between adjacent countries—Austria-Hungary and Serbia in 1914, and Germany and Poland in 1939. Thus, extrapolations as deductions from analyses found in this study are consistent with the historical record.

Relationships with Theories of International Stability and Polarity

These findings suggest certain relationships with theories of international stability expressed by Karl Deutsch and J. David Singer, and by Richard Rosecrance.[19] In their well-known treatment of international stability, Deutsch and Singer argue that the increase in the number of new nations since World War II increases the interaction opportunity of nation-states and in this fashion decreases the share of attention that any great power can direct at another in an intense bipolar confrontation. The authors, however, did not direct their attention to the effect of this interaction opportunity on the number of wars, as is found in the theoretical work of Rosecrance. According to Rosecrance, bipolarity may lead to intense conflicts but fewer wars, while in multipolar systems the number of wars may be greater, but each is of lesser intensity than in the bipolar case. Michael Haas empirically confirmed this understanding of the effects of each system type on international stability.[20]

Now, suppose we combine the formal expression for possible conflicting pairs used by Deutsch and Singer with the concept of a greater frequency of war in multipolar systems proposed by Rosecrance. The expression for the number of interaction opportunities employed by Deutsch and Singer can be used as a measure of the potential for war in a multipolar system with a number of poles less than or equal to the number of independent international

---

[19] Deutsch and Singer, *op. cit.*; Rosecrance, *op. cit.*

[20] Michael Haas, "International Subsystems: Stability and Polarity," *American Political Science Review*, 64 (March 1970), pp. 98–123.

actors.[21] Each actor can have a hostile interaction with any other, as specified by the $N(N - 1)/2$ possible dyadic pairs, and this value should be positively related to the number of wars, as suggested by Rosecrance.

The particular functional form of such a relationship is suggested by the present analysis. It would be unrealistic to assume that *all* of the $N(N - 1)/2$ possible interactions would lead to war. Rather, we should consider only readily available ones such as those specified by alliances or neighboring countries and exclude distant ones, as between Dahomey and Peru. Even the available interactions, however, do not have to lead to war. There is, in fact, an uncertainty operating as to which particular ones of the available inter-acting dyads will experience conflict and possibly war. Thus, we can ask the realistic question of which of the available $N(N - 1)/2$ dyads will experience war under conditions of an a priori uncertainty as to the precise conflicting pairs and an equiprobability for any of the available pairs leading to war. Equiprobability is a necessary assumption here, since on an a priori basis we would have no way of knowing which of the pairs have significantly greater likelihoods of war than others. According to equation (10) this question is answered by[22]

$$\log [\text{number of possible dyads}] = \log \left[\frac{N(N - 1)}{2}\right] \tag{17}$$

where N is the number of available countries, such as bordering nations as in the analysis of power constraints, or alliance partners that might bring a central power into war.

To see the connection between (17) and the present analysis, we expand it and obtain

$$\log \left[\frac{N(N - 1)}{2}\right] = \log N + \log (N - 1) - \log 2. \tag{18}$$

For large enough N, the righthand side of (18) can be approximated as

$$2 \log N - \log 2 \tag{19}$$

or

$$k \log N - k'. \tag{20}$$

Even for smaller values of N, the magnitude of difference between (18) and (19) is not very great. Inspection of (20) indicates that it differs from (10)

[21] Multipolarity, for purposes of treating international conflict behavior, is here understood as a condition existing within a group of nation-states which allows for the possibility of severe conflict or war occurring between any of the dyadic pairs. This view stands in contrast to that of the more hierarchically organized bipolar system that would permit few, if any, major conflicts between subordinate actors, especially within the same bloc.

[22] The base b is omitted from subsequent logarithmic expressions, but is implied for all of them.

only by a constant factor with the functional form exactly the same. Therefore, if we ask a somewhat different research question here than in the analysis of power loss and power constraint, we arrive at the same functional form.

The concept of the uncertainty of which available dyad can lead to war, as suggested by theories of international stability, has a similar outcome to that emerging from the power framework. Theoretically, of course, there are differences in that the alliances and borders as power limitations do not suggest that any available dyad can lead to war; only those relationships concerning alliances, or between a central power and surrounding countries are indicated. In practice, however, for a given value of N, limitations or expansions of the number of dyads available for conflict would not in any way alter the functional form of a logarithmic relationship, but would simply affect the value of the constant k, as explained below.

The lower limit on the number of conflict pairs available for a central power is equal to N in the case of the N number of bordering nations, or some other defining context which includes N number of independent actors. There can be no fewer possible conflicts for a central power than the number of bordering nations available to that power and in this case, k would be equal to unity and k' equal to zero, as in equation (10). Any additional possible interactions adding to the number of conflicting pairs among the bordering nations, for example, will contribute to the value of k whose upper bound is specified by the maximum number of conflicting pairs equal to $N(N - 1)/2$. This value of k is approximately equal to 2, as in the expression (19). Thus, with N fixed, the value of k varies between unity and 2 depending on the number of available dyads, and in no way is the functional logarithmic form affected. The correlations expressed in Figures 3.2 and 3.3, in which $U(X)_{max}$ is equal to log N, therefore, could have been obtained through an alternate approach deriving from theories of international stability.

For each value of N, there is a variable number of possible dyadic pairs, up to and including the value of $N(N - 1)/2$. Now, suppose we allow N itself to vary, not simply in a multipolar condition as before, but over the entire range of values in unipolar, bipolar, and multipolar systems. Each of the polar actors can engage in conflict with any of the others either singly or in hierarchically arranged blocs as in the bipolar condition. Given the results of this study, then, what are the possible consequences of these various systems for international stability?

Figure 3.1 may be useful for our purposes initially because it represents the increase in uncertainty upon supplying additional units to a system. As was indicated in Figure 3.1, the greatest increase in uncertainty—and given the findings of this study, also the greatest increase in the probability of war—appears with the emergence of the second unit, or for our purposes, international pole, and begins to dampen as successively larger numbers of polar actors are added to the system. The existence of relatively strong associations between uncertainty and war in two instances enables us in turn simply to adapt Figure 3.1 into a relationship between polarity and the frequency of war[23] as shown in Figure 3.4.

This plot is consistent with Morton Kaplan's concept of the relative stability of hierarchical or unipolar systems ($N = 1$, $U(x) = 0$, frequency of war $= 0$), and the concomitant instability of systems with larger numbers of actors.[24] The greatest increase in the danger of war would appear upon the initial emergence of a bipolar system, with a somewhat lesser increment when the first or second polar actor is being added to the bipolar setting to form a multipolar system. This largest increase in the probability of war when a bipolar system is formed suggests Organski's concept of the extreme instability inherent in the emergence of a challenger to the dominant nation or bloc in a stratification system.[25] The relationship expressed in Figure 3.4 also is consistent with Haas' finding of a greater frequency of war in multipolar systems than in bipolar ones,[26] although as suggested in the figure, the addition of polar actors beyond the first few would add disproportionately less danger of war than the earlier ones.

In order to test this hypothesis of a logarithmic relationship between polarity and international conflict behavior, descriptions of the polarity of systems, as well as the number of major powers in multipolar systems found in Rosecrance,[27] are used to arrive at the polarity variable. Data

[23] The same logarithmic relationship would exist if the vertical axis were to be expanded or contracted by a constant amount, and so numerical values are omitted for the frequency of war.

[24] See Morton A. Kaplan, *System and Process in International Politics* (New York: Wiley, 1957), pp. 49–50.

[25] A. F. K. Organski, *World Politics*, 2nd ed. (New York: Knopf, 1968).

[26] Haas, *op. cit.*

[27] This relationship is evaluated from the first war listed in the source for the dependent variable—Singer and Small, *Wages of War*, pp. 60–69—to the end of World War II. This later source was used here for purposes of utilizing the most recent published information, while the earlier Singer and Small work, "Alliance Aggregation and the Onset of War, 1815–1945," was employed for the alliance and war analysis because of the presence of both data sets in the same publication, implying similar collection and reliability procedures for both.

The post-1945 period is not yet "closed" with regard to the number of wars that could be experienced and is omitted, as in the rest of the analyses of war. With regard to the polarity variable, a coding decision had to be made with respect to the period 1822–1848 treated by Rosecrance as "quasi-bipolar" in his *Action and Reaction in World Politics: International Systems in Perspective* (Boston: Little, Brown, 1963), p. 246. Given his description of that system, it was given a value of 1.5 on the independent variable. The remaining polarity values are defined numerically in this data source.

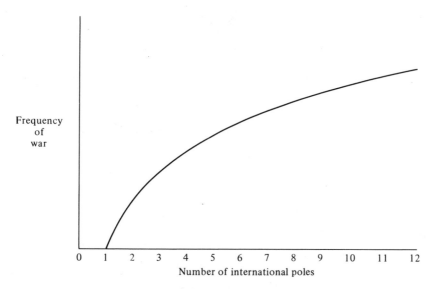

Figure 3.4 **Theoretical Logarithmic Relationship between Polarity and International Warfare**

for the number of wars are found in Singer and Small.[28] Figure 3.5 represents this relationship, which upon inspection conforms rather closely to the one suggested theoretically in Figure 3.4 for the area of correspondence of five international poles.

A chi-square "goodness of fit" comparison between the two was performed. Values of the natural logarithm were calculated for the predicted number of wars based on the number of international poles, and normalized for these data. When these theoretical values were compared to the observed number of wars, a $\chi^2 = 3.346 \, (df = 3)$[29] was found. This value has a probability between 30 and 50 times in 100 of having occurred by chance alone, and so there is no significant difference between the predicted logarithmic and observed values.

As a validity check on this finding, additional data on polarity found in Hopkins and Mansbach were used to predict another set of wars. A $\chi^2 = .835$ $(df = 2)$ was calculated between the observed and predicted frequencies of

---

[28] Singer and Small, *Wages of War*. Only wars involving polar actors were included.
[29] Because of the expected value of zero for the number of wars associated with one international pole, this category was combined with the next largest. As a result, the number of categories was reduced from 5 to 4, and the degrees of freedom from 4 to 3.

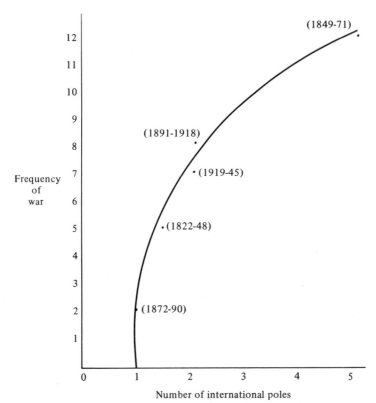

Figure 3.5 **Observed Logarithmic Relationship between Polarity and
International Warfare 1815-1945**

war.[30] By chance alone, the probability of occurrence for this value was
between 50 and 70 times in 100, and again no significant difference was
found between the observed and predicted frequencies. For purposes of
additional comparisons, the numbers of wars were averaged for each polarity
value (the frequencies themselves, not averages, were used in the chi-square
tests) and both the observed averages found in the two sources and the
expected values[31] are found in Table 3.6. The number of poles in the first

[30] These data for polarity are found in Raymond F. Hopkins and Richard W. Mansbach, *Structure and Process in International Politics* (New York: Harper & Row, 1973),
pp. 126–127. As in the previous test, categories were combined because of the zero number
of wars expected for unipolar systems. The total number of categories here is one less
than in the Rosecrance data because of the combination by Hopkins and Mansbach of
two of his periods in the nineteenth century into a single time interval.

[31] The expected values were normalized by multiplying each of them by the constant
factor of 10.

TABLE 3.6.   **Observed and Predicted Frequencies of War, 1815–1945**

Number of poles	Observed frequency of war[a]		Expected frequency of war
(N)	*Rosecrance*	*Hopkins–Mansbach*	$(10 \log_e N)$
1.0	2.0	2.0	0.0
1.5	5.0	—[b]	4.05
2.0	7.5	6.5	6.93
5.0	12.0	17.0	16.09

[a] Observed values are averages for each of the individual time periods.
[b] Hopkins and Mansbach do not list a "quasi-bipolar" system as does Rosecrance.

column are those historically recorded in the two sources for this time period, while the differing numbers of wars in the second and third columns are the result of the variations in lengths of the time spans for each of the unipolar, bipolar, or multipolar periods found in these sources. As can be seen, the relative agreement between theoretical and observed values is consistent with the preceding results of the chi-square analyses. Thus, a deduction from the theory in the form of a logarithmic relationship between polarity and international conflict behavior finds support in the historical data.

Several applications of this interpretation of power, therefore, have led to consistent findings which are significant across the several indicators, and in addition, are consistent with the application of theories of international stability and polarity. The taking on of alliances as increasing the environmental uncertainty of a central power and the existence of borders as fixed uncertainty constraints on the central power are both associated with the onset of international warfare. The similarity in these analyses is that an interconnectedness exists, whether of policy or geography, and serves as an environmental inhibitor of the power of the larger country to make choices and exercise options as it sees fit. A somewhat different type of relationship will now emerge in the treatment of social disorganization in international systems.

IV

Social Disorganization
in International Systems

Whereas in Chapter III we considered the power of nation-states in relation to both their policy and environmental surroundings, in this chapter we analyze the power or control of international systems. Consider for the moment the concept of social disorganization which has been found to be related to the onset of violence. When a disorganizing element is introduced and persists in societies that have existed in a state of relative structural stability, violence may result. In particular, the maintenance of dominance and status orderings in these societies is crucial to their continued stabilization. This principle has been found to pertain to both animal and human societies.[1]

Now consider the concept of social disorganization in relation to international systems. Historically, following Morton Kaplan's treatment, the hierarchical system is most stable, relative to others.[2] The principle of dominance associated with this system applies here, with imperial systems such as

---

[1] For a fairly comprehensive treatment of this subject in relation to aggressive behaviors of both animals and humans, see Elton B. McNeil, "The Nature of Aggression," in E. B. McNeil (ed.), *The Nature of Human Conflict* (Englewood Cliffs, N.J.: Prentice-Hall, 1965), pp. 14–41. Also see Kinji Imanishi, "Social Organization of Subhuman Primates in Their Natural Habitat," *Current Anthropology*, 1 (September–November 1960), pp. 393–407; and E. F. M. Durbin and J. Bowlby, *Personal Aggressiveness and War* (New York: Columbia University Press, 1950).

[2] Morton Kaplan, *System and Process in International Politics* (New York: Wiley, 1957), pp. 49–50.

the Roman Empire exhibiting the greatest relative stability over a long period of time. Instances of dominance-induced stability are relatively infrequent however, and, in fact, a degree of social disorganization and instability ordinarily exists and can be measured.

The international alliance is a common form of social organization in the international system. In a hierarchical or dominance system, all alliances would in fact be generated or controlled by one power. Thus, if there are, for example, four nation-state components of the system, the hierarchical leader would have at least four dyadic alliances, while each of the remaining three countries would likely have no more than one each. In this instance, one could say that the system is highly organized and the state of social disorganization is relatively low. At the same time, the power or control of the system by the dominant actor would be relatively great.

Contrast this state of affairs with the relative social disorganization attendant on the absence of any single actor serving as a hierarchical bloc leader. Each of the four component actors could have as many allies as it wished, and, indeed, at some point in time we might expect all to have an approximately equal number of allies. It is this state of equiprobability with regard to alliances as a prevalent form of social organization that would constitute a state of least power or control of the system by a single actor. The greater the degree of dispersion of alliances among central powers, the smaller the extent of control which can be exercised by any one of them acting alone.

When the mode of organization that we treat is alliance formation, then in at least one sense we are also examining certain aspects of the balance of power. Indeed, within the limits of the subsequent analysis, the terms *social disorganization, powerlessness, equiprobability,* and *balance of power* are equivalent. Powerlessness and equiprobability are identical by definition, since the state of highest uncertainty—the complete equiprobability of alternative outcomes—is the same as the total absence of power exercise or hierarchical control. The balance of power is taken to mean the complete equality (or equilibrium) of power among the elements of an international system.[3] If the number of alliances is used as one measure of power, the equiprobability of alliance formation among central powers is one indicator of the balance of power. Alternatively, the presence of alliance activity by only one central power (with non-central power nations) would be indicative of hegemony.

This is not to exclude from consideration the industrial or popular morale determinants of power; rather, it is meant as a somewhat confined and

[3] For a discussion of the various meanings of the term *balance of power* and its past usage, see Ernst B. Haas, "The Balance of Power: Prescription, Concept, or Propaganda?" *World Politics*, 5 (July 1953), pp. 442–477.

classical view of the balance in the form of alliances. It should also be noted that none of the previous terms refers to homeostatic (equilibrated) control of systems since, as we shall see, a steadily increasing equiprobability in the number of alliances by central powers has been followed by the termination of international systems in either domestic or international violence.

What is proposed is a quantitative description of the continued power loss of international systems. As will be seen, the patterns generally are orderly and quite regular over time. Furthermore, the duration of various systems can be specified by the examination of discrete changes in the power or control of these systems. From a somewhat different perspective, we also will be describing one process in the balance of power with regard to alliances —specifically, a steady convergence of systems to states of almost perfect balance. In this treatment, the increased non-regulation of systems, or a lack of homeostasis, is equivalent to an increased balance in the form of alliances. That is, the balance of power as measured by alliance formation and system regulation may be contradictory concepts when the evidence is examined.

The Calculation of Uncertainty Values

The following analysis is derived conceptually from the treatment of power loss to individual countries in alliance systems, and in method is rather similar to that employed by Charles A. McClelland in his treatments of the Berlin Crises of 1948 and 1961.[4] It has also been applied successfully to the Arab-Israeli Crisis of 1967, the Sino-Soviet dispute of 1969, and the summer crisis of 1914.[5] An earlier analysis of this type was done by John D. Sullivan for the Taiwan Straits Crisis.[6]

These writers employed an indicator of uncertainty to measure the amount of information within a given time period. A greater amount of information flow (in a random sense of molecular bits of information) implies a greater degree of uncertainty as originally suggested by the mathematical information theorists. The categories of information are demands made by one protagonist upon the other, e.g., accede, request, withdraw. Two measures of information

---

[4] Charles A. McClelland, "Access to Berlin: The Quantity and Variety of Events," in J. David Singer (ed.), *Quantitative International Politics: Insights and Evidence* (New York: The Free Press, 1968), pp. 159–186.

[5] Manus I. Midlarsky, Charles J. Wilkins, and Neil R. Andrews, "Periodic Uncertainty and International Crisis: The Arab-Israeli Dispute in Comparative Perspective," in J. D. Ben-Dak (ed.), *Methodologies in Search of Relevance: Assessing Arab-Israeli Conflict Relations* (New York: Gordon and Breach, forthcoming).

[6] John D. Sullivan, "Quemoy and Matsu: A Systematic Analysis," mimeographed (Los Angeles: May 1964).

are used. One is the actual uncertainty (also called absolute uncertainty) as indicated by equation (1) from Chapter III,

$$U(X) = - \sum_{i=1}^{N} p(x_i) \log_b p(x_i).$$

The other is a ratio of the actual uncertainty to the maximum uncertainty, called relative uncertainty, or

$$U(X)_{\text{rel}} = \frac{U(X)}{U(X)_{\text{max}}} = - \frac{\sum_{i=1}^{N} p(x_i) \log_b p(x_i)}{\log_b N}.$$

The ratio varies from zero to unity, or $0 \leq U(X)_{\text{rel}} \leq 1$. When the actual or absolute uncertainty is zero, the ratio $U(X)_{\text{rel}}$ is zero, and when $U(X)$ is at its maximum, the ratio is equal to unity.

Given a number of elements (countries) of a system, the maximum uncertainty states in effect what *could* happen. It defines a maximum state of disorderliness or equiprobability for a system, in contrast to the absolute uncertainty, which describes the *actual* state of disorder. The ratio of the two is defined as the relative uncertainty, and tells us how close the system is to the state of maximum possible equiprobable events. Thus, we will interpret the uncertainty itself as a measure of the dispersion of alliances among the elements of an international system, and the number of such elements or countries involved in central power alliance activity. The relative uncertainty shall be an indicator of the extent to which central powers are each equally likely to enter into alliances. It should be noted that both measures are insensitive to the structure of systems in the form of multipolarity or bipolarity, but not, of course, to unipolarity. However, the concept of power loss implies a non-regulation of the system regardless of its bipolar or multipolar structure, and as will be seen, in the three systems which experience a power loss, the tendency is toward bipolar structures at the end of the life of the system.

Since the central powers are the primary components of the system, and given the previous results on the power loss for individual countries, we are interested in their alternate possible states as measured by their alliance formations. The number of alliance organizations to which a central power belonged within a five-year interval is the basic measure of this analysis. Using the Singer and Small data, values were calculated for the absolute and relative uncertainties within the five-year intervals. If an alliance continued beyond the midpoint of the interval, it was counted toward that country's cumulative effect. This procedure can be illustrated with reference to a single five-year interval, 1840–1844.

TABLE 4.1.   **Number of Alliances and Uncertainty Value for Central Powers, 1840–1844**

Country	Number of alliances	Percent of total	$-p(x_i) \log_2 p(x_i)$
Austria	3	21.43	.4762
England	3	21.43	.4762
France	1	7.14	.2715
Prussia	2	14.29	.4011
Russia	3	21.43	.4762
Spain	1	7.14	.2715
Turkey	1	7.14	.2715
Total	14	100.00	2.6442

Table 4.1 presents the number of alliances, percentages, and the absolute uncertainty equal to the sum of the values in the extreme right-hand column. In this analysis, the logarithmic base is equal to 2, in order to maintain consistency with prior treatments by McClelland and others. The maximum uncertainty is simply the logarithm of the number of central powers—seven in this period—or

$$U(X)_{max} = \log_2 7 = 2.8074$$

and the relative uncertainty is

$$U(X)_{rel} = \frac{U(X)}{U(X)_{max}} = \frac{2.6442}{2.8074} = .942.$$

The large value of the relative uncertainty (close to 1.00) is due to the near equiprobability of each of the central powers having an alliance. Each of these countries had at least one alliance, and none had more than three. If certain of these countries had no alliances in this period and/or one or more had many alliances, then the value of the relative uncertainty would be lower.

The Social Disorganization of Historical Systems

The absolute and relative uncertainties for the central power system are listed for the period 1815–1939 in Table 4.2. Values for the relative uncertainty change not only with values of the absolute uncertainty, but also according to whether or not new central powers are added to the system (e.g., Japan, 1895; U.S., 1899) within a five-year interval. Prior to an analysis of the results, one can ask whether this type of analysis is required in the study of alliance formation, when in fact the number of alliances within a given

TABLE 4.2. **Absolute and Relative Uncertainties, 1815–1939**

Period	Absolute uncertainty	Relative uncertainty
1815–1819	2.24	.797
1820–1824	2.24	.797
1825–1829	2.32	.827
1830–1834	2.50	.891
1835–1839	2.50	.891
1840–1844	2.64	.942
1845–1849	1.84	.656
1850–1854	1.95	.695
1855–1859	1.50	.534
1860–1864	2.52	.841
1865–1869	0.00	.000
1870–1874	1.59	.528
1875–1879	2.20	.732
1880–1884	1.75	.584
1885–1889	2.61	.769
1890–1894	2.50	.832
1895–1899	2.61	.824
1900–1904	2.90	.874
1905–1909	3.03	.913
1910–1914	3.02	.910
1915–1919	1.00	.333
1920–1924	1.79	.598
1925–1929	2.20	.732
1930–1934	2.38	.793
1935–1939	2.58	.860

time period itself might be sufficient. One may not require complex analyses of this type in understanding the relationship between alliances and war. However, by reference to Table 4.2 one can see the difference between the present approach and simply using alliances as a variable. For the years 1865–1869, there were three alliances involving the central power system and for the years 1870–1874, there were also three such alliances. If only values for alliances themselves were used, there would be no difference between the two intervals. However, in the first of the periods only Prussia was involved in all three of the alliances, leading to absolute and relative uncertainties of zero (the hegemony or certainty of a single power alliance dominance),[7] whereas in the second period three central powers were each equally involved in one alliance, leading to an absolute uncertainty of 1.59 and a relative uncertainty of .528. Thus, whereas the number of alliances may indicate national commitments, the two uncertainty measures reflect certain systemic properties not directly indicated by the alliances themselves.

[7] For instances when the number of alliances itself, z, is equal to zero, the convention is adopted that the function $z \log z$ approaches zero as z approaches zero through positive values.

The results for both the absolute and relative uncertainties are graphed in Figure 4.1. Based on secular trends in the data, the curve can be divided into four time periods, three demonstrating highly regular increases and one exhibiting a fairly random decrease. The first three are 1815–1844, 1865–1914, and 1915–1939, whereas the latter period extends from 1845–1864. A decrease in both uncertainty measures occurs after 1914 and may be inferred for the period after 1939 from our knowledge of the system after that year. It should be reemphasized that the time units are five-year intervals and therefore a specific point in time cannot be indicated.

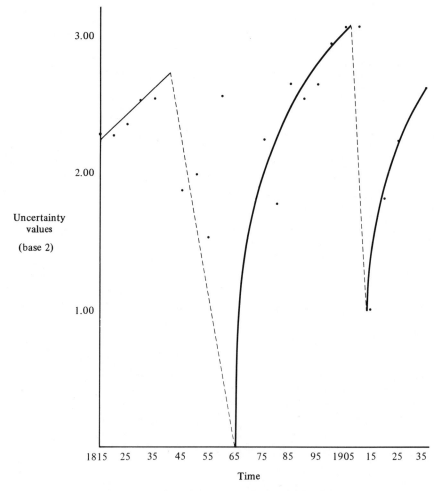

Figure 4.1 **Absolute Uncertainties, 1815–1939**

Let us consider first the two later periods of regular increase. In the years 1865–1914, there is some randomness in the earlier data points which then "settles down" in the later ones until relatively constant values are reached between 1905 and 1914. Historically, the inception of this period may be found in the formation of the German Empire. The Austro-Prussian War of 1866 followed by the Franco-Prussian War of 1870–1871 initiated this period. and, to a certain extent, it may have been dominated by the unification and growth of the German Empire.[8] After World War I, the pattern, if anything, is more regular in its increase of both types of uncertainty.

It may be said that in both periods, the relative uncertainty converges to a value near the maximum (1.00) prior to the onset of both World Wars I and II. One way of approaching these findings is to consider a system of complete equiprobability or, as noted previously, a complete balance of power with regard to alliances. In such a system, each member would have the same probability as any other member of having an alliance. A system of this type also can be seen as one which has achieved a complete balance of power with regard to alliances, since each member is equivalent to every other member in regard to alliance activity.

Figure 4.2 presents the values of absolute uncertainty associated with systems having $1, 2, \ldots, 10$ points of equiprobable activity.[9] The abscissa lists the number of points, N, and the ordinate presents the values of absolute uncertainty (equal to the maximum because of the stipulation of equiprobability). As one moves along the abscissa, the curve records the increase in absolute uncertainty resulting from the addition of new points, all having the same probability of engaging in a common activity—in this instance, alliance formation. The slope of the curve indicates the rate of increase of uncertainty with the addition of new points of equiprobable activity. This curve should then be compared to the portions of Figure 4.1 for the periods 1865–1914 and 1915–1939. Comparisons of the graphs indicate a very strong similarity between the two sections of Figure 4.1 and the theoretical curve, and may be susceptible to the following interpretation.

---

[8] L. B. Namier considers the German domination of this period to have begun even earlier, during the revolutions of 1848: "With 1848 starts the German bid for power, for European predominance, for world dominion: the national movement was the common denominator of the German revolution in 1848, and a mighty Germany, fit to give the law to other nations, its foremost aim." See his "1848: Seed-Plot of History," in Melvin Kranzberg (ed.), *1848: A Turning Point?* (Boston: D. C. Heath, 1959), p. 69. Also see his *1848: The Revolution of the Intellectuals*, from the Proceedings of the British Academy, 30 (London: Geoffrey Cumberlege, 1944).

[9] The numerical values of $\log_2 N$ for this curve are found in E. T. Klemmer, "Tables for Computing Informational Measures," in Henry Quastler (ed.), *Information Theory in Psychology: Problems and Methods* (New York: The Free Press, 1955), pp. 72–74.

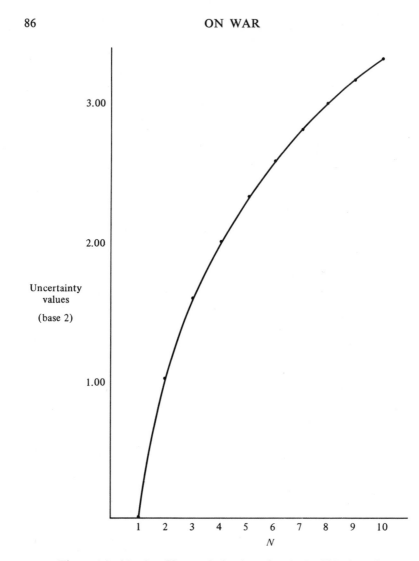

Figure 4.2 **Absolute Uncertainties Associated with N Points of
Equiprobable Activity**

The international systems of the 1865–1914 and 1915–1939 periods behave as if each five-year interval added another point of equiprobable activity to the system; an additional central power became as likely to enter into alliances as all those which had already entered the equiprobable state. By inspection, the slopes of the three curves are virtually identical, thereby indicating a rate of entry for the two time periods roughly equivalent to that for the theoretical curve. One can indeed interchange the time period abscissas for the real-world systems with the number of points N in the theoretical curve, and the figures would remain substantially the same. Thus, if we interpret equi-probability with regard to alliance formation as equivalent to one aspect of the balance of power, then we can say that the rates of convergence to perfect balance of a theoretical system of perfect and regular increase, on the one hand, and the two historical systems, on the other, are virtually identical.

The levels of balance achieved in the pre-World War I and pre-World War II systems, however, are not the same. Given a ten-central-power system in 1914 (see Table 4.1 and Figure 4.2), then the degree of balance was very close to perfect in that system (3.02 actual vs. 3.32 theoretical). In 1939, with an eight-member system, there was less convergence to the maximum (2.58 vs. 3.00) and, by definition, less of a balance among the components. Neverthe-less, the maximum was not too far from being achieved. Another difference between the two plots concerns the very slight drop in the uncertainty values from 1905–1909 through 1910–1914. It may be that the system had reached a point of saturation, whereby the conflict processes involved actually had begun to diminish somewhat in intensity.[10] In Chapter IX a specific compari-son is made between the two periods with regard to the effect of the Bosnian Crisis on the onset of World War I.

These results should be compared with those obtained in Chapter III concerning the logarithmic relationship between international polarity and frequency of war. In that instance, a greater frequency of war was found in multipolar systems than in bipolar ones, but the increase in frequency of war upon the addition of polar actors was dampened as successively larger numbers of actors entered the system. This result was based initially on the uncertainty of which dyadic pair in a multipolar system would result in conflict.

In this chapter, the approach to bipolar conflict in 1914 and 1939 is calcula-ted by means of the uncertainty associated with alliances, with each successive five-year interval adding another power to become entangled in the alliance system. Thus, an enmeshing process takes place and as the uncertainty (alliance dispersion) approaches its maximum value, any incident—an assassi-nation in 1914—could touch off conflict between any of the dyads which,

[10] An alliance saturation dimension was found by Michael Haas in a factor analysis of alliance and polarity data. This dimension groups percentage countries allied and multi-laterality of alliances, and Haas finds that it is associated with destabilizing and longer wars within large international subsystems. If we view the process of alliance saturation as a correlate of the increase of uncertainty, as is done in this study, then Haas' finding and those of this analysis are quite consistent. The two instances of the steady increase of uncertainty beginning in the mid-nineteenth century were both followed by the extreme instability and long duration of the World Wars I and II. See Michael Haas, "Inter-national Subsystems: Stability and Polarity," *American Political Science Review*, 64 (March 1970), pp. 98–123.

in turn, would associate virtually all of the alliance partners in war. Hence, the totality of war occurs at the ends of these periods of uncertainty increase. In the process analyzed in Figure 3.5 (Chapter III), the confrontations were dyadic only and would not allow for this entanglement of all allies. As a result, that analysis did not isolate any particular global conflict as is found here. The multipolar period of 1849–1871 indicated in Figure 3.5 would be illustrative of this incidence of dyadic conflict, without the entangling feature of alliance formation.

The Comparison of Time Periods

We have not yet compared the first of the periods exhibiting steadily increasing alliance-related uncertainty (1815–1844) with two prewar periods of our century which also exhibit this phenomenon. A crucial difference is that the former period did not end in global international warfare. Indeed, this period ends by means of a gradual decrease (1845–1864) of uncertainty, the only one of its type appearing in Figure 4.1. There are at least four possible explanations for this difference: (1) the incidence of primarily dyadic conflicts which did not allow for the large-scale bipolar, hierarchically organized confrontations of later years; (2) a simultaneous internalization of European conflicts in the period 1845–1864 beginning with the revolutions of 1848 and continuing with the unification of Germany; (3) the disappearance of a system regulator in the form of the Concert of Europe; and (4) the colonial expansion of European nations.

As one explanation for the gradual decline in uncertainty values during the period 1845–1864 (i.e., without a major conflagration), the conflicts of the multipolar period were mainly dyadic and did not permit the bipolarization of alliance systems. The wars of Italian unification or early German unification were more localized than in the later period of bipolar confrontations. As a result, the uncertainty values decrease in a random fashion as these sporadic conflicts occur and then reach base values at the end of the unification process, when all alliances have ceased to operate effectively and new ones are about to be formed.

Another reason for the decrease of these values associated with alliances is that the normatively oriented revolutions of 1848 tended to direct the attentions of the monarchies away from intense international conflicts in this period. The incidence of violent threats to the institution of monarchy, as well as to the stability of the international order, served to initiate a period of concern with internal affairs. These upheavals were of a different order of magnitude from the previous revolutions of the nineteenth century. Those of 1820 in Spain and Naples were primarily military in origin, whereas the Greek and Belgian upheavals of a decade later were mainly nationalist in orientation.

The 1830 July Revolution, which elevated Louis Philippe to the throne, was still within the prevailing normative order of monarchical rule. Only the outbreaks in Poland and Italy during this period appeared to challenge the old order, yet in scale were small enough to present little threat to the international *ancien régime*.

The 1848 revolutions were both liberal and nationalist in orientation, and in both of those emphases, and in scope, directly challenged the normative order of European monarchy. As Rosecrance puts it, "They were so successful that they demolished the edifice of traditional conservatism and forced a new conservative synthesis. But the new reactionary program would be very different from the old."[11] This new conservatism oriented the major international actors away from the international system and toward the maintenance of their own regimes. The Concert of Europe could no longer exist primarily as the embodiment of an *international* conservative normative order.

With the end of the Concert, the international system was left without a regulatory device. There was no longer even a quasi-organized and semicoherent organization for the establishment of international norms. Without the established international norms there could not arise challenges to these norms in the form of international warfare. Indeed, this is one possible interpretation of the onset of World Wars I and II. The normative order established by Britain and France was openly challenged by Germany in 1914, and the new organizational embodiment of the Allied order—the League of Nations—was attacked by Hitler in 1939. But whereas the League was destroyed as a regulatory device by international violence, the Concert of Europe effectively disappeared, in large measure, as a product of internal violence. Thus, without a regulator to contend with, the various nations could be concerned with their own internal affairs. Most of the international conflicts took place on a dyadic basis, a situation made impossible in earlier or subsequent periods when regulating measures were present. The extent to which the regulator is present and operative in international systems will be related to the degree of international conflict in Chapter IX. It may be said at this point that a partial regulator may be worse than none at all, for if it cannot effectively enforce its decisions, as in the case of the League, then its activities may only irritate and antagonize a potential opponent to the prevailing normative order.

Another possible reason for a peaceful decline in uncertainty values for the system between 1845 and 1864 lies in the continued existence of a territorial

[11] Richard N. Rosecrance, *Action and Reaction in World Politics: International Systems in Perspective* (Boston: Little, Brown, 1963), pp. 106–107.

focus outside the European continent. Although many of the European powers such as England and France had already acquired the majority of their colonial territories, their attention was still directed in part to the consolidation of rule (e.g., Great Britain in West Africa) and to additional acquisition of territory. The industrialization process accelerated the demand for resources which could be found relatively cheaply in the colonial territories. Thus, to a far greater extent than in the latter portion of the nineteenth century and in the twentieth, an important territorial focus existed outside the European mainland and the central power system. As we shall see, it was the gradual shift of territorial concern back to this system, particularly in Southeastern Europe, that was to serve, in part, as an accelerator of World War I.

A question of the comparability of time periods emerges from the present analysis. We have isolated four time intervals in the period 1815–1939—three of increasing alliance-related uncertainty and one of decrease. Rosecrance, on the other hand, has delineated six systems in the same time span and the dates, although roughly similar in certain instances, differ in others.[12] Whereas we have found one period between 1815 and 1844, Rosecrance finds two intervals within this time span—1814–1822 and 1822–1848—the primary difference between them being the extent to which the Concert was united and effective in dominating European affairs. After 1822, the Concert of Europe ceased functioning as effectively as it previously had, but it did still function as an international regulatory device. A habit of consultation had developed among the major powers of the period which not even the divergence of the British in 1822 at Verona could destroy. It was only with the onset of the revolutions of 1848 that the old Concert could be said to have ceased to exist as a functioning entity.[13]

A period found here, 1845–1864, is roughly comparable to that outlined by Rosecrance—1848–1871. Indeed, the year 1848 probably could also have

---

[12] *Ibid.*, pp. 239–261. Some empirical validity for Rosecrance's dating of historical subsystems is found in a factor analysis of Richardson's data on wars. See Frank Denton, "Some Regularities in International Conflict, 1820–1949," *Background*, 9 (February 1966), pp. 283–296; and Lewis F. Richardson, *Statistics of Deadly Quarrels* (Chicago: Quadrangle, 1960).

[13] For treatments of the Concert, see, for example, René Albrecht-Carrié, *The Concert of Europe* (New York: Walker, 1968); and *idem, A Diplomatic History of Europe Since the Congress of Vienna* (New York: Harper & Row, 1958); Frederick B. Artz, *Reaction and Revolution, 1814–1832* (New York: Harper and Bros., 1934). Specific policies of certain governments with regard to the Concert are found in A. J. P. Taylor, *The Hapsburg Monarchy, 1809–1918* (New York: Harper Torchbooks, 1965); and *idem, Course of Germany History: A Survey of the Development of Germany Since 1815* (New York: Capricorn, 1962); Charles K. Webster, *The Foreign Policy of Castlereagh, 1815–1822* (London: G. Bell, 1925); and in Harold W. V. Temperley, *The Foreign Policy of Canning, 1822–1827* (London: G. Bell, 1925).

been indicated in the present analysis, but the use of five-year periods masks the importance of any single year. (In the present analysis, some time interval greater than one year is needed to calculate the value of alliance-related uncertainty within that interval.) A substantive question, however, relates to whether the endpoint of this period should be dated at 1864, as found here, or 1871, as in Rosecrance's analysis. The former would treat the Austro-Prussian conflict as the beginning of a German-dominated system which ends only in 1914. The latter would emphasize the formation of the German Empire at the end of the Franco-Prussian War. From the perspective of alliance formation and war, the Austro-Prussian War of 1866 is the first major conflict of the period and initiates the time interval of increasing alliance-related uncertainty culminating in World War I. The process of unifying Germany and the later German domination of European interactions form a relatively continuous process from 1866 through 1914.[14] On the other hand, from the viewpoint of diplomatic history, perhaps one would want to specify the new diplomatic period initiated by a victorious and unified Germany in 1871.

Similarly, Rosecrance differentiates between the Bismarckian diplomatic system of 1871–1890 and the system existing after the removal of Bismarck (1890–1914). No such differentiation is found here, primarily because even in the post-1890 period the alliance system continued to relate to the perceived threat of German industrial growth and colonial expansion. Whether in the form of a near hegemony of diplomatic interaction prior to 1890, or in the form of a growing conflict between Germany, on the one hand, and France and Russia, on the other, after 1890 the entire period can be said to have been concerned with the "problem" of Germany. This analysis thus indicates the continuity of the period beginning with the first major war clearly connected with German unification, and the onset of World War I. The last period of this analysis, 1915–1939, is virtually identical to Rosecrance's.

It should be noted that the only period of a gradual decrease of alliance-related uncertainty (1845–1864) corresponds with the same period described by Rosecrance as multipolar and one in which disharmony prevailed. The withdrawal of each of the central powers to their own domestic and foreign

---

[14] As has been indicated, Namier, *1848*, and *Revolution*, would place the origins of this process at an even earlier point in time, sometime around 1848. Also see Taylor, *Course*. Other treatments of the 1848 revolutions are to be found in C. Edmund Maurice, *The Revolutionary Movement of 1848–1849* (New York: G. P. Putnam, 1887, republished 1968); George Woodcock (ed.), *A Hundred Years of Revolution: 1848 and After* (London: The Porcupine Press, 1948); Priscilla Robertson, *Revolutions of 1848: A Social History* (Princeton, N.J.: Princeton University Press, 1952); and in George Fasel, *Europe in Upheaval: The Revolutions of 1848* (Chicago: Rand McNally, 1970).

concerns exclusive of close associations with other powers led to a dissolution of the pre-1845 system. As indicated by theory and research findings,[15] a greater number of wars may occur in multipolar than in bipolar systems, yet the duration of wars occurring in the latter systems will be greater. Although several wars did occur during the mid-nineteenth-century period, such as the Austro-Sardinian of 1848–1849 and the Crimean of 1853–1856, the intensities of these wars, as measured by the number of persons killed or their duration as a temporal measure, are not nearly as severe as wars of wider scope, such as World Wars I and II. Moreover, with the exception of the Crimean War, none of the wars occurring in this period included more than two central powers. The dyadic nature of these wars in regard to central powers contrasts sharply with the subsequent global wars of the twentieth century. It also may be a reflection of the general lack of commitment of central powers to each other during this period, as indicated by the decrease in alliance formation and alliance-related uncertainty.

It is possible that the honoring of broad commitments among central powers in 1848 may have, in fact, ended these commitments and thus prevented later widespread international conflicts. The Russian intervention in Hungary, the French in Italy, and the Prussian in the various Germanic states represented a clear manifestation of the will to maintain an essentially conservative monarchical order in Europe. But it was a new conservative synthesis that resulted from 1848 and destroyed the Concert of Europe. The old order had been conservative and dynastic but international in scope. A conservatism and monarchism were characteristic of the post-1848 period as well, yet emphasized nationalism and separate action.[16] It was more than a half century later, with the onset of World War I, that once again the result of honored commitments would be felt in the form of international political violence.

If the interventions of 1848 represented the internal violence resulting from honored commitments in the nineteenth century, then the Indochina wars of the 1960's and 1970's may represent a similar experience for the twentieth century.[17] As of this writing, these wars have not ended and a relatively long time period subsequent to them might be required to ascertain whether their effects will dissipate the alliance system and its uncertainties existing prior to

[15] See Richard N. Rosecrance, "Bipolarity, Multipolarity, and the Future," *Journal of Conflict Resolution*, 10 (September 1966), pp. 314–327; and M. Haas, *op. cit.*, pp. 119–121.

[16] See Rosecrance, *Action and Reaction*, p. 107.

[17] For a thorough analysis of patterns of change in contemporary European history, including the problems of internal and external violence, see Raymond Aron, *Peace and War: A Theory of International Relations*, trans. R. Howard and A. B. Fox (New York: Praeger, 1966), chap. 11. Also of interest here is the treatment of bipolar and multipolar systems, found in chapter 5 of this work.

1960. It is clearly too soon to determine whether the internalization of conflict in Vietnam bears any comparison to the internalization of conflict in the European states in 1848. Nevertheless, if we interpret correctly the role of internal conflict in 1848 as having in part replaced the intense external variety and, in addition, if the current Indochina experience represents a similar honoring of international commitments in the form of intervention in civil strife, then perhaps the present international system will experience some future stability. Although the wars in Indochina may have represented a power loss for the primary central power involved—the United States—and indeed may have been disastrous for her, from the perspective of the international system, these wars may have led to future internal preoccupations on the part of great powers such that large-scale international war may be less probable.

Thus, we have examined the condition of an increasing power loss or powerlessness over time, which in the international system may be understood as a form of increasing social disorganization. This has occurred under conditions of an equiprobability of alliance formation whereby each power is as likely as any other to enter into an alliance. A state of balancing is achieved which approximates complete disorganization of the international system. This situation stands in contrast to a hierarchically organized, relatively stable system. In this sense, the balance of power is a form of social disorganization whose end result is war at the close of two major time periods (1865–1914, 1915–1939) analyzed here. The closer the approximation of the system to perfect balance, the greater the likelihood of major global conflict.

Alliances among nations take place as a form of international interaction at the systemic level. Once they exist, they are essentially independent of specific national attributes, despite the later consequences of alliance formation which may accrue to the nation-state. The status inconsistency of nations, on the other hand, is explicitly dependent upon the internal achievements of nations. The inconsistency between an achieved status and an ascribed status conferred by the international system is a condition which straddles the boundary between the nation-state and international system, and which constitutes a type of constraint on uncertainty reduction. We turn in Chapter V to an analysis of the relationship between status inconsistency and international war.

V

Status Inconsistency and International War

With the treatment of social disorganization, our analysis of the international system itself is now completed, and we can turn to the boundary between the system and nation-state as the focus of analysis. The concept of status inconsistency as an inability to exercise power was theoretically treated in Chapter II. Now it can be considered empirically as a boundary effect.

It was suggested in the prior analyses that if a nation has developed certain capabilities in the form of internal achievements and yet cannot employ these abilities for its own benefit, then power exists which is subject to constraint. The ascription of importance by one nation to another is an illustration of a process occurring within the system which is for the most part outside the control of the nation being ranked. Its own power in the form of achievement within the state cannot be used to influence directly the ascription process, and as a result of this constraint on the capabilities of nations, political violence may result. This discrepancy between processes internal to the nation-state (*achievement*) and processes external to it (*ascription*) has direct antecedents in the study of international relations.

Quincy Wright, in his classic studies of war, refers to the tension between societal changes internal to the nation-state and elements of the international system which may be inconsistent with these changes.[1] The Treaty of Versailles and the League Covenant established certain standards with regard to the

---

[1] See Quincy Wright, *A Study of War* (Chicago: The University of Chicago Press, 1942), pp. 380–382.

future of a disarmed and emasculated Germany, as well as the illegality of armed aggression. According to Wright, Germany, Italy, and Japan revolted against the "public law" of their time, and this revolt constituted a challenge to the Western powers which ultimately led to war.

A Structural Framework

This concept of an inconsistency among elements within a larger framework also is found in the work of Johan Galtung.[2] He conceives of a set of actors (nations, groups, or individuals) whose membership constitutes a stratification system. The concern here is with the origins of international warfare; thus, the following discussion refers to a set which consists only of nations.[3] According to Galtung's theory, each nation may occupy a position relative to every other nation, based on rank with respect to certain variables.

Consider three nations which are ranked on five variables. Following Galtung's usage, let T symbolize the "topdog" and U the "underdog" for each of the variables. To be sure, T and U are, in reality, likely to be points on a continuum; nevertheless, for the sake of simplicity and clarity, we can treat them as dichotomies. Let one nation be "topdog" on all five variables, a second nation "topdog" on four of the five variables, but "underdog" on one of them, and a third nation "underdog" on all five.

Figure 5.1 schematically outlines this condition. Each of the nations now has a variable profile, and the behavior of each nation may be dependent on this profile. If we examine conflict as a possible behavioral outcome, then three possibilities exist. A desire for change and an attendant conflict may originate primarily from nation 1, the complete "topdog," or from nation n, the lowest-ranked nation, or from the second-ranked nation with a mixed profile.

The first-ranked nation may initiate conflict in the sense that it seeks to augment what it already has. Great Britain, in the nineteenth century, engaged in the conquest and acquisition of colonies despite the existence of an already formidable colonial establishment and what many would regard as a first-ranked status in that time period. Similarly, the French also acquired colonies and established an imperial set of relationships with the "underdog" nations. Thus, the first-ranked nation may initiate conflict with respect to

[2] Johan Galtung, "A Structural Theory of Aggression," *Journal of Peace Research*, 1 (no. 2, 1964), pp. 95–119.

[3] In this discussion, the nation-state is the focus of analysis. However, any social grouping, including alliances, may be substituted. See Manus I. Midlarsky, *Status Inconsistency and the Onset of International Warfare* (Evanston, Ill.: Ph.D. diss., Northwestern University, 1969).

Variables

		1	2	3	4	5
	1	T	T	T	T	T
	2	T	T	T	T	U
		,	,	,	,	,
Nations		,	,	,	,	,
		,	,	,	,	,
	n	U	U	U	U	U

Figure 5.1 **Galtung's Theory Applied to Three Nations and Five Variables**

nations which occupy a much lower rank, but this form of conflict behavior seldom leads directly to war.

The lowest-ranked nations often do not have the capability to prevent the encroachments of the first-ranked nations, and whatever conflict results generally is localized, of low intensity, and of short duration. With respect to the second possibility—that of conflict originating from the bottom-ranked nation—the country which occupies the lowest rank in this stratification system seldom initiates conflict with the highest-ranked nation. Lacking the capabilities to wage effective warfare and a consequent lack of incentive for such conflict, the nation lowest on the hierarchy most likely seeks an accommodation with the "topdog."

The nation of mixed profile is the third possible source of conflict behavior which results in international warfare. This form of conflict behavior generally involves a *desire for change* in the stratification system and often constitutes a *challenge* to the first-ranked nation. Nation 2, which occupies the first rank on four of the five variables, is a probable candidate for the initiation of a challenge to the first-ranked nation: Its capabilities are almost equivalent, and it may have the capacity to displace the "topdog." Moreover, it may be motivated to initiate such a challenge primarily due to its state of inconsistency. The second-ranked nation most likely casts the dominant nation as its point of reference and, therefore, may be reminded continually of its state of inconsistency. This nation might also be subjected to differential treatment whereby the dominant nation demands and receives the majority of rewards the system has to offer, leaving only a small share to the second-ranked nation. Thus, the nation of mixed profile may have to adjust the inconsistency and impose a forced correspondence between the consistent elements of its profile and the one exception. This attempt at a change in its condition may assume the form of a challenge to the dominant nation and might lead to war.[4]

[4] It is also possible to reorient the framework such that the challenge to the dominant nation is in the form of a challenge to the international norms established by that nation.

The Status Inconsistency Hypothesis

This account of Galtung's framework does not refer to *specific* variables which might be crucial to the onset of international warfare. This framework is essentially without meaning unless it is given specific content. The previous discussion of the boundary between the nation-state and international system, as well as Wright's reference to the "tension" between these levels, indicate that perhaps the variables might be chosen from both. Selection of variables which pertain only to characteristics internal to the nation-state, makes it difficult to establish the link between internal changes and a potential challenge to the dominant power. These changes may be effected internally without reference to external processes. There is no need to challenge the dominant nation. On the other hand, the choice of only system variables makes the framework exist without reference to those internal capabilities which may be essential to the conduct of effective warfare. Both the capabilities of nations and systemic constraints probably are necessary for the construction of a valid explanation of war.

At the system level, ascribed status is one aspect of international relations suggested in sociological theory, and refers here to the relative position or rank of a nation as perceived by other nations.[5] That is, the status of a particular nation depends on the perceptions and behavior of other states with respect to that nation. This form of status may be contrasted with *achieved status*, which is dependent entirely on processes internal to the nation-state and which may increase the capability of that nation to wage effective warfare. Now, if, in Figure 5.1, the second-ranked nation is an "underdog" with respect to its ascribed status, but is a "topdog" on measures of achievement (variables 1–4), then it may be said to experience a status inconsistency which might lead to war.

In an analogous fashion, some sociological and anthropological writings suggest that social conflict is largely a product of unresolved inconsistencies in societal development. James C. Davies, for example, suggests that major revolutions often are a consequence of a gap between "achievement" in the form of economic or political development and "expectations," where expectations refer to the population's predictions (or ascription) of the future behavior of governmental elites.[6] Robert A. LeVine proposes that inter-

[5] See Galtung, *op. cit.*, p. 103; Max Weber, *The Theory of Social and Economic Organization*, trans. A. M. Henderson and Talcott Parsons (New York: The Free Press, 1947); and Talcott Parsons, *The Social System* (New York: The Free Press, 1951).
[6] James C. Davies, "Toward a Theory of Revolution," *American Sociological Review*, 27 (February 1962), pp. 5–19.

group conflict may be a consequence of the inconsistency between social changes resulting from the modernization process and the demands of tradition.[7] The rapidity of environmental change combined with the reluctance of traditional leaders to abandon "consummatory" value systems indeed may act as a condition of conflict in transitional societies.[8]

Gerhard Lenski specifically formulates the concept of status inconsistency to account for the tendency of individuals or groups to seek social change, often by expressing preferences for liberal political alternatives.[9] Rather than emphasizing the vertical dimension of status within hierarchies, as do the earlier works of Max Weber and Pitirim Sorokin, Lenski is concerned primarily with the inconsistencies *across* status dimensions.[10] He finds that the greater the inconsistencies among the four attributes of ethnicity, occupation, education, and income, the greater the political liberalism of the respondents. Irwin W. Goffman deals with the concept of status inconsistency in much the same fashion and finds a relationship between the degree of inconsistency among these variables and preference for change in the distribution of power.[11]

Early in the development of the theory, writers such as Elton F. Jackson, in his own work and in collaboration with Peter J. Burke, examined an alternate possible effect of status inconsistency.[12] Instead of studying the externalization of the effects of inconsistency in the form of projection onto the polity or society, Jackson and Burke considered the effects of the inconsistency on internalization in the form of stress symptoms. Uncertainties as to what the individual can expect from others, and what they can expect from him, are suggested as explanations of the relationship between status inconsistencies and internal stress. The frustration at experiencing contradictory expectations from others and not being able to satisfy all of them, with the possibility of negative sanctions being imposed, also is posited by Jackson as a possible cause of the stress symptoms.[13]

---

[7] Robert A. LeVine, "Anthropology and the Study of Conflict: An Introduction," *Journal of Conflict Resolution*, 5 (March 1961), pp. 3–15.

[8] David E. Apter, *The Politics of Modernization* (Chicago: The University of Chicago Press, 1965), pp. 22–33.

[9] Gerhard E. Lenski, "Status Crystallization: A Non-Vertical Dimension of Social Status," *American Sociological Review*, 19 (August 1954), pp. 405–413.

[10] See Weber, *op. cit.*; and Sorokin, *op. cit.*

[11] Irwin W. Goffman, "Status Consistency and Preference for Change in Power Distribution," *American Sociological Review*, 22 (June 1957), pp. 275–281.

[12] See Elton F. Jackson, "Status Consistency and Symptoms of Stress," *American Sociological Review*, 27 (August 1962), pp. 469–480; and Elton F. Jackson and Peter J. Burke, "Status and Symptoms of Stress: Additive and Interaction Effects," *American Sociological Review*, 30 (August 1965), pp. 556–564.

[13] Jackson, *op. cit.*, pp. 469–470.

Certain difficulties, however, have been found in the use of status inconsistency as an explanation for the desire for change. In one study, Brent Rutherford performed an exhaustive analysis of the relationship between status inconsistency and political liberalism.[14] He found little relationship between these variables, but some small positive relationships were found between status inconsistency and both presidential vote and political participation for urban residents. However, even these relationships disappeared after controlling for socioeconomic status. Rutherford's findings have added importance because of his use of a national sample in contrast to Lenski's more restrictive sample drawn from the Detroit area. Furthermore, it has been suggested that Lenski's finding of a relationship between status inconsistency and political liberalism may be the result of a confound with ethnicity, whereby only persons who were status inconsistent and at the same time low in ethnicity exhibited tendencies towards political liberalism.[15] Other studies have failed to find any relationship between status inconsistency and anti-black prejudice, or have failed to replicate Lenski's findings.

Another difficulty with studies using status inconsistency is the problem of identification.[16] Given a variable which is a composite function of two or more primary variables, under certain circumstances it is difficult to determine whether the inconsistency variable or one or more of the primary variables is principally responsible for the discovered relationship. Moreover, the use of a linear measure may not be justified in certain cases where in fact an interactive or multiplicative term should be used.

The problems concerning the lack of significant relationships appear to be resolvable by suggesting that the concept of status inconsistency may be

[14] Brent M. Rutherford, *Social Status Consistency as an Explanatory Concept in Political Behavior Research* (Evanston, Ill.: Ph.D. diss., Northwestern University, 1968).

[15] A general argument that Lenski failed to differentiate adequately between the main effects of status and "inconsistency" effects is found in Robert E. Mitchell, "Methodological Notes on a Theory of Status Crystallization," *Public Opinion Quarterly*, 28 (Summer 1964), pp. 315–325. The possibility of a confound with ethnicity is given empirical support in Donald Treiman, "Status Discrepancy and Prejudice," *American Journal of Sociology*, 71 (May 1966), pp. 651–664. For studies which attempted to replicate Lenski's finding but failed to do so, see William F. Kenkel, "The Relationship between Status Consistency and Politico-Economic Attitudes," *American Sociological Review*, 21 (June 1956), pp. 365–368; and K. Dennis Kelly and William J. Chambliss, "Status Consistency and Political Attitudes," *American Sociological Review*, 31 (June 1966), pp. 375–382.

[16] See the following articles by Hubert M. Blalock, Jr., "The Identification Problem and Theory Building: The Case of Status Consistency," *American Sociological Review*, 31 (June 1966), pp. 375–382; "Status Inconsistency, Social Mobility, Status Integration, and Structural Effects," *American Sociological Review*, 32 (October 1967), pp. 790–801; "Tests of Status Inconsistency Theory: A note of Caution," *Pacific Sociological Review*, 10 (Fall 1967), pp. 69–74; and "Status Inconsistency and Interaction: Some Alternative Models," *American Journal of Sociology*, 73 (November 1967), pp. 305–315.

applicable in specific contexts and under specified conditions. David R. Segal found that a more liberal preference does indeed exist among status inconsistents when their low ascribed status is visible to others, or under conditions of extreme political relevance of a nonvisible lower status (e.g., certain orthodox religions).[17] Leonard Broom and F. Lancaster Jones also did not find a generalized effect of status inconsistency on voting behavior, but did find certain effects of specific types of inconsistency. These writers have argued that the effect of status inconsistency on interpersonal behavior varies with the importance or prestige of ascribed status in a given society.[18]

Research on the effects of simultaneous occupancy of inconsistent status positions thus has a long and detailed history primarily in the field of political sociology. Virtually all of this research, however, has been directed at assessing the effects of inconsistencies on the behavior of individuals. Only recently has attention begun to be directed to the question of the status inconsistency of nations. In certain respects the resort to war is analogous to the desire for change or "liberal" political preferences in national politics. Given the relative lack of alternatives for stating peaceful preferences for change in international politics, wars among nations may reflect the desire for change in some normative system. In particular, World Wars I and II can be interpreted in this light. The norms established by the Allies prior to World War I and institutionalized in the League of Nations may have been unacceptable to the Central and Axis Powers, and therefore in both instances violent attempts at change occurred. As we shall see, the relative status inconsistencies of both groups of nations prior to their respective conflicts may be closely related to the onset of these wars.

Other formulations are relevant to the relationship between status inconsistency and the onset of war. A. F. K. Organski, for one, has suggested that there are occasional challenges to the international order that exist at any point in time.[19] The primary vehicle by which the challenger attains his position of prominence is industrialization. By means of a rapid positive rate of change over time, the challenger rapidly approaches the dominant position of the more mature, slower developing power. The rate of increased attributed importance to the challenger may be considerably lower than the rate of

[17] David R. Segal, "Status Inconsistency, Cross-Pressures, and American Political Behavior," *American Sociological Review*, 34 (June 1969), pp. 352–359.

[18] Leonard Broom and F. Lancaster Jones, "Status Consistency and Political Preference: The Australian Case," *American Sociological Review*, 35 (December 1970), pp. 989–1001.

[19] A. F. K. Organski, *World Politics*, 2nd ed. (New York: Knopf, 1968), pp. 338–376.

achievement. Indeed, the dominant power (or powers) would attempt to decrease the attributed importance of the challenger through its own network of interactions with other nations.

Power and achieved status are seen as virtually identical by Organski, and as noted in Chapter II, if the power cannot be used for the benefit of an actor, political violence may result. Two recent studies tend to support this view. J. David Singer and Melvin Small, employing path analysis, found that the "peace through parity" model of international politics is less valid than the idea of a closing gap (parity) between dominant power and challenger as an antecedent of war.[20] A study of Nazli Choucri and Robert C. North also examines aspects of the competitive model of challenger versus dominant power.[21] They find that such a model, which incorporates interactions among competitive powers leading to perceptions of threat and violence, is a better explanation of 1870–1914 conflict data than models which assume a non-competitive stance.

More directly in the realm of status and international politics are studies by Raymond Tanter and R. J. Rummel.[22] Their studies deal with generalized relations between status and international political behaviors. Tanter, using the concept of status inconsistency and its operational referents as the primary explanatory variable, treats the relationship between status and influence attempts in the period 1963–1966. Two of his findings are, first, there is no linear additive relationship between status inconsistency and influence attempts; and second, within a negative status-inconsistent group, the relationship between status variables and influence attempts increased when controls for political system were employed. Rummel's work is more oriented to the synthesis of theories rather than their application. He combines the substantive elements of status theory with the mathematical structure of field theory and generates a set of axioms and theorems. Among Rummel's conclusions are that field theory, with additional status interpretations, leads

[20] J. David Singer and Melvin Small, "Capability Distribution and the Preservation of Peace in the Major Power Sub-System, 1816–1945" (Paper delivered at the 1970 Annual Meeting of the American Political Science Association, Los Angeles, Calif., September 7–12).

[21] Nazli Choucri and Robert C. North, "The Determinants of International Violence," *Papers, Peace Research Society (International)* (1969), pp. 33–63. Also, by the same authors, "International Dynamics, 1870–1970: In Search of Peace Systems" (Paper presented at the 1970 Annual Meeting of the American Political Science Association, Los Angeles, Calif., September 7–12).

[22] Raymond Tanter, "Status and Influence Attempts in International Politics" (Paper delivered at the 1969 Annual Meeting of the American Political Science Association, New York City, September 2–6); and R. J. Rummel, "A Status–Field Theory of International Relations," (Paper presented at the Peace Research Society [International] Conference, Vienna, Austria, August 29–30, 1971).

to the same behavioral prediction of "status-dependent" international behavior as does status theory alone.

Studies dealing explicitly with the concept of status inconsistency in relation to war are those of Michael Wallace and Maurice A. East.[23] Wallace uses measures of status inconsistency at the level of the international system and, with a fifteen-year lag, finds relationships between status inconsistency and the duration (nation-months) of international warfare. In further research, Wallace finds certain persisting relationships between status inconsistency and battle fatalities in the period 1850–1964. East has found similar relationships among four measures of status discrepancy and international conflict in the period 1946–1964. Thus, the theoretical approach of status inconsistency in the explanation of international warfare already has some empirical validation.

International Status in Historical Perspective

To this point, the chapter has outlined a theoretical framework providing references to research on status inconsistency applied to individuals and to research on its relationship to war. A next step is to illustrate the importance of international stratification. In the contemporary international system, as suggested by Gustavo Lagos, there exist status differentials among nations.[24] The newly independent nations of Asia and Africa, as well as their more economically underdeveloped counterparts in Latin America, stress the economic distance between themselves and the more developed nations.

Irving Louis Horowitz also considers the gap between the Third World countries and the developed nations of both the West and the Communist world.[25] In his view, much of the military competition between East and West takes place in the territory of the developing countries primarily because of their vulnerability and concomitant low status. However, this form of stratification might be an artifact of the contemporary period with its proliferation of new nations and might not necessarily be relevant to prior historical periods. Since this study is concerned with the period 1870–1945, it would do

[23] Michael D. Wallace, "Power, Status, and International War," *Journal of Peace Research*, 8 (no. 1, 1971), pp. 23–35; and *idem*, "Status, Formal Organization, and Arms Levels as Factors Leading to the Onset of War, 1820–1964," in Bruce M. Russett (ed.), *Peace, War, and Numbers* (Beverly Hills, Calif.: Sage Publications, 1972), pp. 49–69. Also see Maurice A. East, "Stratification in the International System: An Empirical Analysis," mimeographed (Denver: Graduate School of International Studies, University of Denver, December 1968).

[24] Gustavo Lagos, *International Stratification and Underdeveloped Countries* (Chapel Hill: University of North Carolina Press, 1963), pp. 3–30.

[25] Irving L. Horowitz, *Three Worlds of Development* (New York: Oxford University Press, 1966).

well to indicate the importance of international stratification throughout recent European history.

One of the earliest historical references to stratification among European nations is the dual list of sovereigns attributed to Pope Julius II in 1504. The list refers first to the order of European monarchs and then to the ranking of princes and republics.[26]

Ordo Regum Christianorum

Imperator	Caesar
Rex	Romanorum
Rex	Franciae
Rex	Hispaniae
Rex	Aragoniae
Rex	Portugalliae
Rex	Angliae
Rex	Siciliae
Rex	Scotiae et Rex Ungariae
Rex	Navarrae
Rex	Cipri
Rex	Bohemiae
Rex	Poloniae
Rex	Daniae

Ordo Ducum

Dux	Britanniae
Dux	Burgundiae
Dux	Bavariae
Dux	Saxoniae
Marchio	Brandenburgensis
Dux	Austriae
Dux	Sabaudiae
Dux	Mediolani
Dux	Venetiarum
Duces	Bavariae
Duces	Franciae et Lotharingiae
Duces	Borboniae
Dux	Aurelianensis
Dux	Januae
Dux	Ferrariae

[26] Sir Ernest Satow, *A Guide to Diplomatic Practice*, 3rd ed., rev. by H. Ritchie (London: Longmans, Green, 1932), pp. 23–24.

In one case, there is an apparent attempt to compensate the British for their relatively low status in the order of monarchies, by according them first rank in the order of princes and republics. Even in the early sixteenth century, Britain was a rising power—this attempt at compensation may have been due in part to a recognition of her power. In two instances there are ties in the status orderings, one for each of the two stratifications.

Status may be conferred from "above," as in this example of a stratification system constructed by the Papacy. However, in the normal process of interaction between nations, the diplomat is the person accorded the status reserved for a given nation. The respect he receives is really that which is shown his country and the insults directed at him are intended for the country he represents.[27] Thus, the treatment accorded a diplomat is often indicative of the status of his country, and disputes between diplomats may be symptomatic of status conflicts between nations.

As indicated by the *Ordo Regum Christianorum*, France and Spain, respectively, occupy the third and fourth status positions among European monarchies. Galtung's framework leads us to expect that conflicts over status might occur between the two countries. And indeed the sixteenth and seventeenth centuries were replete with such conflicts. For example, at the wedding of the Crown Prince of Denmark in 1633, a dispute arose between the French and Spanish ambassadors over the seating arrangement. The French ambassador informed the Danish ministers that he would give the Spanish ambassador the opportunity of choosing the most honorable place at the table, and once having made the choice, the French ambassador would throw out the Spaniard and take the place himself. To avoid trouble, the Spanish ambassador did not appear at the ceremony.

There also was an incident in London in the year 1661, when the new Swedish ambassador made his formal entry into the city. A violent dispute broke out between the French and Spanish resident ambassadors and their armed coachmen as to who should follow in the place of honor behind the Swedish ambassador. The Spanish coachmen defeated their French counterparts and took the desired position. When Louis XIV heard of the incident he expelled the Spanish ambassador to France and demanded that de Watteville, the Spanish ambassador to London, be punished. Moreover, Louis XIV demanded that Spanish ambassadors should yield places of honor to the French at all foreign courts and "In case of a refusal a declaration of war was to be notified."[28] The Spanish largely acceded to the request.

With the dissolution of the Holy Roman Empire in 1806, even its nominal

[27] Hans J. Morgenthau, *Politics Among Nations: The Struggle for Power and Peace*, 4th ed. (New York: Knopf, 1967), p. 71.

[28] Satow, *op. cit.*, pp. 25–26.

precedence as the first among European states was hardly tenable, and the diplomatic equality of all soverign states was recognized. Prior to this date, arguments had been put forward regarding the equality of all nation-states. Gustavus Adolphus of Sweden had asserted this position at the Congress of Westphalia and was supported by Queen Christina of Denmark. At the formation of the Quadruple Alliance, Britain argued for the equality of nation-states.

Despite frequent assertions of equality, however, and the nominal equality of sovereignties after 1806, status considerations are still a reality of international politics. Sir Ernest Satow has noted that a nominal equality and adherence to democratic forms of government hardly "lessen the importance attached by states to the maintenance of their position *vis-à-vis* other states"; and the status considerations which had motivated France, Spain, and the Papacy centuries earlier are equally relevant in modern times.[29] Countries such as the Soviet Union which have expressed an ideological commitment to international equality are quite conscious of the importance of status.

At the Potsdam Conference in 1946, Truman, Churchill, and Stalin, the leaders of the three great powers, could not agree on the order of entry into the conference room. It was eventually decided that all three should enter simultaneously through separate doors. In 1946, when the foreign minister of the Soviet Union was placed in the second row at a victory celebration in Paris while the ministers of the other great powers sat in the first, he left the celebration in protest. The Soviet Union had in the past endured many diplomatic slights from the Western powers, but with its recent victory over Germany in the East, the U.S.S.R. would insist on a prestige concomitant with its new-found national power.[30]

The United States, of course, was not immune to status concerns, even in the late nineteenth century. The American delegates to the First Peace Conference at The Hague in 1899 were unhappy at being seated at a table under the letter *E* for États-Unis. At the Second Peace Conference in 1907, it was discovered that the name "Amérique" was also acceptable in the French lexicon, and as a result, the United States could have seating precedence over all of the Latin American republics and many of the European powers as well.

Some Illustrations of Contemporary Warfare

A number of examples may serve to illustrate the status inconsistency of a nation prior to a major conflict. Perhaps the three outstanding instances of modern warfare are the Franco-Prussian War of 1870–1871, and World

[29] *Ibid.*, p. 30.
[30] Morgenthau, *op. cit.*, p. 72.

Wars I and II. Each of these wars, at the time of their occurrence and again in the light of historical evaluation, is important for later political and historical development. With respect to our framework, each of these examples exhibits the phenomenon of status inconsistency prior to the occurrence of the conflict. The Franco-Prussian War was apparently the product of Bismarck's attempt at German unification. Yet, it appears that the status inconsistency of Prussia together with the German principalities was a condition of this conflict.

Prior to 1870, Germany was not yet unified; its status as a military and economic power was relatively low when compared with England and particularly with France. French was the diplomatic language of Europe, and the memories of Napoleonic greatness, as well as the acquisition of vast colonial territories in the mid-nineteenth century, tended to enhance French status. Hence, on a comparative basis (and all meaningful judgments on status are by necessity relative), the Germans tended to enjoy a low level of ascribed status.

Nevertheless, their level of achievement was relatively high. Germany was reaching what has been called the "take off" stage of economic growth, and economic development was increasing at a rapid rate.[31] Moreover, the Prussian bureaucracy, always a highly efficient organization, had reached new levels of effectiveness in organizing the state machinery. The Prussian military also had experienced a rapid rate of development in the years following the Napoleonic Wars.

Thus, an inconsistency existed between Germany's achieved and ascribed status prior to the challenge to the dominant nations. This challenge by Bismarck was inherent in his attempts at German unification. A long-standing policy of the French had been that a set of weak, disunified principalities should exist on her eastern border. Moreover, the very emergence of a united Germany constituted a challenge to the perpetuation of French continental dominance. With a population slightly larger than that of France and with a higher birth rate, a unified Germany would offer an even greater challenge.

The history of the international system prior to World War I also manifests a similar process. Despite the even greater economic, administrative, and military development of Germany after 1871, her ascribed status was still largely inconsistent with her level of achievement. A measure of ascribed status in this period was the extent to which a European country obtained overseas colonies, and in this attempt at an increase in ascribed status, Germany was consistently blocked by the Anglo-French coalition. Moreover,

[31] W. W. Rostow, *The Stages of Economic Growth: A Non-Communist Manifesto* (New York: Cambridge University Press, 1960).

the British had uncontested naval supremacy, and the German challenge took the form of rapid naval development, which became intolerable to the British. Although World War I may have been the *immediate* product of the conflict between Serbian nationalism and Austrian attempts at maintaining the Hapsburg Empire, the status inconsistency of the German Empire may have been a long-term antecedent of this conflict.

The period prior to World War II also exhibits elements of status inconsistency on the part of Germany. Shorn of her colonies and treated as a pariah by the dominant Anglo-French coalition, Germany's level of status ascription was at a new low. George F. Kennan describes how the victorious Allies shunned German diplomats at Geneva and generally excluded her from the major international policy-making conferences of the period.[32] This treatment was clearly inconsistent with Germany's power potential which, under Hitler, was experiencing a rapid rate of development. This status inconsistency may have led Germany to challenge the dominant system, whose dictates were embodied in the Treaty of Versailles and the League Covenant.

Figure 5.2 shows the status inconsistency of a nation-state. The ascribed status emanates from an international system consisting of diplomats as well as international organizations and conferences.[33] The achieved status of a nation is determined solely by internal characteristics such as economic development or communications growth. (The specific variables employed are discussed in a subsequent section.)

At this juncture, something in the nature of a caveat is in order. The sample of wars extends only until 1945, and it may be argued that the subsequent emergence of nuclear weapons fundamentally has altered the nature of international conflict. Whereas conventional (non-nuclear) warfare allows individual nation-states the option of openly declaring war if all avenues of conflict resolution fail, the existence of nuclear weapons in both East and West severely limits this option. The immense destructive power of nuclear weapons and the potential consequences of a military engagement are so great that the superpowers could not lightly engage in direct open warfare. Partly as a result, nation-states in the postwar period resort to subversion and other methods of initiating internal conflict as a means of implementing their policies.[34]

---

[32] George F. Kennan, *Russia and the West under Lenin and Stalin* (New York: Mentor, 1960), pp. 198–212.

[33] The difficulties in operationalizing the concept of international ascription are many and will be treated at a later point in this chapter.

[34] For a detailed treatment of subversive activities by the major powers of both East and West, see Paul Blackstock, *The Strategy of Subversion: Manipulating the Politics of Other Nations* (Chicago: Quadrangle, 1964).

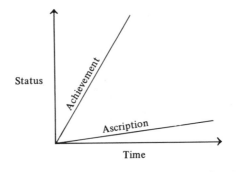

Figure 5.2 **The Status Inconsistency of a Nation-State**

The initiation of internal conflict thus replaces foreign conflict as a means of goal attainment for the foreign policies of the major international actors. Indeed, Samuel P. Huntington has proposed that in the mid-twentieth century, an inverse relationship may exist between domestic and foreign conflict behavior due to the emergence of nuclear weapons and attendant doctrines, such as that of "la guerre révolutionnaire." [35]

However, even if one accepts the validity of the preceding arguments, they do not militate against the relevance of status inconsistency as an explanation of contemporary international warfare. Granted the impracticality of an open military confrontation and its substitution by internal warfare, it may be argued that most of the major internal wars of the contemporary period—those involving a confrontation between the major powers—have been a product of the status inconsistency experienced by at least one of these powers. A large percentage of these internal wars has occurred around the periphery of China. The single large-scale conventional military engagement of the postwar period—the Korean War—involved Chinese troops as well as other forms of military aid. The Indochina conflict already has exhibited many of the properties of conventional warfare. To be sure, Chinese troops had not openly entered the war, yet it would be difficult to deny the Chinese role in support of this conflict.

An examination of recent Chinese history reveals that China experienced

[35] The doctrine of "la guerre révolutionnaire" arose as a product of the war in Indochina prior to 1954, and the Algerian rebellion. French political observers recognized that these insurrections were primarily internal, yet they bore the imprint of support from Communist countries. This doctrine therefore was applied to any internal war in which the insurgents employed both guerrilla warfare and psychological warfare and, in addition, received external Communist support. See Samuel P. Huntington, "Patterns of Violence in World Politics," in S. P. Huntington (ed.), *Changing Patterns of Military Politics* (New York: The Free Press, 1962), pp. 17–50.

perhaps the most severe status inconsistency of any major power in the postwar period. With a population approaching 750 million persons, a large and well-disciplined army, a rapid rate of economic growth (despite periodic setbacks), and a highly centralized administration, China's rate and level of internal achievement were exceedingly high relative to the earlier part of this century. Yet, her rate and level of ascribed status were low. Without a seat in the United Nations, and without diplomatic representatives from several Western nations, China's ascribed status appeared inconsistent with her actual achievements. If the major powers, in particular the United States, had been willing to accord China an ascribed status consistent with her achievements, it is conceivable that much of this conflict behavior might have been significantly reduced. Thus, although the fundamental character of contemporary warfare may have undergone a transformation, nevertheless much of domestic conflict and even conventional foreign conflict behavior may be attributed, in part, to considerations of status inconsistency.

The Variables

This discussion is concerned with the explanation of three principal characteristics of war—the frequency, magnitude, and severity of international warfare. This is a departure from the analyses in Chapters III and IV, which dealt only with frequency as a dependent variable. It will be recalled that the framework in Chapter II was specified initially for the explanation of the frequency of political violence, and a principal operationalization—alliance-related uncertainty for the nation-state—was statistically related only to the frequency of war. This procedure was appropriate in that instance because of the nature of both theory and data. The uncertainty represents a power loss or lack of control over events *prior* to the conflict: it would be difficult to argue that uncertainty itself should be *theoretically* (although it may be correlated empirically) associated with characteristics of the conflict, such as magnitude as a temporal measure or severity as indicated by the number of combatants killed. The data for the independent variables also justified this approach. Variables such as frequency of alliance or time spent in alliance for the continuous case lend themselves readily to mathematical manipulations of the type described in Chapter III. Given the explicitly probabilistic interpretation of the independent variables suggested by the framework, they should initially be related only to other variables with specific probabilistic interpretations such as the frequency of violent events.

Status inconsistency is a form of the prevention of uncertainty reduction and, therefore, is a type of power loss or powerlessness; however, it is not susceptible to the same types of interpretation as is the treatment of alliance-related uncertainty. It can be argued that the type of uncertainty existing in the case of status inconsistency could be *theoretically* related to the magnitude and severity of international warfare. The greater the inconsistency over a long period of time, the greater may be the desire to rectify it at whatever cost in lives or time spent in war. Decision makers in a high status-inconsistent nation may be conscious of the inconsistency and consequently disturbed by it.[36] This situation stands in contrast to the probable lack of awareness of a power loss in the instance of alliance-related uncertainty. Given the likelihood of a consciousness in nations of high status inconsistency, the decision makers then could carry their negative feelings into the conflict itself and affect its magnitude and severity. In this sense of the possibility of anger as an intervening variable between status inconsistency and war, the perceived inconsistency of nation-states by their own decision makers may bear similarities to the frustration–aggression approach to the study of political violence. However, a principal component of status inconsistency—the achievement of nations as a form of ability—is not suggested by frustration–aggression theory; therefore, the concept of an inconsistency between achievement and ascription should not be considered an outcome of this approach.

It may also be possible to relate status inconsistency to the characteristics of war because of the nature of the data. As will be seen, the measurement of status inconsistency is in the form of a continuous disparity between two conditions, achievement and ascription, and is not based on the frequency of events, as in the case of alliance-related uncertainty. Thus, we are seeking to explain not only the frequency of international political violence, but also its magnitude and duration.

A further distinction between the present analysis of status inconsistency and the previous ones concerns the time period of analysis. Whereas in the earlier treatments the entire 1815–1945 interval was employed for the dependent variable, here it is 1870–1945. This reduction in time span is necessitated by problems of data availability. The time series used to construct the independent variables are based on data (and sources) which for the most part did not exist prior to 1850 and are available for the majority of countries only after 1870. Therefore, in order to employ a longitudinal form of analysis to explain warfare during the period for which data are available, the time period for the dependent variables is shortened to 1870–1945.

The *frequency* of war is the number of wars a nation experienced during the

---

[36] George F. Kennan, *op. cit.*, details how the Soviets and Weimar Germans were often snubbed by Western diplomats in the post-World War I period and the possible embittering effect on these persons. The discriminatory treatment of the Japanese at the 1922 Washington Naval Conference may be another example of this type of behavior.

TABLE 5.1.   Values of the Dependent Variables, 1870–1945

Country	Years in war	Years in war vs. major	No. of wars	No. of wars vs. major	Battle deaths[a]
Argentina	0.0	0.0	0	0	0.0
Austria (-Hungary)	4.4	4.3	2	1	1200.0
Belgium	4.3	4.3	2	2	95.3
Brazil	0.8	0.8	1	1	0.1
Bulgaria	6.3	5.8	4	2	74.0
Chile	4.8	.0	1	0	3.0
Czechoslovakia	.0	.0	0	0	.0
Denmark	.0	.0	0	0	.0
England	10.4	10.2	3	2	1178.0
Finland	3.5	3.5	2	2	82.0
France	6.6	6.5	4	3	1700.0
Germany (Prussia)	10.7	10.5	4	3	5340.0
Greece	6.1	1.9	6	2	68.1
Guatemala	.2	.0	2	0	1.2
Holland	.1	.1	1	1	6.2
Hungary	3.6	3.6	1	1	40.0
Italy	10.0	8.2	5	2	737.0
Japan	16.1	9.5	7	3	1350.3
Luxembourg	.0	.0	0	0	.0
Nicaragua	.2	.0	1	0	0.4
Norway	.2	.2	1	1	1.0
Paraguay	7.0	.0	1	0	50.0
Peru	4.5	.0	1	0	10.0
Poland	.1	.1	1	1	320.0
Portugal	2.7	2.7	1	1	7.0
Rumania	4.6	4.5	3	2	636.5
Russia	10.0	8.8	6	3	9415.0
Spain	1.0	.0	2	0	7.0
Sweden	.0	.0	0	0	.0
Switzerland	.0	.0	0	0	.0
Turkey	10.0	5.8	7	3	575.4
United States	5.8	5.3	4	2	423.0
Yugoslavia (Serbia)	4.8	4.3	4	2	491.5

SOURCE: Abstracted from J. David Singer and Melvin Small, "National Alliance Commitments and War Involvement, 1818–1945," in J. N. Rosenau (ed.), *International Politics and Foreign Policy: A Reader in Research and Theory*, rev. ed. (New York: The Free Press, 1969), pp. 518–521, 528–529, for the period 1870–1945. The time period and mode of tabular presentation made this the preferred source.
[a] In thousands.

period 1870–1945. This variable is a measure of a nation's propensity to engage in violent conflict. According to the theoretical framework, the greater the status inconsistency experienced by a nation, the greater the number of wars engaged in by that nation. A high degree of status inconsistency may act as a goad to decision makers who may feel that the only available corrective to this inconsistency lies in international warfare.

The second of our dependent variables concerns the *magnitude* of international warfare. As defined by Singer and Small, this variable is virtually identical with duration and is the number of years each nation participated in a given war.[37] As indicated by the theory, a greater degree of inconsistency between achieved and ascribed status prior to a given war leads to increased participation by a country in that war. The inconsistency provides the impetus for participation, and the greater the inconsistency, the greater the motivation for increased participation—hence, an increased duration.

Similar reasoning applies to the third dependent variable, the *severity* of international conflict. This variable is synonymous with intensity, and is the number of battle-connected deaths resulting from the conflict. It may be argued that for a given country, the greater the number of persons killed as a direct result of the war, the greater its intensity of participation. The Soviet Union, for example, has an extraordinarily large number of persons killed, or high severity and intensity of participation, whereas Argentina has relatively few battle-connected deaths, which suggests a relatively low intensity of participation.

Two additional dependent variables are included for the sake of completeness. These are the number of wars versus major powers, and years in war versus majors. Major powers may be identified among the entire set of nations, and the frequency, as well as the magnitude, of war versus these countries might be of interest. If international warfare is a conflict over the dominant norms of the international system, then it is likely that the conflict over these norms is directed at certain major powers. The Treaty of Versailles and the League Covenant are instances of legally embodied norms which were established by the major powers of that period—Britain and France. World War II may have been a challenge to these norms and the major powers which supported them. Table 5.1 presents the values for the dependent variables for countries included in the analysis.[38] Certain countries are

[37] J. David Singer and Melvin Small, "The Frequency, Magnitude and Severity of International War, 1815–1945" (Ann Arbor: Mental Health Research Institute, University of Michigan, August 1965), p. 14.

[38] Other writers, such as Michael Haas, do not employ the data collected by Singer and Small, but use war data compiled by Wright and Richardson. For the purpose of analyzing international stability, Haas is undoubtedly correct in using these sources. However, given the intention of this study in explaining certain characteristics of war, it was decided to use the Singer and Small data for the following reasons. First, each of the sets of data developed by Wright and Richardson is relatively incomplete with regard to certain variables of interest in this study. Wright includes the frequency and duration of war, but not severity in the form of battle deaths for specific nations participating in specific wars. Richardson, on the other hand, tends to emphasize battle casualties for the wars themselves, but not for the specific nations involved in these wars. Second, both Wright and Richardson include wars which are not strictly international in scope, such as wars to defend civilizations or purely internal wars. Third, Singer and Small's data

omitted from this tabulation because of the lack of data on the independent variables. These problems in data availability are discussed in the last section of this chapter.

The independent variables are achieved and ascribed status. The first of these, the achievement variable, consists of *centralization* and *capability*. The former is chosen because of its relevance to conflict–cohesion hypotheses formulated by theorists such as Georg Simmel and Lewis Coser; it includes those aspects of internal development which tend to bring an increasing number of persons under the control of a central authority.[39]

The unification of Germany was primarily a process of centralization, in that the independent German principalities were brought under the control of the Prussian authority at Berlin. Both the Russian and Chinese Revolutions may be viewed as centralizing processes, in light of the centralization needs of socialized economies and the authoritarian reorientation of social processes. Indeed, centralization may be a condition of the second achievement category, capability. In order for a country to wage war effectively or even to consider the possibility of war, it must have effective control of matériel, a centralized means of military recruitment, and the loyalty of a significant proportion of the population. Without a centralized control of transportation and communication, or a high degree of urbanization, such conditions would exist only partially, and the potential of a country to wage effective war would be impaired.

Consider for the moment the need for effective transportation and communication facilities. The raw materials for armaments construction and the armaments themselves could not be transported to areas as necessary. Troops could not be transported, and the logistics dependent upon effective communication would be virtually immobilized. Prior to World War I, both Germany and Russia built railroad tracks and telegraph lines which aimed

---

compilation in part constitutes a refinement of these prior efforts, and in this way may be superior to both. See Michael Haas, "International Subsystems: Stability and Polarity," *American Political Science Review*, 64 (March 1970), pp. 98–123; Quincy Wright, *The Study of War*, pp. 641–665; and Lewis F. Richardson, *Statistics of Deadly Quarrels* (Chicago: Quadrangle, 1960), pp. 32–111.

In addition, the term *major powers* will be used to denote a group of countries which is not quite identical with the previous central power system. In the present analysis, we are concerned with wars *against* major powers (not initiated *by* major powers); therefore, only holders of power which could clearly determine the norms of international systems and thereby give rise to challenges to these norms are included. Spain and Turkey are excluded from the major powers, and this category consists of the remainder of those countries previously termed central powers (see Table 3.1).

[39] See Georg Simmel, *Conflict and the Web of Group-Affiliations*, trans. Kurt H. Wolff and Reinhard Bendix (New York: The Free Press, 1955), pp. 17–20, 98–107; and Lewis Coser, *The Functions of Social Conflict* (New York: The Free Press, 1956), pp. 33–48, 87–149.

at the other's heartland, thus facilitating troop movement in the eventuality of war. Similarly, urbanization may supply the conditions of a speedy and effective mobilization of troops and matériel. Moreover, the presence of this variable may be effective in insuring the sustained loyalty of the population. The socialization and propagandization of populations may be facilitated when the population is concentrated in urban areas, whereas rural areas with few administrative links to a central authority are potential (and often actual) sources of rebellion which may reduce the unity of the state.[40] Such unity may be necessary for the effective conduct of a major conflict. Thus, the three variables, transportation, communication, and urbanization, constitute operational measures for the concept of centralization.[41]

The notion of capability stems principally from Quincy Wright's field theory of international relations and R. J. Rummel's adaptation of it.[42] Capability is defined by those societal conditions and processes which directly enhance the state's potential for waging successful warfare. A. F. K. Organski points to economic development as a primary source of the state's potential for the conduct of war.[43] Measures of rates of change in economic development, as well as population growth, act as operational referents for this variable.[44] Essentially, this concept of capability is concerned more directly with the

[40] See William Kornhauser, "Rebellion and Political Development," in Harry Eckstein (ed.), *Internal War* (New York: The Free Press, 1964), pp. 142–156, especially pp. 146–149.

[41] The term *centralization* in its operational form here refers to a form of "mobilization potential." In choosing the three measures of transportation, communication, and urbanization, the purpose of the analysis is to determine the effect of availability of persons and matériel on international warfare. As such, these measures are intended to ascertain the extent to which a country has effectively mobilized its resources in the event of war. Of course, the concept of centralization can, and often does, refer to the dispersion of resources in society. That is, how the means of transportation, communication, or urbanization are distributed throughout the country. Although dispersion measures often are of interest in the study of internal politics and, in particular, internal violence (e.g., Gini Index of Inequality), they may be of less importance in the analysis of international warfare. The availability of human and material resources in the form of a "mobilization potential" might be a more adequate concept in this context, especially in the light of the confrontation of armies at the battle front, a process which occurs in international warfare, but not necessarily in internal war.

[42] See Quincy Wright, *The Study of International Relations* (New York: Appleton-Century-Crofts, 1955), pp. 531–569; and R. J. Rummel, "A Field Theory of Social Action with Application to Conflict Within Nations," *General Systems: Yearbook of the Society of General Systems*, vol. 10 (1965).

[43] Organski, *op. cit.*, pp. 199–200, 211–215.

[44] The concept of capability also has other interpretations. Harold and Margaret Sprout, for example, employ a functional analysis of capability wherein the functions of intelligence, decision making, means provision, means utilization, and resistance to demands are seen as aspects of national capability. See their *Foundations of International Politics* (Princeton, N.J.: Van Nostrand, 1962), pp. 167–177. Stephen B. Jones provides another interpretation of capability in which the availability (potential) of these resources is central to the analysis, as it is, in fact, in the treatment of *centralization* or *mobilization potential* in this study. See his "The Power Inventory and National Strategy," in James

TABLE 5.2. **Operational Measures for the Achievement Variable**

Centralization			Capability	
Transportation	*Communication*	*Urbanization*	*Economic development*	*Population*
Railroad mileage	Telegraph Telephone Mail flow	Number of persons in cities	Gross national product	Number of persons

capacity to wage war, in contrast to the centralization variable, which may be interpreted as a condition of capability. Table 5.2 presents the measures chosen for each of the variables.

A few comments are in order concerning the adequacy of each of these measures. The use of railroad mileage as a measure of transportation may be appropriate for the time period under investigation. In the late nineteenth and early–middle twentieth centuries, paved highways and air traffic were not yet primary means of transportation. In particular, the transportation of matériel employed in international warfare was generally by means of railroad, and the extent to which a country was centralized with regard to transportation capacity might be measurable by means of railroad mileage.

Although a single measure may be appropriate for the transportation variable, the choice of a solitary measure for communication would be inapplicable. Throughout the time period under investigation, at least three forms of communication were employed. These are telegraph, telephone, and mail flow. Despite the fact that during different segments of this time period, one or the other of these forms of communication was more prevalent, it would be difficult to assume that any one form was employed exclusively.

N. Rosenau (ed.), *International Politics and Foreign Policy* (New York: The Free Press, 1961), pp. 254–267.

The analysis of capability here is specific to economic development and population, as suggested by A. F. K. Organski, *op. cit.*, pp. 148–153. One can narrow the field even further by specifying only those capabilities directly related to the conduct of war. Examples are the number of combat-related aircraft, proportion of defense expenditures, and numerical size of the armed forces. However, the inclusion of only these variables will not account for factors such as agricultural production, which may be equally relevant to the conduct of modern warfare (e.g., food shortages in Germany in 1917–1918). Data for GNP are found in Colin Clark, *The Conditions of Economic Progress*. 3rd ed. (London: Macmillan, 1957), while values for urbanization and population are given in *The Statesman's Yearbooks* and the *United Nations Demographic Yearbook* (1952). Railroad mileages are found in the statistical publications of the Union Internationale des Chemins de Fer (1927–1938). Data for telegraph and telephone are found in the statistical publications of the Bureau Internationale des Administrations Télégraphiques (1871–1940; 1893–1940), and the American Telephone and Telegraph Company (1914–1930). Mail flow data are given in the statistics of the Universal Postal Union (1878–1940).

Thus, all three are appropriate as measures of the communication variable.[45]

The third of the centralization variables—urbanization—is the size of the urban population. Other alternatives, such as a ratio of urban to total population, might appear to be acceptable; however, such a measure might not reflect the meaning of the centralization concept in this study. This concept refers to the availability and potentiality for mobilization of large numbers of individuals.[46] Therefore, it is the absolute number of individuals residing in urban areas which is relevant. A ratio of urban to total population might conceivably be high, even if the absolute number of urban residents were small (small urban population/small total population). Conversely, a large urban population might be reflected by a small urbanization ratio (large urban population/large total population).

With regard to the measures of capability, economic development is represented by gross national product, and population by the total number of persons residing in a given country. Economic development might also be represented by other variables such as those pertaining to increased industrial capacity. However, gross national product is a *comprehensive* measure of economic output, and data for this variable are available as early as the mid-nineteenth century. Variables such as output of electricity or the production of heavy industry are generally available only from the early part of the twentieth century. Finally, population is the number of persons residing in a given country, a rather direct operational measure which has few alternatives.

The second of our independent variables is the status ascribed to a nation by elements of the international system. Ascribed status may be seen as identical to the importance attributed to a given nation by other nations, and the number and rank of diplomats sent to that nation by all other nations

[45] Karl Deutsch has emphasized the importance of communication variables in the understanding of political phenomena. See, for example, his "Shifts in the Balance of Communication Flows: A Problem of Measurement in International Relations," *Public Opinion Quarterly*, 20 (Spring 1956), pp. 143–160; and *The Nerves of Government: Models of Political Communication and Control* (New York: The Free Press, 1963).

[46] The potentiality for mobilization does not pertain only to the physical induction of persons into armed forces. It also refers to doctrinal mobilization under the auspices of a political cause or ideology. In addition, more careful control of large populations is possible within a highly mobilized setting.

The reasoning with regard to the operationalization of this variable is similar to that employed in the interpretation of the concept of centralization (see note 41 above). The availability of persons, or "mobilization potential," as the result of urbanization is of greater interest here than measures such as a comparison of urban and rural populations which an urbanization ratio might provide. The latter method perhaps might be more germane to an investigation of internal violence, but not necessarily of international warfare. The absolute number of persons available for doctrinal or physical mobilization is of interest in the present context primarily because the confrontations between armies at the battle front would be more dependent on availability for mobilization than on specific patterns of population dispersion within countries.

may be a measure of ascribed status. As indicated previously, the diplomat is the vehicle through which status may be expressed. If nation A is not perceived to be important to the interests of nation B, then it seems likely that the number of diplomats sent to A by B will be smaller, and the rank lower than diplomats sent by B to some other country with higher status. Thus, the number and rank of diplomats received by a country acts as a measure of the ascription variable.

The measurement of ascribed status by the number and rank of diplomats received was suggested by Singer and Small and I have used it elsewhere.[47] Clearly, there are alternative measures in this instance. The number of international conferences attended by a country, as well as the frequency with which these conferences were held in a nation's capital, might act as an alternative measure. However, an examination of data of this type reveals that despite the appropriate use of such a measure for the nineteenth century, it becomes increasingly inapplicable for the twentieth century. Many of the important international conferences of the nineteenth century, such as the Congress of Paris in 1856 or the Conferences of London in 1867 and 1871, indeed were indicative of the host country's status. After the two Peace Conferences at The Hague (1899, 1907), and the attendant expansion of the international system, relatively "neutral" capitals were chosen as sites for international gatherings. Brussels and Geneva became increasingly prominent as host capitals, with London, Paris, and Berlin chosen less frequently.

Another possible measure for ascribed status might be the number of international organizations to which a nation belonged. However, a similar

[47] See J. David Singer and Melvin Small, "The Composition and Status Ordering of the International System: 1815–1940," *World Politics*, 18 (January 1966), pp. 236–282. A study of instability employs status and competence as predictors of the diffusion of instability. The number and rank of diplomats received are used to measure status. See Manus Midlarsky, "Mathematical Models of Instability and a Theory of Diffusion," *International Studies Quarterly*, 14 (March 1970), pp. 60–84. For other uses of data on diplomatic exchange, see Chadwick F. Alger and Steven J. Brams, "Patterns of Representation in National Capitals and Intergovernmental Organizations," *World Politics*, 19 (July 1967), pp. 646–663.

The diplomatic data as published by Singer and Small are collected for the period 1815–1940 and are published for five-year intervals within this period. The primary data source is the *Almanach de Gotha*, and where it is incomplete or unreliable it is supplemented by other sources which are listed in Singer and Small, "Composition," pp. 251–252. The score for each country for a given year is compiled by assigning 3 points to each ambassador or equivalent assigned to that country from all other countries, and 2 for each minister, minister resident, or envoy. Chargés d'affaires or equivalents receive 1 point. Using this system, France, for example, in 1869 received a score of 57, England, a score of 51. The authors also convert the data to composite standardized scores and, in addition, provide a list of weighted status orderings. Since standardizations were performed explicitly in certain portions of the present study or were included within the correlational procedures, it was decided to employ the original scores.

problem exists with regard to the choice of this variable. Although during their early history these organizations maintained a rather selective membership, with the turn of the century and in particular the Hague Peace Conference of 1907, many more nations were invited to join. To be sure, organizations such as the Universal Postal Union maintained an explicit ordering of nations based on the amount of dues each had to pay to the organization, but "status" orderings of this kind were rare among international organizations. Thus, if either or both of these additional measures were chosen, there would be a serious risk of creating insensitive measures, particularly with regard to the twentieth-century segment of this time period. In order to maintain a constant sensitivity of the status measure throughout the period under investigation, the use of the number and rank of diplomats received is a preferred alternative.

Measurement of the Independent Variables

The question arises as to the specific forms of measurement to be employed here. This problem is particularly important in this context because of the seventy-five-year time period. Cross-sectional analysis, in which the *level* of variables is measured at given points in time, appears to be a possibility, yet the choice of certain points in time to the exclusion of others may be open to serious question. In addition, there exists the problem of choosing a time lag between independent and dependent variables. It can be argued that the effect of an independent variable on the dependent characteristics of war might not be immediate but may require a period of time to mature. The same questions which arise in the choice of a given point in time to conduct a cross-sectional analysis also apply to the choice of a given time lag. This problem is not serious when the time period under analysis is short, although for a seventy-five-year period it might be crucial.

Given the problems inherent in the choice of a cross-sectional analysis for this study, the use of a modified form of longitudinal analysis seems to be appropriate. The particular analysis employed here first measures the rates of change of the independent variables for the entire time period, and then relates them to the dependent characteristics of war. The necessity for choosing certain points in time over others is eliminated and the whole time interval can be utilized for the data analysis.[48] Aside from the elimination of certain difficulties, however, there are positive advantages to be gained through the

---

[48] It is possible to aggregate data over a relatively long period, but this is practical only when the data refer to discrete events such as the number of wars or battle deaths. For the independent variables of this study, the aggregation over time of variables such as GNP or railroad mileage would not be appropriate.

use of an analysis over time. As Otis Duncan indicates, the inferences derived from a longitudinal analysis are more generalizable than those from a cross-sectional analysis.[49] Because of the limitations imposed on the latter by the choice of discrete points in time, the inferences are relative only to these points and may not be relevant to others.

Certainly, however, there are difficulties with longitudinal analyses which must be taken into account. The first is not directly relevant to this study, but because of the prominence of this criticism in the statistical literature, at least brief mention should be made of it. A longitudinal analysis involves time series data and as such may depart from the assumptions underlying inferences derived from correlations. It is assumed that each item in the sample is drawn independently and in a random fashion from all others. A time series may not conform to this assumption since each point in the series may correlate with a preceding or subsequent point. When there is a significant degree of association between each point in the time series and a succeeding point in that series, then there is a significant autocorrelation effect.[50] Because the assumptions of random sampling may not have been met, the correlation coefficients between two such time series may not be stable from one time period to the next.

Although this is a common criticism of time series analysis, it is not directly applicable to the present context. The purpose of this study is the use of time series data to obtain measures for rates of change over time. These rates of change are then related to the characteristics of war, which are not in the form of time series, but are expressed as aggregate measures of the frequency, magnitude, and severity of war summed over the time period 1870–1945.[51] Thus, the correlations between time series which might exhibit instability from one time period to another are not obtained in this study.

A limitation of time series analysis which indeed is applicable to this study is imposed by the problem of data availability. Data are collected from the mid-nineteenth century, and the data sources often exhibit gaps in time for which values may not be obtained. The rates of change over time, therefore, are sometimes based on a relatively small number of values. However, even

[49] Otis D. Duncan, Ray P. Cuzzort, and Beverly Duncan, *Statistical Geography: Problems in Analyzing Areal Data* (New York: The Free Press, 1961), pp. 160–161.

[50] Mordecai Ezekiel and Karl A. Fox, *Methods of Correlation and Regression Analysis: Linear and Curvilinear* (New York: Wiley, 1959), p. 327.

[51] The use of rates of change measures for the independent variables and aggregate measures for the dependent variables deserves comment. Under certain circumstances, it might be advisable to use rates of change measures for both. However, many of the countries in the analysis experienced only one or two wars in this time period, and the calculation of regression coefficients could not be carried out for these cases. In addition, the problem of autocorrelation effects in two or more time series to be related with one another is eliminated by the procedure chosen here.

with a small number of values, if the data points are spread over a relatively large segment of the time period, the probability of obtaining an unstable time series is significantly reduced.

A modified form of longitudinal analysis having been chosen, it remains to determine the quantitative means by which the analysis is carried out. A concern with rates of change over time suggests the possiblity of using the regression coefficient as a measure of change. This statistic is a least-squares measure of the slope of a line and has been used in a prior analysis of the relationship between rates of change of economic development and revolulution.[52] When data points are obtained in time series form, the regression coefficient constitutes a measure of the time rate of change of the series. Although percentage change might be an alternative, the regression coefficient makes better use of the data than would a percentage change measure.

Data Collection

The data were collected for the time period 1860–1940. This is not to say, however, that all variables could be obtained for all countries over the entire time interval. Data were obtained most easily for the European countries, as well as the United States and Japan, with varying degrees of success for other countries.

The obtained data are subject to error of various kinds. Regarding reliability error, for example, there are at least two possible courses of action. The first entails the inclusion of data from all possible sources, in which case the time series would have been relatively complete for many countries. However, the reliability of the time series might have been jeopardized seriously by this approach. Indeed, even when a single source was employed in the construction of a time series, inconsistencies resulted in the series.[53] When two sources are used for a single series, the probability of error is significantly increased, and if a third or fourth data source is employed, then the reliability of that series cannot be guaranteed.

The second alternative, which was chosen for this analysis, involves the use of not more than two sources for each time series. The reliability errors associated with this alternative are of a somewhat different variety. Although each of the time series does not suffer from a confusion of data sources, still

[52] Raymond Tanter and Manus Midlarsky, "A Theory of Revolution," *Journal of Conflict Resolution*, 11 (September 1967), pp. 264–280.
[53] Even a single source such as the *United Nations Statistical Yearbook* may contain inconsistencies in recording time series data. An illustration of the use of time rates of change of economic development is found in Tanter and Midlarsky, *op. cit.*; and inconsistencies in the recording of time series were found in data sources such as the *U.N. Yearbook*.

the choice of a small number of data sources effectively limits the number of data points which can appear in a single series. As a result, each of the series may be relatively insensitive to fluctuations of short duration, but will generally capture larger trends over long periods of time. Moreover, discontinuities in the data which might appear due to a variety of sources, might be partially eliminated.

A serious problem in data collection arises due to a combination of data availability and the vagaries of history itself. For many of the countries in the statistical universe, data simply are not available from any source known to this writer (e.g., Ethiopia, Saudi Arabia). Consequently, these countries are not included in the analysis. British Commonwealth nations such as Australia, Canada, and New Zealand only recently established independent diplomatic corps, and an insufficient number of data points exist for the reliable measurement of ascribed status. These countries, therefore, are also omitted. In addition, certain countries for which data on achieved status are available (e.g., Brazil, Chile) began recording pertinent data at a relatively late date in their own histories. Britain and France have aggregate data available from the mid-nineteenth century or earlier, but others, such as many of the Latin American countries, have systematic records beginning only in 1920 or 1933.

Another issue in data collection arises from the relative recency of independence of some countries and the disappearance of others. Czechoslovakia, Finland, and Poland, for example, became independent as a result of World War I, and data availability generally does not extend before that time. Austria-Hungary disappeared as a political entity after World War I and the regression coefficients for its time series are calculated only up to 1919. The case of Yugoslavia is rather unique in that its predecessor, Serbia, provided the political and economic nucleus for the new state, and both are treated as forming a single time series.

Given these inconsistencies of history and data availability, two criteria are that a minimum of seven data points and a maximum of seventeen points are necessary for a time series to enter this study. The average number of data points per time series for each variable is approximately twelve, which is equivalent to one data point for every seven-year period. Although more values could be included by referring to additional data sources, this might result in the gross reliability error mentioned earlier.

The regression coefficients for the independent variables are based on the time series data.[54] For each country and its time series, there is a starting date

---

[54] Two issues are involved in the calculation of regression coefficients over this time period. The first involves the points in time when certain nations experienced war. In a few cases, the data for the independent variables are extended for a short time period after the war occurred. This was done to maximize the number of points per time series,

depending on data availability and the country's history. Where possible, the starting date is set at 1860 or before, to allow for at least ten years prior to the beginning of the period under analysis.

Only one of the variables—communication—is a composite measure and is constructed as follows.[55] The source for data on telephone messages presents the values as urban and inter-urban telephone communication. The two forms are added, and this summed value is added to the values for telegraph and postal communication; the result is divided by three. Thus, the communication variable is a mean value for all three forms. Now it may be argued that each of these types of communication should be evaluated separately. However, an analysis of the individual measures reveals that technological change over this time period apparently led to variations in the employment of different modes of communication. The telegraph came into use in the late nineteenth century, but with the passage of time the telephone was adopted increasingly as the standard form of communication in the twentieth century. Thus, a decline in the use of one form of communication over time does not necessarily imply that people are communicating less, but that other modes of communication are used more. A measure which takes all three into account is probably of greater validity than one which relies on only one mode. The statistical tests of the status inconsistency hypothesis are now carried out in Chapter VI.

---

but as a result, certain values of the regression coefficients are based, in part, on a time period subsequent to the war. In these instances, the calculated values are extrapolations, in which it is assumed that the rates of change are relatively constant over this time period.

The second issue concerns the possibility of splitting the time period into nineteenth- and twentieth-century segments, as Singer and Small did in their "Alliance Aggregation and the Onset of War, 1815–1945," in J. D. Singer (ed.), *Quantitative International Politics: Insights and Evidence* (New York: The Free Press, 1968), pp. 247–286. However, these writers dealt with a longer time period (1815–1945), as opposed to the shorter (1870–1945) period of this study. The choice of this alternative would not be practical here.

[55] The F value for the ratio of mean square linear regression to mean square error and deviations was checked for each of the regression coefficients. In approximately 80% of cases the F ratios were significant. For the coefficients which exhibit nonlinear trend, it was noted that those based on a greater number of values are more nearly linear. Thus, it may be concluded that if more data were to be obtained, then nearly all of the time series would exhibit significant linear trends and that the assumption of linearity is tenable for the calculation of the regression coefficients. Even for the few cases which exhibit "sine" wave patterns, the assumption of linearity may be applicable within the context of this study. We are interested here in overall rates of change over this time period, not necessarily in periodic rises and declines. On the other hand, fluctuations of this type may have some bearing on the war experiences of nations, although this is not specifically investigated in this study.

CHAPTER

VI

Tests of the Status Inconsistency
Hypothesis

═══════════════════════════════

The history of the status inconsistency hypothesis in the literature is not one of complete validation or rejection, and given the sometimes contradictory findings, a rather complete test is offered here. As will be seen, the incremental process of prediction, explanation, and specification offers the best possibilities for exploring the validity domain of this relationship. However, in order to approach the problem initially, certain face validity considerations should be addressed by means of descriptive statistics.

Some Descriptive Statistics

As a result of the considerations of Chapter V, the regression coefficients as measures of rates of change for achievement and ascription are now the independent variables used in the explanation of the characteristics of international warfare. (Throughout succeeding portions of this chapter, whenever a variable is referred to only by name, e.g., population or urbanization, it means the rate of change over time of that variable.) Recall that achievement consists of capability and centralization. The two components of achievement are related to ascription, and the composite expression is employed in the explanation of the characteristics of war. We now seek a measure of status inconsistency to assess the face validity of this concept in the construction of hypotheses for the explanation of war.

In certain of the earlier studies employing this concept, status inconsistency was defined in terms of discrepancies across all variables used as measures of status. Lenski, for example, selected a sample of individuals and coded them into categories based on income, education, occupation, and ethnicity.[1] Cumulative percent scores were calculated for each individual and deviations from the mean were taken. Each of the four deviations was squared and added to the squared values of the other three; the square root of the resulting value was subtracted from 100.

Lenski's purpose, as in certain other studies of this type, was to determine an *overall* inconsistency or status integration. In this analysis, however, we are concerned with a specific type of inconsistency—that between achieved and ascribed status. To this extent, we are not concerned with differences among *all* variables, as was Lenski in his earliest work. A further difference pertains to the use of measures such as the cumulative percent scores which tend to group the data.

Frequently, in studies of status inconsistency when data are initially in the form of coded categories, they are then related to each other by means of dichotomous, rank order, or other non-interval data forms. These procedures generally lead to a loss of information in situations where the data initially are interval. Given the presence of interval data, as is the case in this study, methods which lead to comparability among measures (as do rank order measures) and still maintain the original information and distribution intact would tend to be preferable to other approaches.

For descriptive purposes initially, we standardize each of the variables ($\bar{x} = 0$, $s = 1$) and take the differences between standard scores for achieved and ascribed status. Each of the individual measures of achievement is subtracted from the measure of ascription and means are taken for capability and centralization. Thus, the measure of capability inconsistency is the average of the differences between rates of change in economic development and population, on the one hand, and rate of diplomatic representation, on the other. Similarly, the differences between the rates of the separate measures of centralization (transportation, urbanization, communication) and the rate of ascription are averaged into one measure of centralization inconsistency. In each case, a positive sign indicates achieved status greater than ascribed, a negative sign represents ascribed status greater than achieved. Values close to zero would indicate an "equilibrium" condition of high status consistency. These values are presented in Table 6.1.

To ascertain whether there is indeed any face validity to the relationship between status inconsistency and war experience, it might be useful to group

[1] See Gerhard Lenski, "Status Crystallization: A Non-Vertical Dimension of Social Status," *American Sociological Review*, 19 (August 1954), pp. 405–413.

TABLE 6.1. **Standard Scores for the Inconsistency Variables**

Country	Centralization	Capability
Argentina	.252	−.148
Austria (–Hungary)	.238	.058
Belgium	−.235	−.410
Brazil	.246	1.108
Bulgaria	−.567	−.625
Chile	−.107	−.099
Czechoslovakia	−3.564	−4.093
Denmark	.147	.021
England	1.260	.585
Finland	−1.225	−1.399
France	.933	−.030
Germany (Prussia)	1.270	1.079
Greece	.270	.225
Guatemala	.096	.191
Holland	.038	−.071
Hungary	−.394	−.667
Italy	.063	.115
Japan	1.175	1.567
Luxembourg	−1.241	−1.306
Nicaragua	.085	.047
Norway	−.701	−.807
Paraguay	.282	.237
Peru	.082	.123
Poland	−3.890	−2.867
Portugal	.134	.153
Rumania	.048	.630
Russia	2.006	3.490
Spain	−.008	−.160
Sweden	.261	.028
Switzerland	−.145	−.286
Turkey	.398	−.501
United States	4.895	3.664
Yugoslavia (Serbia)	.012	.515

countries according to their mean values of status inconsistency. In this fashion, it may be possible for certain countries, to "fall" together and stand in contrast to others which may exhibit different international behavioral characteristics. Table 6.2 presents such a breakdown of nations for the total system. The first column presents countries with inconsistency values greater than 1.000, meaning that the achieved status of these nations is substantially greater than their ascribed status. The opposite is true for countries in the second column. Here, the ascribed status of nations is considerably larger than achieved, as indicated by the column heading of −1.000. Finally, countries with a fair balance between rate of achievement and rate of ascription are included in column three. In this instance, the difference between the

TABLE 6.2.   Categorization of Nations on Extreme Inconsistencies

Greater than 1.000 (positive inconsistency)	Less than −1.000 (negative inconsistency)	Lying between −.100 and +.100 (consistency)
	(a) *Centralization*	
England	Czechoslovakia	Guatemala
Germany (Prussia)	Finland	Holland
Japan	Luxembourg	Italy
Russia	Poland	Nicaragua
United States		Peru
		Rumania
		Spain
		Yugoslavia (Serbia)
	(b) *Capability*	
Brazil	Czechoslovakia	Austria (–Hungary)
Germany (Prussia)	Finland	Chile
Japan	Luxembourg	Denmark
Russia	Poland	France
United States		Holland
		Nicaragua
		Sweden

two status forms does not differ substantially from zero, and these countries may be said to demonstrate status consistency.

If, prior to the systematic analysis, we accept a "reputational" approach to the categorization in Table 6.2, then there does appear to be some face validity to the use of the concept of status inconsistency. All of the entries in the first column are larger countries with some reputation for the initiation of international violence. There would be little argument concerning the presence of Germany, Japan, Russia, or the United States, and England's nineteenth-century experience would tend to justify its presence at least in the category for centralization inconsistency. Brazil's appearance in the category for capability inconsistency is a possible anomaly, although her population growth during this period was very great and had the strongest effect on placing Brazil in this category.

The entries in the second column are, for the most part, relatively newly independent nations in this time period. To some extent, their presence in this column is an artifact of recency of independence. When countries such as Czechoslovakia or Poland attained independence, some of the older European countries (e.g., France) rushed to provide them with the maximum of diplomatic prestige in order to effect new alliances. Thus, the rate of ascription of these countries was extremely high after World War I, whereas their rate of achievement was approximately the same, leading to greater ascription than achievement. However, their very newness and a concomitant vulnerability, in a sense, places these countries at the opposite end of an international violence spectrum from those countries found in the first column. Czechoslovakia, Finland, and Poland were formed from defeated or weakened European empires. Once having been part of empires, these countries may have been viewed as fair game for reincorporation or at least some territorial aggrandizement. Indeed, by the end of World War II, each of these countries was forced to cede some territory to the victorious Soviet Union. Had Nazi Germany emerged triumphant in Europe, as the heir to the other major empire involved, at the very least it, too, would have made heavy territorial demands. Thus, whereas the countries in the first column may have tended to behave aggressively in their international postures, those in the second column may have been victimized by these same behaviors.

Perhaps the only distinguishing feature of the entries in the third column is the relative absence of very large or very new countries. Italy does appear in the category for centralization consistency and Austria-Hungary in that for capability consistency. However, both countries essentially were weak allies of stronger powers and by themselves did not behave aggressively toward larger opponents. The same may be true for France, particularly in the later portion of this period, and may account for its presence in the category for capability consistency. The remainder of these countries may have been for the most part pacific, with countries such as Holland, Nicaragua, Spain, Denmark, and Sweden found in the third column. Thus, we may infer some plausibility for the use of status inconsistency as an explanation of international warfare. We turn now to a statistical analysis of the separate components of status inconsistency and their relationships to the onset of war.

Methodological Considerations

There are five separate inconsistency variables, three for centralization and two for capability. In order to infer certain systematic relationships among the independent and dependent variables, we employ multiple regression analysis. Assuming the ordinary circumstances of a moderate degree of statistical independence among the predictors, the use of this method in itself would be satisfactory. It could answer the three primary questions often asked in a research design of this type: (1) the degree of statistical *prediction* afforded by the set of predictors taken simultaneously in a multiple regression equation; (2) the extent to which *explanation* is afforded by the statistically independent effect of a separate variable such as a high achieved–low ascribed status inconsistency; and (3) *specification* of which predictors bear the strongest relationships to the criterion.

The use of a multiple regression equation ordinarily provides statistical prediction in the form of predicted values of the criterion which then are associated with the observed values by means of the multiple correlation coefficient. Beta weights indicate the extents of association between the predictors and criterion, as well as directions of relationships: the magnitudes of these statistics specify which are the most important variables in accounting for the variance of the criterion.

Two factors in this study prevent the use of this procedure in the standard way. The first is that we seek to determine the unique effect of status inconsistency apart from the effects of the status variables themselves. When a variable such as status inconsistency is defined as a function of two or more status variables within the same system of equations, it becomes virtually impossible to disentangle the main effects of the status variables from the inconsistency. The fundamental problem of the number of unknowns exceeding the number of equations then arises.[2]

The best approach thus far to the resolution of this problem for aggregate or survey data appears to be a dummy variable scheme for the predictors within a multiple regression analysis. Separate categories are constructed for the extreme inconsistencies (high achieved–low ascribed, high ascribed–low achieved) and these are allowed to vary independently from the status variables. The omission of the moderate inconsistency categories (e.g., high achieved–neutral ascribed) introduces a simplifying assumption necessary for solution. In the subsequent test of the status inconsistency hypothesis, this method is further elaborated.

Despite the ability of the dummy variable scheme to distinguish among the effects of the status variables on the one hand and the inconsistency effects on the other, it does not resolve the second of the methodological problems—multicollinearity. When the predictors in a multiple regression analysis are highly intercorrelated, the problem of specification arises. The high values of the correlation coefficients can lead to unreliability of the beta coefficients and in certain cases to sign reversals.[3] Thus, it becomes impossible to specify

[2] Hubert M. Blalock, Jr., has treated this problem at length in various articles. See, for example, his "The Identification Problem and Theory Building: The Case of Status Inconsistency," *American Sociological Review*, 31 (February 1966), pp. 52–61; "Tests of Status Inconsistency Theory: A Note of Caution," *Pacific Sociological Review*, 10 (Fall 1967), pp. 69–74; and "Status Inconsistency, Social Mobility, Status Integration and Structural Effects," *American Sociological Review*, 32 (October 1967), pp. 790–801.

[3] There are many treatments of the multicollinearity problem in the sociological literature and, in particular, in economics. Among these are Robert A. Gordon, "Issues in Multiple Regression," *American Journal of Sociology*, 73 (March 1968), pp. 592–616; Donald E. Farrar and Robert R. Glauber, "Multicollinearity in Regression Analysis: The Problem Revisited," *Review of Economics and Statistics*, 49 (February 1967), pp. 92–107; Karl A. Fox, *Intermediate Economic Statistics* (New York: Wiley, 1968), pp.

reliably the magnitude of a predictor's relationship with a criterion or even the direction of the relationship if the intercorrelations are sufficiently high. In instances when the intercorrelation is less severe, some reliability can be achieved in parameter estimation. However, even here the model can be extremely sensitive to changes in model specification and sample size. The results of one study, then, although perhaps reliable within their own domain of inquiry, may not generalize to another of very great similarity but having some variation in measurement and sample coverage.

Given the two major problems of ascertaining the independent variation of the inconsistency effect and that of multicollinearity, we choose separate procedures for each of the several aspects of the test of the status inconsistency hypotheses. For purposes of *prediction alone*, the problems of independent inconsistency effects or multicollinearity need not concern us. The regression equation for prediction is valid whatever the interrelationships among the independent variables. As Wonnacott and Wonnacott have commented with regard to collinear predictors, "For prediction purposes, it does not hurt provided there is no attempt to predict for values of X and Z [predictors] removed from their line of collinearity. But structural questions cannot be answered—the *relation* of Y [criterion] to either X or Z cannot be sensibly investigated."[4]

Thus, our first step is to construct an equation for the limited purpose of ascertaining the predictive power of the status inconsistency hypothesis solely within the domain of variation specified by the sample and variables.

Prediction

For purposes of prediction, in contrast to the illustrative descriptive statistics used previously, we employ ratios of the achievement variables to the measure of ascription. Ratios are chosen in order to minimize reliability problems that would appear in the use of difference measures which are subject to random fluctuations.[5] A further advantage is the deflation of

256–265; J. Johnston, *Econometric Methods* (New York: McGraw-Hill, 1963), pp. 201–207; David S. Huang, *Regression and Econometric Methods* (New York: Wiley, 1970), pp. 149–158; Arthur S. Goldberger, *Econometric Theory* (New York: Wiley, 1964), pp. 192–194; and Potluri Rao and Roger L. Miller, *Applied Econometrics* (Belmont, Cal.: Wadsworth, 1971), pp. 46–52. A recent application of these concepts to the explanation of political violence is found in Douglas A. Hibbs, Jr., *Mass Political Violence: A Cross-National Causal Analysis* (New York: Wiley, 1973).

[4] Ronald J. Wonnacott and Thomas H. Wonnacott, *Econometrics* (New York: Wiley, 1970), p. 61.

[5] An excellent discussion of the attenuation of the reliability of correlations when the data are in the form of difference scores is found in Quinn McNemar, *Psychological Statistics*, 3rd ed. (New York: Wiley, 1962), pp. 155–158.

extreme values by the division process, a feature that would be lacking in the case of subtraction.[6] Although the use of ratios does not introduce the problem of decreased reliability, it does raise the issue of spurious correlation—relationships between the measures that essentially are artifacts of the ratios and do not arise from properties of the variables themselves. However, since we are interested solely in relationships between the predictors and criteria for purposes of *prediction*, and ratios are not constructed for the dependent variables, this problem does not apply in this case. What does derive from the use of ratios is the knowledge of certain properties of the ratios as estimates of controlled relationships.[7]

Each of the predictors consists of a rate of achievement variable, economic development, population growth, urbanization, transportation, and communication growth, divided by rate of ascription in the form of the number and rank of diplomats received. The criteria are the variables which pertain to the frequency, magnitude, and severity of international war. The greater the value of the status inconsistency ratio, the greater is the excess of achievement over ascription. Small values of the ratio indicate an excess of ascription over achievement; values very close to unity suggest a balance between achievement and ascription. Prior to the construction of the ratios, all independent variables were put into standard score form to provide for the comparability needed to carry out the division process.

Multiple regression solutions were then calculated and the multiple correlation coefficients, as well as the associated F ratios for the inconsistency variables, are found in the first two rows of Table 6.3. The values of all the coefficients are significant at $p < .01$. In all instances, the squares of the multiple correlation coefficients explain more than half of the variation, and in four of the five cases account for more than 80% of the variation.

[6] For a treatment of the advantages of ratio scores, including deflation of extreme values, as well as several of the disadvantages, see Edwin Kuh and John R. Meyer, "Correlation and Regression Estimates When the Data Are Ratios," *Econometrica*, 23 (October 1955), pp. 400–416. Also see Hibbs, *op. cit.*, pp. 46–56.

[7] It is known that including a variable in the denominator of a ratio is the same as controlling for the influence of that variable, when certain assumptions are met. Thus, if P is the correlation between x/z and y/z, then in order to have $P = r_{xy \cdot z}$, the following assumptions must hold: (1) The coefficient of variation—the ratio of the standard deviation to the mean—for z should be small; (2) x and y should be linear homogeneous functions of z. In addition, given the relationship between multiple and partial correlation, and having these assumptions met, it can be shown that the multiple correlation coefficient using ratios is the same as that without ratio construction, but with the denominator variable included separately as a predictor. Since we are here not using ratios for the criteria (war variables), the equivalence for multiple correlation does not apply. However, for partial correlations among the predictors (as ratios) alone, it does apply and provides some perspective on the interrelationships among them. See Kuh and Meyer, *op. cit.*, pp. 401–405.

TABLE 6.3. **Multiple Correlation Coefficients and *F* ratios for the Inconsistency and Achievement Variables**

	Years in war	Years in war vs. major	Number of wars	Number of wars vs. major	Battle deaths
			(a) *Inconsistency*		
R	.76	.91	.91	.95	.92
F	10.03**	12.22**	13.20**	23.92**	15.19**
			(b) *Achievement*		
R	.89	.80	.71	.67	.87
F	12.83**	5.83*	3.19*	2.54	10.33*

* $p < .05$.
** $p < .01$.

It may be objected, however, that prediction as good as is obtained here could be the result of the achievement variables alone, without reference to ascription. From a theoretical perspective, the international system may be entirely dependent on behaviors internal to the nation-state. Thus, if the primary components of achievement are specified, then all relevant behaviors, including ascription, are specified (e.g., ascription as a result of economic development). In this view, there exist no systemic behaviors of importance; the role of diplomatic exchange may be merely determined by protocol and/or chance. If this is valid, then empirically we should find no essential difference between the previous results and multiple regression solutions based on the achievement variables alone. The predetermined nature of protocol allocation of attributed importance or chance variations in the number and rank of diplomats received should not give rise to any improvement of the inconsistency measures over achievement.

The multiple correlation coefficients for the five achievement variables are found in the lower portion of Table 6.3. With the exception of the first criterion, years in war, all of the multiple regressions for the inconsistency variables account for larger proportions of the variation than do the achievement variables. In one instance, the results for the achievement variables alone do not reach significance, whereas in the inconsistency analysis, the results are significant for all of the criteria.

The beta weights for both the inconsistency and achievement variables are presented in Table 6.4. As can be seen, the structures of explanation are roughly comparable, with some differences in the directions of association for urbanization and communication. However, the standard errors for the coefficients in both analyses are unacceptably high. If the criterion that a beta coefficient should be greater than twice its standard error is used, none of the predictors in either analysis consistently meets this standard of reliability

TABLE 6.4.   **Beta Weights for the Inconsistency and Achievement Variables**

Criteria	*Economic development*	*Population*	*Transport-ation*	*Urbaniza-tion*	*Communi-cation*
			Predictors		
(a) *Inconsistency*					
Years in war	1.34	—	−1.36	−.36	1.09
Years in war vs. major	4.37	−2.81	−1.34	−.61	.81
Number of wars	7.02	−4.04	−1.23	−2.28	.87
Number of wars vs. major	6.78	−4.47	−1.13	−1.52	.56
Battle deaths	.68	−.29	−.06	.87	−.67
(b) *Achievement*					
Years in war	2.48	−1.39	−.35	.29	−.81
Years in war vs. major	.26	−.44	−.16	1.15	−.39
Number of wars	2.69	−1.08	−.52	−.35	−.52
Number of wars vs. major	1.20	−.63	−.31	.61	−.49
Battle deaths	.28	.11	−.04	1.29	−1.20

across the various multiple regression solutions. The problem of the "tipping" effect or that of the "bouncing beta" also is evident.[8] The zero order correlation coefficients between the predictors and criteria are positive in all cases, yet we see mostly negative beta weights in at least three of the five predictors. In general, the weakest predictors in the zero order analysis will be most susceptible to sign reversals. This is the case here for transportation and population, whereas economic development and communication, which bear stronger relationships in the zero order analysis, demonstrate positive associations with the characteristics of war.

Another way of viewing the problem of sign reversals is by means of the notion of a suppressor variable. If a variable bears a weak relationship to the criterion but has a strong influence on another predictor, then that variable may qualify as a suppressor in that it can "suppress" certain non-explanatory elements within the first predictor. Suppose, for the sake of illustration, that the predictor x_1 is composed of five elements, and a second predictor x_2 consists of two elements, both of which are included within the domain of x_1. Now, if the two elements common to both x_1 and x_2 have no explanatory power with regard to the criterion y, then the subtraction or suppression of these elements increases the predictive power of x_1. The removal of these irrelevant elements by means of a negative beta weight attached to x_2 tends to increase the value of the multiple correlation coefficient,

---

[8] See, for example, Gordon, *op. cit.*, pp. 595–597; and Farrar and Glauber, *op. cit.*, pp. 203–205. Even the values of the multiple correlation coefficients can be affected and have demonstrated instability from one analysis to the next.

since only those elements relevant to the explanation of y now remain.[9] Within the present context, transportation bears the weakest zero order relationships to the criteria and at the same time consistently has negative beta weights. Therefore, it may qualify as a suppressor variable.

Although the concept of a suppressor variable may help explain the tipping effect in certain instances, it does not in any way alleviate the reliability problem in the form of high standard errors of the beta weights. Nor is the suppressor variable susceptible to precise interpretation because, in most cases, we do not know what is suppressed and what remains associated with the criterion. Thus, we turn to other means of determining the effect of status inconsistency on international warfare.

Interaction Effects: Explanation

We have thus far ascertained the predictive power of the concept of status inconsistency based on percentages of variance explained by the inconsistency variables in comparison with the achievement variables alone. However, we have not yet indicated which of the two types of status inconsistency, centralization or capability, is more important. Nor have we indicated which of the two conditions high achieved–low ascribed or high ascribed–low achieved is superior in explanatory power. Finally, and most important, we seek to determine whether indeed there exists a statistically independent effect of status inconsistency entirely apart from the effects of the status variables themselves. In order to carry out these purposes, we turn to a dummy variable scheme.

This form of analysis can be specifically tailored for the comparison of additive versus interactive effects. In the present instance, we want to know the proportion of variance contributed by the *interaction* between achieved and ascribed status, over and above the additive contributions of the status variables themselves. As Broom and Jones indicate in connection with their analysis of voting behavior, "For the purposes of assessing the status consistency thesis, however, the critical question is not how much of the total variation can be explained, but whether a regression equation including terms for status inconsistency explains significantly more of the total variance in voting behavior than one restricted to terms for the status variables themselves."[10] In this technique we can incorporate the continuous status variables

[9] Particularly good discussions of the effects of suppressor variables are found in McNemar, *op. cit.*, pp. 185–187; and Gordon, *op. cit.*, pp. 611–612.

[10] Leonard Broom and F. Lancaster Jones, "Status Consistency and Political Preference: The Australian Case," *American Sociological Review*, 35 (December 1970), p. 994. The use of dummy variables for the analysis of interaction emerges from econometrics

with discrete categories formulated for the inconsistencies between achievement and ascription.[11] Separate assessments are made for the centralization and capability variables because we had already treated the overall predictive-explanatory power of the status inconsistency concept and now seek to determine separate contributions of component elements.

The measure of centralization inconsistency is constructed by averaging the separate inconsistencies for rates of development in transportation, urbanization, and communication. Similarly, a measure of capability is constructed by taking an average of rates of economic growth and population increase. The range of each composite measure was calculated and then divided into three equal numerical parts, thus dividing the cases into three status conditions—high achieved–low ascribed, neutral achieved–neutral ascribed, and high ascribed–low achieved. This was done for both centralization and capability inconsistencies. For computational purposes, the neutral–neutral categories were omitted because of a simplifying assumption necessary for solution.[12] If a country fell into one of the two extreme inconsistencies, it received a value of 1, and if it did not fall into that category it received a zero. Thus, the data on the two types of inconsistency are in the form of 0's and 1's and the two dummy variables (high achieved–low ascribed, high ascribed–low achieved) were analyzed together with the continuous variables for both centralization and capability.[13]

The results, in the form of increased percentage variance explained over and above the additive effects of the status variables, are presented in Table 6.5. These values are all significant at $p < .05$ with the exception of the value for "deaths," which verges on significance. We can thus directly infer that a statistically independent interaction effect on war experience may be attributed to status inconsistency. However, we cannot yet make firm conclusions as to the effect of each of the individual status inconsistency categories.

---

and has been developed for sociological analysis in works such as Otis D. Duncan, "Residential Areas and Differential Fertility," *Eugenics Quarterly*, 11 (June 1964), pp. 82–89; and *idem*, "Methodological Issues in the Analysis of Social Mobility," in Neil J. Smelser and Seymour M. Lipset (eds.), *Social Structure and Mobility in Economic Development* (Chicago: Aldine, 1966), pp. 51–97. The first direct application of this method to the analysis of status inconsistency is found in Elton F. Jackson and Peter J. Burke, "Status and Symptoms of Stress: Additive and Interaction Effects," *American Sociological Review*, 30 (August 1965), pp. 556–564.

[11] The combination of dummy variable predictors with continuous ones is found in Goldberger, *op. cit.*, pp. 222–224; and Huang, *op. cit.*, p. 168.

[12] See Duncan, "Residential Areas," p. 85; Jackson and Burke, *op. cit.*, p. 558; and Blalock, "The Identification Problem," pp. 59–60.

[13] The dummy variables for centralization and capability are combined in a single equation for each of these characteristics of war, as in Wonnacott and Wonnacott, *op. cit.*, pp. 74–75.

TABLE 6.5. **Proportions of Explained Variance Added by the Dummy Status Inconsistency Variables**

	Years in war	Years in war vs. major	Number of wars	Number of wars vs. major	Battle deaths
Added variance	.20	.13	.28	.23	.09
F ratio	8.10**	6.12*	7.94**	6.82**	4.83

* *p* < .05.
** *p* < .025.

The standard errors still are unacceptably high (the beta coefficients are smaller than twice their standard errors) and evidence of sign reversals are found in the beta coefficients.

Multicollinearity Problems: Specification

In order to ascertain the precise effects of each category we must somehow break the multicollinearity deadlock. One means of alleviating the problem is by the acquisition of additional information. If, for example, the data are in the form of time series, and multicollinearity exists, then the estimation of beta coefficients for one or more of the predictors by means of cross-section data may help to mitigate the problem. However, several problems are associated with this procedure. One is that cross-section and time series analyses often measure different processes, whereby the variation across different units of a system may be the result of different influences rather than variation within the same unit longitudinally. Related to this is the problem of sizeable differences in the variances of measures when they are taken over time or in cross-sections.[14] In the present study, our theoretical focus is rate of change over time, so that if this type of data is abandoned, then the particular influence specified by the theoretical framework would be lost. A second alternative would be to live with this poorly conditioned data. However, given the high standard errors and in particular the sign reversals, the option of remaining with the present results is unacceptable. Therefore, we turn to a third alternative—restructuring the data so that the multicollinearity is

[14] One can employ cross-sectional data in addition to longitudinal in order to break the multicollinearity deadlock by means of this supplementary information. However, aside from the fact that time series and cross-sectional data often measure different things, there arises the fundamental problem of differing variances in the two sets of data which may yield different conclusions. See Edwin Kuh and John R. Meyer, "How Extraneous Are Extraneous Estimates?" *Review of Economics and Statistics*, 39 (November 1957), pp. 380–393.

reduced to acceptable levels, subject to the constraint that the results are meaningful within the original theoretical framework suggested by the status inconsistency concept.

Given the high intercorrelations among the estimates of rate of achievement, there may exist a common uniformity among them. If this be the case, then we would expect a data reduction technique such as factor or cluster analysis to isolate this common trend component among the achievement variables. In addition, if ascription as measured by diplomats reflects a different regularity among the data, it also should appear separately. The same argument would hold for one or more of the status inconsistency measures if indeed it measured something different from achievement and ascription. Were we then to obtain a set of underlying dimensions, the scores on the dimensions could be secured for each country and these scores used to replace the original set of multicollinear data.[15]

It must be understood that this process opts for the data reduction approach to the problem of multicollinearity, in contrast to either the addition of new data or the maintenance of the original data set. Now, it may be argued that a reduction of the data by means of finding the most highly collinear data subsets, as in a cluster analysis, might lead to new variables of great artificiality. A factor or cluster can be simply a linear combination of variables which has no political meaning. As such, its use could not in any way contribute to substantive conclusions concerning the status inconsistency concept. However, when many measures of achievement exist, reducing them to one single component may be not only permissible, but desirable as a means of removing redundant elements, much as a "true" score is obtained from several different measures of the same trait by means of a path analytic or other data-reducing technique.[16]

The removal of redundant elements to arrive at some underlying "true" score may have some methodological justification. In the test of a status inconsistency hypothesis it may also have important *theoretical* justification. In prior research on status inconsistency, when the proportions of variance explained in the dependent variable by the status variables have been separated into additive and interactive components, it has been found generally

[15] A suggestion for the use of factor analysis as a means of alleviating the multicollinearity problem is found in Marilynn B. Brewer, William D. Crano, and Donald T. Campbell, "Testing a Single-Factor Model as an Alternative to the Misuse of Partial Correlations in Hypothesis-testing Research," *Sociometry*, 33 (March 1970), pp. 1–11, especially pp. 8–9.

[16] A treatment of the concept of "true score" in path analysis is found in Charles E. Werts and Robert L. Linn, "Path Analysis: Psychological Examples," *Psychological Bulletin*, 74 (September 1970), pp. 193–212, especially pp. 193–195. Also see Farrar and Glauber, *op. cit.*, pp. 96–98.

that the additive effects of the status variables predominate. Thus, in one explanation of symptoms of stress, Jackson and Burke found that the additive effects of the status variables accounted for 58% of the variance, while inclusion of the interactive effects added another 18%. (In a second analysis, using a different model, the interactive effects explained 9% of the variance in stress symptoms, in addition to the additive effects.)[17] Broom and Jones, in the voting analysis for the Australian Labor Party, were able to explain at most an additional .8% of the variance through the addition of a variety of status inconsistency terms.[18] In both the Jackson–Burke and Broom–Jones studies, the status inconsistency terms were statistically significant but did not appreciably enhance the overall explanatory power of the analysis. If we consider the nature of the specific status variables, however, it may be reasonable to suppose that the mode of analysis used considerably under-estimated the explanatory powers of the inconsistency terms in comparison with the status variables.

In the Jackson and Burke study, the status variables are occupation, education, and a racial-ethnic term. The Broom and Jones work treated education, occupation, and income as achievement variables and religion as the ascribed status variable. The question can be asked as to the extent to which these variables are suggestive of independent sociologically operative status considerations. To be sure, income or education provides a rank ordering of individuals in terms of unit (dollar, pound) monetary income or years of formal education, and so in a strict sense these are status variables insofar as they provide societal orderings of persons relative to one another. If one seeks to explain the variance in certain individual or collective behaviors based on these orderings per se, one can do so providing that no additional meaning is attached to any of these variables. Thus, each of the status variables separately can serve as a predictor in a multiple regression equation, as was done in both of these status inconsistency studies.

On the other hand, if income or occupation is taken to mean a form of achievement, and race or religion is treated as a form of ascription, then we might ask if indeed these variables should be treated as separate status orderings. Aside from the issue of overlap between them, in their conjoint representations of, say, achievement, there is the issue of the extent to which these variables are actually indicative of the concept of achievement. In certain instances, high income may indicate inherited wealth or the returns on investments made many years before. Long years of education may be the

[17] Jackson and Burke, *op. cit.*, pp. 561–563.
[18] Broom and Jones, *op. cit.*, p. 998. This value is considerably smaller than those found in the Jackson and Burke study because of the large amount of within-groups (individual) variation that was allowed to enter into the analysis.

product of parental influence at exclusive institutions, rather than the product of the individual's own efforts. Thus, variation in these status forms may be due to factors other than achievement. Consequently, it may be appropriate to consider the extent of *common variance* among these variables as a measure of overall achievement (or another way of saying socioeconomic status). That proportion of the variance which is not held in common by three variables such as income, occupation, and education may represent unique status factors other than that which is of primary interest.

Of additional importance is the fact that in examining the empirical validity of the status inconsistency hypothesis, the high achieved–low ascribed status generally appears to be most strongly related to behaviors such as liberal vote or helping behavior.[19] In order to examine further the effects of this condition, or indeed any other combination of various status forms, one must treat achievement or ascription as unitary variables, which would imply the use of the common variance among several variables, each measuring some different form of achieved status.

By using the common or "true" score variances for achievement, ascription, and status inconsistency, we will be able to avoid much of the multicollinearity which has clouded the results thus far, and provide a comparison of the proportions of variance explained by the status variables themselves in comparison with the status inconsistency effects.

A cluster analysis is employed here to determine the areas of maximum collinearity in the data. Given the relatively small number of variables, and the existence of the inconsistency categories in the data, a factor analysis would impose certain stringent requirements on these data which very likely could not be met. The use of the cluster analysis requires no assumptions concerning the nature of the data. The particular form of cluster analysis we are employing aims at "discovering a minimal number of composites among a collection of variables or objects. The composites can replace the full array of variables or objects without loss of generality, in the sense that the reduced set will reproduce the intercorrelations among the full array."[20] Furthermore, we do not require an orthogonal solution to the analysis such as would be employed in many factor analytic studies. The importance of orthogonality, although desirable in many instances, might introduce an undesirable element of artificiality. Hence, an oblique solution is preferred

[19] See, for example, David R. Segal and David Knoke, "Social Mobility, Status Inconsistency and Partisan Realignment in the United States," *Social Forces*, 47 (December 1968), pp. 154–157; and Manus and Elizabeth Midlarsky, "Additive and Interactive Status Effects on Altruistic Behavior," *Proceedings of the Eightieth Annual Convention*, American Psychological Association, 1972, pp. 245–246.

[20] Robert C. Tryon and Daniel E. Bailey, *Cluster Analysis* (New York: McGraw-Hill, 1970), p. 30.

TABLE 6.6.   **A Cluster Analysis of the Status and Status Inconsistency Variables**

Variable	h^2	Factor coefficients		
		I	II	III
1. Economic development	1.03	.99	−.10	.16
2. Population	.77	.85	.11	−.17
3. Transportation	.97	.93	.06	−.32
4. Urbanization	.99	.94	−.06	.32
5. Communication	.79	.89	.00	.01
6. Diplomats	.95	.04	.96	−.18
7. Centralization inconsistency	.92	.72	−.63	.09
8. Capability inconsistency	.94	.71	−.65	−.06
9. High ascribed–low achieved (centralization)	.72	−.22	.82	−.04
10. High achieved–low ascribed (centralization)	.72	.68	−.12	.50
11. High ascribed–low achieved (capability)	.67	−.28	.73	.25
12. High achieved–low ascribed (capability)	.52	.67	−.18	.20
Percent common variance		63.2	30.3	6.6

in order to allow for the actual clusters of collinearity to emerge, whatever the degree of statistical independence among them. This solution is presented in Table 6.6.

The first cluster most clearly represents the achievement variable and explains the greatest proportion of the variance. Predictably, the second cluster reflects the ascription variable—diplomats—while the third has as its highest loading the high achieved–low ascribed centralization inconsistency. Thus, the three essential components of the theory, achievement, ascription, and status inconsistency, are reflected by each of the clusters. To this extent, the original framework has been preserved by the analysis, and scores on these dimensions can be used in further multiple regressions.

Note that the high achieved–low ascribed centralization inconsistency loads somewhat more highly on the first cluster representing achievement than on the third. In an analysis which seeks orthogonal partitioning of the variables into separate factors this, of course, would be undesirable because the variable in question would not have a unique "home." However, in this case we are not concerned with maintaining the uniqueness of a particular variable, which in itself may represent several distinct components, but in obtaining separate clusters that are relatively independent from one another.

In the dummy variable analysis, the unique interaction effect was partialed out and indeed found to bear significant relationships with the characteristics of war, albeit under the confounding effects of multicollinearity. Here, rather than being concerned solely with the issue of interaction and introducing some unreliability, we allow the overlap in order to represent the

TABLE 6.7.   **Multiple Regression Solutions for the Factor Scores**

	Years in war	Years in war vs. major	Number of wars	Number of wars vs. major	Battle deaths
Beta weights—achievement	−.21	−.05	−.08	−.04	.02
Beta weights—ascription	−.16	−.03	−.17	.05	−.10
Beta weights—centralization inconsistency	(.81)	(.76)	(.54)	(.73)	(.56)
Multiple correlation coefficient	.76	.74	.57	.68	.62
F ratio	13.03**	11.60**	4.75**	8.29**	6.01**

Parentheses indicate that the beta weight is more than twice its standard error.
** $= p < .01$.

more realistic state of achieved and ascribed conditions existing simultaneously and not compartmentalized into separate interaction categories.

As is pointed out elsewhere in this chapter, neither ordinary human beings nor decision makers in nation-states should necessarily have their status dimensions and interactions among them treated wholly apart from one another, especially under conditions wherein the same individual is simultaneously comparing both status dimensions. The oblique solution allows for the possibility of clusters of correlated variance, and the first cluster incorporates that part of the inconsistency measure more strongly associated with achievement, leaving the status inconsistency to be represented in the third cluster. This last cluster can then be understood as indicating that portion of the inconsistency measure not associated either with achievement or ascription.

Factor scores were obtained for each country on each of the clusters, and the results used as the independent variables in the analysis of war. Table 6.7 presents the multiple correlation coefficients along with the respective F ratios, as well as the beta weights for each of the three clusters. The results are significant at $p \leq .01$ for all of the multiple regression equations. Of even greater importance are the findings for the status inconsistency dimension which reflects the high achieved–low ascribed status inconsistency for centralization. Not only does this dimension have the largest values of the beta weights, indicating the strength of association with war, but all of these beta values are at least twice the values of their respective standard errors. This extent of reliability is indicated in Table 6.7. by means of parentheses. Thus, in addition to the strength of association for the status inconsistency, controlling for the achieved and ascribed statuses, there exists, moreover, reliability of explanation for the first time in several multivariate analyses. This reliability resulted from the breaking of the multicollinearity deadlock by means of the cluster analysis.

Some Interpretive Comments

The analysis in this chapter has indicated the predictive power of the status inconsistency concept, as well as its statistical independence in the explanation of international warfare. The problem of specification has been satisfied, in part, by the cluster analysis yielding the high achieved–low ascribed centralization inconsistency as being not only positively associated with war, but also giving consistently reliable beta coefficients. The reasons for the salience of the high achieved–low ascribed category in the explanation of war follow from the earlier theoretical reasoning concerning this form of status inconsistency as leading to uncertainty or the prevention of uncertainty reduction. Decision makers acting for their countries internalize the status inconsistencies of their respective nation-states. If the nation has a high rate of achievement, but a concomitant attributed importance does not follow from this achievement, then the decision makers may behave as frustrated individuals or experience uncertainties as to the precise position or status of the countries they represent. These ambiguities may then lead to international violence as an effort to resolve once and for all the anomalous state generated by the status inconsistencies.

Less clear perhaps is the reason for the greater importance of the centralization inconsistency. Surely capabilities in the form of economic development or population are important forms of achievement and would be expected perhaps to bear even stronger relationship, via an inconsistency, with the characteristics of war. However, the greater explanatory power and greater reliability of centralization inconsistency perhaps indicates the greater sensitivity of this variable as a predictor of war.

Consider the component measures which comprise the centralization variable—transportation, urbanization, and communication. In contrast to variables such as GNP and population, which constitute the capability variable, the centralization components may be more indicative of societal factors that are involved directly in the industrialization process and, therefore, in national power. Gross national product includes non-industrial variables, and population growth is only in part affected by the industrialization process. The growth of railroad networks, communication vehicles such as telegraph and telephone, and even urbanization are more directly dependent on qualitative technological change and quantitative implementation. As such, they may be more closely related to the modern components of national power. Since a status inconsistency may be understood as a type of incapacitation of the exercise of power, then it becomes understandable why the centralization inconsistency may have greater importance in the explanation of war.

Urbanization may have an additional importance in that it may provide the setting for a common discourse required for contemporary nationalistic sentiment—perhaps a condition of modern warfare. The importance of this variable is indicated not only by the fact that it is one of the components of centralization, but also by a zero order analysis of dummy achievement variables. When dummy variables were constructed for each of the achievement variables and related individually to the characteristics of war, the category *high urbanization* consistently bore the strongest relationship to war experience.[21] This finding provides validation for the salience of one of the components of centralization inconsistency.

Another more direct validation of the conclusions of this study comes from an experimental analysis of the effects of achieved-ascribed inconsistencies on aggressive attitudes and helping behavior.[22] Aside from remedial procedures of the type employed here, the only other way to avoid the confounding effects of multicollinearity is to have direct control of the independent variables in an experimental situation. In this fashion, the problem is avoided because of the nearly complete independence of one variable from another in a properly constructed research design.[23] The results of this experimental test of the effects of status inconsistency on aggressive attitude found that the high achieved–low ascribed inconsistency was strongly associated with aggressive attitude, and in both first- and second-order interaction analyses explained approximately 15% of the variance, in comparison with some 2% and 14%, respectively, for the main effects of status. Thus, the effects of status inconsistency in this experimental study individually exceed the linear status effects, as they do in the results of the cluster analysis and subsequent multiple regressions.

In the current analysis, in order to specify the importance of the centralization variable in the high achieved–low ascribed category, the entire variable set had to be restructured by a cluster analysis. Although these operations led to the specification of one of the components of status inconsistency as important for the explanation of war, it did not entirely break the multi-

[21] The value of this correlation is $r = .73$. This statistic cannot be interpreted in the same manner as a Pearson product-moment correlation coefficient, but still provides a measure of association between a dichotomous and continuous variable, as would a biserial correlation coefficient.

[22] Midlarsky and Midlarsky, *op. cit.* A detailed theoretical treatment which argues for the use of unitary concepts of achievement and ascription is found in Steven Box and Julienne Ford, "Some Questionable Assumptions in the Theory of Status Inconsistency," *Sociological Review*, 17 (July 1969), pp. 187–201, especially pp. 195–197.

[23] The percentage variance held in common by the experimental analogues of achievement and ascription was at most equal to .03%. See Midlarsky and Midlarsky, *op. cit.*, p. 245.

collinearity deadlock. For one, it became virtually impossible in a multiple regression analysis to specify which particular component variable (e.g., population or urbanization) was more closely associated with war. Second, a reliable explanation was found for only one dimension—centralization inconsistency—in the multivariate analysis of the scores obtained from the cluster analysis. Given the degree of collinearity among these predictors, perhaps it is indeed impossible to obtain any greater distinctions among them as to explanation and reliability. However, it should be recognized that this general approach of restructuring the data and in this fashion resolving multicollinearity may have limitations, and that beyond a certain level of intercorrelation, the several collinear variables are to all intents and purposes statistically the same variable. Nothing further can or should be done to attempt separations or distinctions.

Perhaps this form of restructuring the data to alleviate multicollinearity works best when there is a theoretical framework to be preserved and the restructuring process indeed preserves essential elements of the original theory. Variables chosen initially for theoretical relevance are still maintained in close to their original form even after restructuring. In the present analysis, the three dimensions which emerged from the cluster analysis are achieved status, ascribed status, and a status inconsistency dimension relating to centralization. These results enabled us to evaluate the two separate types of inconsistency in relation to achievement and ascription—the two other variables of importance suggested by the theory. On the other hand, if the restructuring had yielded results which discarded the original theory or produced dimensions without political meaning, this approach to the resolution of multicollinearity would have been of little use.

From any perspective employed in this analysis, then, the status inconsistency concept is of importance. The extent of prediction is strongly increased by the use of measures predicated on this concept, and the statistical independence of an inconsistency effect is substantiated in the dummy variable multiple regression analysis. However, the *extent* of importance of status inconsistency may depend in part on the definition of what constitutes status. If each of the variables, economic development or population, is taken in itself to mean a status ordering, then the addition of the status inconsistency measures does not appreciably enlarge the proportion of variance explained, although what is explained is statistically significant and independent from the linear status effects. Yet, if one employs a more inclusive concept such as achievement or ascription and obtains dimensions for each, removing much of the redundancy of the individual achievement variables, then the status inconsistency dimension explains more of the variance than do either achievement or ascription.

The status inconsistency concept, therefore, may be of greater importance than was previously considered, and the multicollinearity problem of redundant status dimensions in prior studies may have tended to obscure the importance of certain types of status inconsistency. In addition to the substantive findings which derive from this study, there are strong methodological implications for the study of sociopolitical phenomena which carry with them interactive and collinearity problems.[24] The stepwise procedure of treating prediction, explanation, and specification in separate analyses appears superior to the conventional single multivariate treatment. Future studies of similar phenomena may provide further tests of the utility of this approach. Thus, the treatment of status inconsistency and war has concluded the first half of our analysis of the effects on political violence of the boundary between the nation-state and international system. Now we turn to the effect of this boundary on domestic instability.

[24] For a comprehensive discussion of the problems inherent in analyzing nonadditive relationships, and some ingenious solutions, see Hayward R. Alker, Jr., "The Long Road to International Relations Theory: Problems of Statistical Nonadditivity," *World Politics*, 18 (July 1966), pp. 623–655.

VII

The Diffusion of Instability

We have established that a significant proportion of the variance in international warfare is a consequence of the interaction between certain changes internal to the nation-state and ascriptive elements of the international system. The status inconsistency analysis of the preceding chapter demonstrated how phenomena occurring at the boundary between the nation-state and the international system can affect the war experience of nations. These findings suggest that war as a form of political violence external to the nation-state is a consequence, in part, of systemic characteristics. A question asked in the following analysis is the extent to which *internal* violence also may be understood as arising from elements of the international system.

There may occur a diffusion of instability from one country to the next whereby a coup in one country may, in part, result from a coup which took place in a neighboring country at an earlier point in time. In this view, the boundary of the nation-state is permeable to external influences such that the international system can directly affect the domestic instability of nation-states.

This analysis is drawn both from the mathematics of "contagious" probability distributions,[1] and a psychological theory of imitation. However, in the literature of psychology, the term *imitation* implies specific psychological mechanisms, although it also is treated as a generic term which includes the

---

[1] The mathematics of contagious distributions is treated in William Feller, "On a General Class of 'Contagious' Distributions," *Annals of Mathematical Statistics*, 14 (December 1943), pp. 389–400; and in his *An Introduction to Probability Theory and Its Applications*, vol. 1 (New York: Wiley, 1957).

somewhat different processes of behavioral contagion, social pressures, and conformity, as well as social facilitation.[2] Therefore, to avoid the implication that we are here treating any specific psychological mechanisms, as well as to avoid confusing generic (imitation) and specific (contagion) effects, the term *diffusion* is employed. The definition consequently does not imply the existence of a specific mechanism, but rather an aggregate process which may be susceptible to systematic analysis.

Both the mathematical and statistical diffusion analyses of instability are dependent on the following theoretical foundation: coups and revolutions are fundamentally different phenomena, and whereas the revolution may arise from profound and widespread societal discontent,[3] the coup is largely the result of small-group decision making such as that found in a military clique. The elite–mass gap in many societies may be large enough to preclude the influence of mass effects on elite decision making. Latin American societies, for example, may be highly stratified with relatively impermeable barriers separating the elite from the remainder of society.[4] In nation-states of this type, the impermeability of such barriers might prevent large-scale discontent and societal processes such as economic development from affecting the form and direction of governmental policy and whatever instability processes exist. Given the existence of barriers of this type, the elite can remain isolated from the remainder of society and, therefore, the decision making of this group also would be unaffected by mass societal processes or behavior. Thus, the most productive level of analysis for the study of coups may not be the mass society itself, but rather the small group of individuals constituting the elite, often the military, which actually is capable of initiating the coup.[5]

Although a group of this type may be largely unaffected by mass behavior, it can be affected by processes external to the nation-state. Thus, the barriers separating groups within nation-states may actually be less permeable than the boundaries separating nation-states. The military in Latin American

[2] See Ladd Wheeler, "Behavioral Contagion: Theory and Research," in Edward C. Simmel, Ronald A. Hoppe, and G. Alexander Milton (eds.), *Social Facilitation and Imitative Behavior* (Boston: Allyn and Bacon, 1968), pp. 189–215.

[3] Works which treat the distinction between coups and revolutions are Crane Brinton, *The Anatomy of Revolution* (New York: Vintage, 1952); Lyford P. Edwards, *The Natural History of Revolution* (Chicago: University of Chicago Press, 1927); and James C. Davies, "Toward a Theory of Revolution," *American Sociological Review*, 27 (February 1962), pp. 5–19. Also see Raymond Tanter and Manus Midlarsky, "A Theory of Revolution," *Journal of Conflict Resolution*, 11 (September 1967), pp. 264–280; and Manus Midlarsky and Raymond Tanter, "Toward a Theory of Political Instability in Latin America," *Journal of Peace Research*, 4 (no. 3, 1967), pp. 209–227.

[4] Lyle N. McAlister, "The Military," in John J. Johnson (ed.), *Continuity and Change in Latin America* (Stanford: Stanford University Press, 1964), pp. 136–160.

[5] For a treatment of levels of analysis in international politics, see J. David Singer, "The Level-of-Analysis Problem in International Relations," *World Politics*, 14 (October 1961), pp. 77–92.

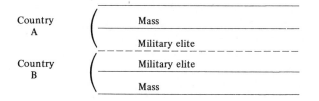

Figure 7.1   **Boundary Permeability in Regard to Military Intervention**

countries, for example, may tend to identify with their counterparts in neighboring countries more closely than with elements of the mass in their own country. The occurrence of military coups in these countries may then be more susceptible to influences from these neighboring military elites. If a coup is initiated by a military elite, this event might be repeated by the neighboring military. In sum, a regional international system consisting of component nation-states and behaviors occurring within and between them constitutes a source of domestic instability for nation-states within that region. The boundaries of nation-states may be relatively permeable, while barriers between mass and elite within countries could be less penetrable. This process is diagrammed in Figure 7.1.

Probabilistic Models of Randomness and Diffusion

As a first approach to the examination of this phenomenon, we consider a macroscopic analysis which can indicate the existence of a diffusion effect attributable to an observed military intervention. If such an effect did not exist, then coups in Latin American or Sub-Saharan African countries would occur as random processes. The unique domestic processes internal to each country would determine the occurrence of coups such that a random distribution of coups would emerge for each geographic region considered. Two assumptions which would be met by such a process are: first, the probability of the occurrence of a given number of coups is independent of the number of coups which occurred in an earlier interval; second, each coup occurs at random, independently of all the rest. The two basic assumptions, and others, are incorporated into the Poisson model of a probability distribution. Essentially, the occurrence of events is random, and independent of all others over the time period and region of analysis.[6]

---

[6] This set of assumptions, plus others which are primarily of mathematical importance, is derived from B. V. Gnedenko, *The Theory of Probability*, trans. B. D. Seckler (New York: Chelsea, 1963), pp. 330–331. Also see Thornton C. Fry, *Probability and Its Engineering Uses* (Princeton, N.J.: Van Nostrand, 1965), p. 243; and Feller, *Probability Theory*, p. 400.

If P_{it} is the probability of being in state i during the time interval $(0, t)$ and $e^{-\alpha t}$ is an exponential function, then the Poisson can be written

$$P_{it} = \frac{(\alpha t)^i e^{-\alpha t}}{i!}.$$

Since t often represents a fixed time interval, it can be treated as a constant and set equal to unity for convenience, resulting in the ordinary form of the Poisson

$$P_i = \frac{\alpha^i e^{-\alpha}}{i!}.$$

In this form of a Poisson frequency distribution, α is the number of events expected to occur—the mean of the distribution.

In contrast to this approach stands one based on interconnections among units such that events are not random and independent of one another, but instead depend on events of the same type in neighboring countries or at earlier time periods. This view is the same as the diffusion of instability from one country to the next, or through time. In the random model, the probability of passing from one state to the next (*transition rate*) is constant for all countries under consideration since they are all essentially the same and independent of each other. The transition rate refers to the probability of passing from the state of having no coups to that of having a single coup. A constant transition rate means that the probability of passing from the state of having i number of coups to $i + 1$ is the same as that of passing from $i + 1$ to $i + 2, \ldots,$ to $i + n$. However, if the probability of a coup increases with observing another country experiencing a coup, then the transition rate is not constant, but is dependent on the domestic instability of other countries. A similar variable transition rate results from the country's own history of instability acting as a spur to further instability. This "coup proneness" may also yield the same distribution. A subsequent analysis will distinguish between these two sources of a variable transition rate.

If there are successive states of having $0, 1, 2, \ldots, i$ number of coups, then each country can have a transition rate from 0 to 1 coups $(q_{0, 1})$; 1 to 2 $(q_{1, 2})$; or, in the general condition of going from i to $i + 1$ number of coups, there would be a transition rate of $q_{i, i+1}$. These transition rates can be defined in terms of an initial value which receives additional increments for the effects either of experiencing a history of instability in the past or of observing coups which take place in neighboring countries. Thus, if

$$q_{0, 1} = \alpha$$

then

$$q_{1,2} = \alpha + \beta$$
$$q_{2,3} = \alpha + 2\beta$$

and, in the general condition

$$q_{i,i+1} = \alpha + i\beta.$$

The beta (β) term can be considered a measure of the extent of diffusion in which each element has an increasing transition rate subsequent to the first occurrence of a coup. The derivation of the equation of the Poisson with diffusion leads to the equation[7]

$$P_i = \frac{e^{-(\alpha+i\beta)}\alpha(\alpha + \beta)\cdots\{\alpha + (i - 1)\beta\}(e^{\beta} - 1)^i}{i!\,\beta^i}$$

where, as before, t has been set equal to 1. The value of beta is defined as

$$\beta = \ln\frac{\sigma^2}{\mu}$$

in which the symbol ln stands for the natural or Naperian logarithm, and

$$\alpha = \frac{\mu^2\beta}{\sigma^2 - \mu}$$

where μ and σ^2 are the mean and variance, respectively.

Comparisons of the Two Models

A comparison of these models in regard to "goodness of fit" to the number of coups can indicate which of the assumptions concerning the occurrence of instability has greater empirical support: that of the randomness, associated with the Poisson and the concomitant domestic sources of instability, or the diffusion process, implied by the second distribution and the associated conclusion regarding the sources of domestic instability found in the international system.[8] In the following analysis, the two models are applied to the

[7] For the mathematical derivations closest to those verbally described in this chapter, see James S. Coleman, *Introduction to Mathematical Sociology* (New York: The Free Press, 1964), pp. 288–314. The mathematical development directly leading to the expression for the Poisson with diffusion used here is found on p. 312. Although less simplified algebraically than other forms, this expression was found to be more convenient to use in the calculation procedure. For a second derivation of the Poisson, see Gnedenko, *op. cit.*, pp. 300–335; and Feller, *Probability Theory*, pp. 400–402.

[8] In order to determine if each of these models is applicable, as well as to determine the superiority of one over the other, a statistical test of significance such as chi-square might appear appropriate. However, the number of predicted countries in each category is small, in many cases less than five, and the chi-square test therefore cannot be applied. While some of the categories could be combined, this would lead to the loss of information, and a concomitant reduction in the power of the test.

occurrence of Latin American coups in a spatial distribution of n_i countries having i number of coups within a probability space conceptualized as having governmental units which experience instability either of the random variety or subject to diffusion effects.[9] Latin America presents a useful "laboratory" for the comparison of both models because of the relative prevalence of instability there.[10] A later application of the analysis to Sub-Saharan African coups is done for substantially the same reasons.

Table 7.1 presents the comparison of fit for the two distributions in the

[9] This is done in a fashion analogous to the examination of other social phenomena. It may be objected that since the Poisson and its modified versions assume continuity of the spatial parameter, these models may not be applied to a non-continuous "country space" composed of discrete and unequal territorial entities. However, it is not necessary to conceive of the probability space here as composed entirely of countries with unequal boundary configurations. The *governments* of nations experience coups, not their entire territorial units, and the probability space is more adequately conceptualized as a continuous one in which governments exist and experience instability. Governments can enter any of the states of having 1, 2, ..., i number of coups, just as individuals exist in a continuous space and experience accidents, exhibit consumer preferences, or engage in any of the other processes normally represented by a Poisson distribution over space. See Coleman, *op. cit.*, pp. 291–308; Feller, *Probability Theory*, pp. 149–154; and Emanuel Parzen, *Modern Probability Theory and Its Applications* (New York: Wiley, 1960), pp. 251–258. All of these works include the Poisson probability law as applied to spatial distributions. The majority of illustrations in both Coleman and Feller, for example, are applications of the Poisson over space.

[10] The data for Latin American coups are from Martin C. Needler, "Political Development and Military Intervention in Latin America," *American Political Science Review* 60 (September 1966), p. 619, as follows:

Successful insurrections took place during the period (1935–1964) in *Argentina*: June 1943, February 1944, September 1955, and March 1962; *Bolivia*: May 1936, July 1937, December 1943, July 1946, May 1951, April 1952, and November 1964; *Brazil*: October 1945, August 1954, November 1955, and April 1964; *Colombia*: June 1953 and May 1957; *Costa Rica*: March 1948; *Cuba*: March 1952 and January 1959; *Dominican Republic*: September 1963; *Ecuador*: August 1935, October 1937, May 1944, August 1947, November 1961, and July 1963; *El Salvador*: May 1944, October 1944, December 1948, October 1960, and January 1961; *Guatemala*: July 1944, October 1944, June 1954, and March 1963; *Haiti*: January 1946, May 1950, and December 1956; *Honduras*: October 1956 and October 1963; *Nicaragua*: June 1936; *Panama*: October 1941, November 1949, and May 1951; *Paraguay*: February 1936, August 1937, June 1948, January 1949, September 1949, and May 1954; *Peru*: October 1948 and July 1962; *Venezuela*: October 1945, November 1948, and January 1958.

One correction was made: a value for Peru was changed from October 1949 to October 1948.

This set of data includes revolutions such as Cuba 1959 and Bolivia 1952. Although these are not comparable to the coup or "palace revolution," they were maintained in the set of data to illustrate the growing participation of civilian groups in Latin American instability and the inhibitory effect found in the later time period.

Perhaps diffusion effects would be even better illustrated by an analysis of attempted coups. However, these are extremely difficult to determine, partly because of the tendency of threatened elites to accuse the opposition of an attempted coup even when no such plot ever existed.

TABLE 7.1. **Number of Latin American Countries Having *i* Number of Coups, 1935–1964**

i number of coups	n_i number of countries	Poisson with diffusion $\alpha = 2.22, \beta = .447$	Poisson $\alpha = 2.80$
0	3	2.2	1.2
1	3	3.9	3.5
2	4	4.2	4.8
3	3	3.5	4.5
4	3	2.5	3.1
5	1	1.6	1.7
6	2	1.0	0.8
7	1	0.5	0.3

time period 1935–1964. This is a rather long period, thirty years, which includes a total of fifty-six coups that occurred in seventeen of the twenty Latin American countries independent throughout this time period. The first two columns list the number of countries n_i which had *i* number of coups. The third and fourth columns present the predicted values of n_i number of countries associated with the *i* number of coups for both the Poisson and the Poisson with diffusion. It can be seen that both models provide a relatively good fit to the data, and that the Poisson with diffusion is superior to the Poisson. If, as a rough measure of applicability, we compare the difference between observed and predicted values for both models, the Poisson yields a sum of deviations between observed and predicted values equal to 7.3, whereas the Poisson with diffusion produces a sum of deviations of 5.0.

This somewhat greater applicability of the Poisson with diffusion should not be taken at face value, and without the introduction of added distinctions. The assumption underlying the diffusion effect may hold better in one time period than in another. Recall that basic to the notion of diffusion is the concept of a small group of leaders who are susceptible to the influence of a modeling effect. This susceptibility depends, in large measure, on the relative freedom of this group from mass influence. A time period in which such influence is at a minimum would be one in which the diffusion effect could operate with maximum consequences. Conversely, a period in which the elite–mass gap is closing would likely be one in which the diffusion process could not operate very effectively.

It has been argued by Needler, as well as by Midlarsky and Tanter, that the form of Latin American instability may have been undergoing a change in emphasis during the thirty-year period under investigation.[11] Whereas the

[11] Needler, *ibid.*; and Midlarsky and Tanter, *op. cit.*, pp. 218–219.

military may have been predominant in the initiation of coups in the earlier portion of this period, various civilian groups, particularly in urbanized areas, may have become more involved in Latin American instability during the latter part of this time frame. Put another way, the elite–mass gap in relation to Latin American instability may have been steadily closing during the latter interval such that the second half of the entire thirty-year period would have considerably more mass involvement in Latin American instability than the first half. In relation to our concern for a diffusion effect, the first half of the time period under examination should exhibit stronger diffusion effects than the second.

Table 7.2 presents a comparison of the diffusion model with the random Poisson applied to the two halves of the time period. The first two columns list the number of countries which had i number of coups, whereas the second two present, respectively, the predicted values of the Poisson with diffusion and the Poisson.

The diffusion model provides a relatively good fit for the earlier time period; the random Poisson is not nearly as good. For the later time period, neither model is as good as for the earlier period. It should be noted that the value of beta, a measure of the degree of diffusion, is negative for the years 1950–1964. This indicates that rather than a diffusion effect during this later period, there may have existed an inhibitory effect, particularly when this value is compared to the positive one for the earlier interval (1935–1949).

To provide a comparison with the Latin American experience, the random and diffusion models also were applied to the occurrence of Sub-Saharan

TABLE 7.2. **Number of Latin American Countries Having i Number of Coups**

i number of coups	n_i number of countries	Poisson with diffusion	Poisson
1935–1949		$\alpha = 1.12, \beta = .490$	$\alpha = 1.45$
0	7	6.5	4.7
1	5	5.8	6.8
2	4	3.7	4.9
3	1	2.0	2.4
4	2	1.0	0.9
5	1	0.5	0.3
1950–1964		$\alpha = 1.58, \beta = -.324$	$\alpha = 1.35$
0	5	4.1	5.2
1	5	7.7	7.0
2	8	5.7	4.7
3	2	2.1	2.1

African coups in the time period 1963–1967. A value of beta equal to $-.083$ was calculated for the African countries and is sufficiently close to zero to discount any diffusion effects. The applicability of the Poisson to Sub-Saharan African coups, as seen in Table 7.3, suggests that in contrast to Latin America, coups in this African region may meet the fundamental assumptions of randomness embodied in the Poisson process.[12]

Before we can conclude, however, that the diffusion effect exists at least in the earlier Latin American time period, we must also consider an alternate hypothesis of heterogeneity, which also would lead to the applicability of the Poisson with diffusion. The increment beta, added to the transition rate in the construction of this model, not only may be due to a diffusion of instability from one country to the next, but also may be a product of differences in coup proneness such that countries which have greater propensities for instability would tend to "imitate" their own unstable past. It is these differences between countries with regard to propensities toward instability that constitute the hypothesis of heterogeneity.

TABLE 7.3.   **Number of Sub-Saharan African Countries Having i Number of Coups, 1963–1967**

i number of coups	n_i number of countries	Poisson
		$\alpha = .615$
0	14	14.1
1	8	8.6
2	4	2.7

NOTE: Through April 1967.

[12] This region is defined as Sub-Saharan Africa, and excludes North Africa, the Sudan, South Africa, Rhodesia, and all colonial dependencies. The following successful coups occurred in the time period 1963–April 1967: *Burundi*: July 1966 and November 1966; *Central African Republic*: January 1966; *Congo (Brazzaville)*: August 1963; *Congo (Kinshasa)*: November 1965; *Dahomey*: October 1963 and December 1965; *Ghana*: February 1966; *Nigeria*: January 1966 and July 1966; *Sierra Leone*: March 1967; *Tanzania*: January 1964 (Zanzibar); *Togo*: January 1963 and January 1967; *Uganda*: February 1966; *Upper Volta*: January 1966. This time period was chosen to insure that the vast majority of Sub-Saharan African countries were already independent, thus allowing for the *possibility* of diffusion. A successful coup in the Congo (Kinshasa) in September 1960 was, therefore, omitted. The entire set of twenty-six countries (including those which had no successful coups) is composed of all Sub-Saharan African nations independent at least since 1962. The data are drawn from the *New York Times*, and cross-referenced with *Deadline Data on World Affairs* and *Facts on File*. Further data are found in William R. Thompson, *Explanations of the Military Coup* (Seattle: Ph.D. diss., University of Washington, 1972).

Heterogeneity or Diffusion

There are essentially two methods for determining whether heterogeneity or diffusion exists. The first is suggested by an analysis of correlations between the number of coups experienced by countries in successive time intervals. This constitutes an examination of whether the countries each show the same pattern of instability over time, but different from each other (heterogeneity), or tend to imitate other countries (diffusion).[13] The second approach follows from the tests of hypotheses emanating from the theory of diffusion. The latter method is deductive in that the verification of an assumption or postulate concerning diffusion is dependent upon tests of relationships which derive from the original assumption. Both methods are employed in the subsequent analysis.

The first test of differentiation between heterogeneity and diffusion is essentially that of determining whether there exist constant probabilities for countries to experience coups. Under the assumption of heterogeneity, a given country has the same probability of having a coup in two successive time intervals, but this probability differs from one country to the next. On the other hand, a diffusion effect would lead to a variable probability of coups because this probability would not depend on a unique property of domestic politics, but on uncontrolled occurrences in neighboring countries. In the case of heterogeneity, then, the constant probability of a coup would lead to a high (and significant) correlation between the frequency of coups occurring in adjacent time intervals. When a diffusion effect is present, the variable probability would result in a lower (and non-significant) correlation between coups occurring in successive time intervals.

The diffusion effect appeared strongest in the period 1935–1949, which was divided into two equal non-overlapping intervals—1935–1941, and 1943–1949. No coups occurred in the year 1942, and it was omitted to assure equality of length for the intervals. A product-moment correlation coefficient of $r = .44$ ($N = 20$) was calculated between the coups in the two intervals.[14] Since we are dealing with a universe of Latin American countries, rather than a random sample, significance levels are not strictly applicable.[15] However,

[13] For a brief but comprehensive treatment of the Poisson with diffusion and the hypothesis of heterogeneity see Feller, *Annals*. Other more extensive treatments may be found in Ethel M. Newbold, "Practical Applications of the Statistics of Repeated Events, Particularly to Industrial Accidents," *Journal of the Royal Statistical Society*, 90 (1927), pp. 487–547; and in Ove Lundberg, *On Random Processes and Their Application to Sickness and Accident Statistics* (Uppsala, Sweden: Almqvist and Wiksell, 1964).

[14] See Feller, *Annals*, p. 398; and Newbold, *op. cit.*, pp. 498, 500–506, and 533–534.

[15] If the data here were obtained as random samples, then one would test the hypothesis of heterogeneity by calculating an *expected* value for the correlation coefficient between

as in the previous analyses of war, they may be stated as a basis for comparison, as well as to provide some criterion of acceptability, albeit an imperfect one. This value of the correlation coefficient is non-significant at our criterion level of $p < .05$.[16]

An additional value of the product-moment correlation coefficient was calculated only for Latin American countries that experienced coups in this period. Our concern here is to determine whether diffusion or heterogeneity exists. As such, the inclusion in the calculation of the above coefficient of those countries which were stable might have obscured the specific processes of instability that are present. The omission of countries which experienced no coups in the period 1935–1949 could yield a value of the correlation coefficient which is more directly related to instability. This value of the correlation coefficient is $r = .23$ ($N = 13$), and also is nonsignificant at $p < .05$.

An assumption basic to the notion of heterogeneity, that of a constant probability for each country, appears to lack empirical support. Moreover, the occurrence of a total of eight coups in the earlier time interval (1935–1941) contrasts sharply with twenty-one which took place in the second interval (1943–1949). A diffusion effect could account for this increase, whereas heterogeneity would seem a less likely explanation.

We may tentatively conclude that the diffusion of instability in this period may be a more tenable explanation than heterogeneity. However, the moderately positive value of the correlation coefficient when stable countries (in this period) are included indicates that perhaps a combination of heterogeneity and diffusion leads to the better fit of the modified Poisson. As a result, we shall proceed further and examine the hypotheses which emanate from the conclusion that diffusion indeed exists. If the tests of these hypotheses provide added confirmation for the inference of diffusion, then the alternative hypothesis of heterogeneity may be rejected with even greater confidence.

---

events in the two successive intervals. The calculation of this coefficient would be based upon the existence of a compound Poisson distribution, which consists of a sum of a set of numbers, each following a separate Poisson series. However, since our data represent the entire population of coups in a given period, this procedure would be inappropriate, and the *actual* value of the correlation coefficient is calculated. See Al. A. Tchouproff, "On the Mathematical Expectation of the Moments of Frequency Distributions," Part II," *Biometrika*, 13 (1920–1921), pp. 283–295, especially pp. 284–285. Also see Newbold, *op. cit.*, p. 521, and pp. 533–534.

[16] The tabled value for $N = 20$ at the .05 level is .444. Since the calculated value is $r = .439$, it must be considered nonsignificant. The fact that the two values are so close to one another argues for further explorations of this hypothesis, and are carried out in subsequent sections of the chapter. Significance levels for the product-moment correlation coefficient can be found in George W. Snedecor, *Statistical Methods* (Ames, Iowa: Iowa State College Press, 1946), p. 351.

Qualitative Inferences: A Theory of Diffusion

Our inference of diffusion is qualitative and, therefore, not susceptible to a mathematical test of deduction such as that found in certain forms of classical physics. Nevertheless, we can still examine the validity of tests of hypotheses generated by a theory of diffusion. Such a theory exists in the psychological literature with regard to imitative behavior among individuals. Because, as previously indicated, coups may be initiated by small groups of individuals such as a military leadership or a few members of a civilian elite, a theory pertaining to the psychology of individuals may have greater applicability than a theory based upon large-scale societal processes.

Perhaps the most important element of a theory of diffusion is the existence of a "model" or prototype.[17] The prototype exhibits certain behavior patterns and an observer matches these behaviors. Three types of effects may then occur: (1) a modeling effect—the exact behavior patterns of the prototype are copied by the observer; (2) an inhibitory effect which may be caused by an aversion to the behavior pattern exhibited by the prototype; and (3) a disinhibitory effect—certain inhibitions in the observer are reduced by the observation of certain behaviors exhibited by the prototype.[18] In the analysis of coups, the last of these may be difficult to determine and to distinguish from the modeling effect itself. Therefore, we will deal only with the first two possibilities.

It will be recalled that the diffusion effect for Latin American coups appeared in the years 1935–1949, rather than in the later period of 1950–1964. A positive value of beta was calculated for the earlier time period and, as indicated, may be considered a measure of the degree of diffusion. For the later period, on the other hand, a negative value was computed, which may indicate that some form of inhibition was present, although its exact nature is difficult to determine. Perhaps an increased participation of civilian groups in the political processes of the later period may have acted to inhibit the military from acting as it chose. Certain modernizing elites may have developed strong inhibitions against military intervention, perhaps as the result of observing the amount of coup activity in the earlier period and in neighboring countries. In any event, the two possible effects—the matching of the proto-

---

[17] In the psychological literature, the term *model* is employed. However, to avoid confusion with the use of model to mean abstract representation, we will henceforth use the term *prototype*. For an explicit reference to diffusion effects by a Latin American specialist, see Edwin Lieuwen, *Arms and Politics in Latin America* (New York: Praeger, 1960), p. 125.

[18] Albert Bandura and Richard H. Walters, *Social Learning and Personality Development* (New York: Holt, Rinehart, 1963), ch. 2, especially pp. 60–79.

type's behaviors and inhibition—may be reflected in the two time periods of Latin American coups.

Having found some correspondence between our treatment of Latin American coups and two aspects of a theory of diffusion, we next introduce certain variables which might tend to increase the extent of diffusion. These variables may be divided into two categories: (1) the characteristics of the prototype; and (2) the characteristics of the observer. Among the characteristics of the prototype which have been cited as eliciting greater degrees of diffusion are status and competence.[19] Prototypes with higher status have been shown to elicit a greater extent of diffusion than those with lower status. Similarly, prototypes which exhibit a higher degree of competence to the observer also have elicited greater amounts of diffusion.

The characteristics of the observer also are important in determining the extent of diffusion. Observers who are more likely to exhibit diffusion effects are those who are higher in measures of dependency, lower in self-esteem, and who perceive themselves as similar to the prototype.[20] The relationship between dependency and diffusion arises from the fact that those who are more dependent upon others may be less able to find innovative solutions to particular problems. Dependency implies the existence of multiple relationships, such that innovation by the observer may disturb any one of these relationships. Matching the prototype's behaviors might, therefore, be a simpler solution and one that might lead to the stability of existing relationships. In a similar fashion, it may be argued that those who rank lower on measures of self-esteem might be less capable of finding innovative solutions and would, consequently, find the diffusion effect more suitable as a problem-solving alternative. Finally, the similarity between the observer and prototype might induce the observer to generalize his condition and to perceive that the prototype may have experienced a similar set of problems which apparently were resolved by the initiation of a coup.

[19] A study that relates the status of the prototype to the degree of psychological imitation is Monroe Lefkowitz, Robert R. Blake, and Jane S. Mouton, "Status Factors in Pedestrian Violation of Traffic Signals," *Journal of Abnormal and Social Psychology*, 51 (November 1955), pp. 704–706. The effect of competence is treated by Milton E. Rosenbaum and Irving F. Tucker, "The Competence of the Model and the Learning of Imitation and Nonimitation," *Journal of Experimental Psychology*, 63 (February 1962), pp. 183–190.

[20] For the effects of dependency, see Leonard F. Jakubczak and Richard H. Walters, "Suggestibility as Dependency Behavior," *Journal of Abnormal and Social Psychology*, 59 (July 1959), pp. 102–107. Self-esteem in its relation to psychological imitation is treated by Donna M. Gelfand, "The Influence of Self-Esteem on Rate of Verbal Conditioning and Social Matching Behavior," *Journal of Abnormal and Social Psychology*, 65 (October 1962), pp. 259–265. The similarity of the observer to the prototype is dealt with in Eugene Burnstein, Ezra Stotland, and Alvin Zander, "Similarity to a Model and Self-Evaluation," *Journal of Abnormal and Social Psychology*, 62 (March 1961), pp. 257–264.

The characteristics of both prototype and observer may comprise the core of a theory of diffusion. Viewed from another perspective, they constitute a set of deductions which were derived from our mathematical analysis. If it is found that relationships exist between the extent of diffusion and the characteristics of both prototype and observer, then additional evidence will have been provided for our inference of diffusion; moreover, we will have established certain relationships among variables which may serve as explanations for the occurrence of coups in these regions. However, it is not possible to test both sets of relationships due to the requirement of brevity and the limited suitability of operational referents for our variables. Thus, we will test only the relationships between the characteristics of the prototype —status and competence—and the extent of diffusion.

Status and Competence as Predictors of Diffusion

In our analysis, the status of the prototype is defined as the status of each nation which experienced at least one coup in the time period under investigation. Each of these countries constitutes a prototype for all of the others, and the extent of diffusion may be measured by counting the number of coups which occurred during a fixed time interval subsequent to the occurrence of each coup. For both Latin America and Sub-Saharan Africa, this time interval is set equal to one year. Status itself can be measured by the number and rank of diplomats received by each nation from all other nations. Although other measures of status might be employed, such as size, population, or level of economic development, this measure was chosen as perhaps most indicative of each nation's standing in the international community. Diplomatic status is a compound measure which reflects attributed importance and therefore may subsume the other measures of status. Since status is an ordinal variable, the data are presented in the form of a rank order, and an appropriate statistical test is a Spearman rank correlation coefficient. The values for diplomatic status are those published by J. David Singer and Melvin Small and are for the year 1940.[21]

Table 7.4 presents the rank order of Latin American countries with respect to the degree of diffusion and status. A high rank for a given country on the extent of diffusion means that a relatively large number of countries experienced coups within a one-year period subsequent to the occurrence of a coup within that country. Since the mathematical analysis indicated that strong

[21] J. David Singer and Melvin Small, "The Composition and Status Ordering of the International System: 1815–1940," *World Politics*, 18 (January 1966), pp. 236–282; the data are found on p. 264. An examination of the effects of status orderings on the origins and characteristics of war is found in Manus Midlarsky, *Status Inconsistency and the Onset of International Warfare* (Evanston, Ill.: Ph.D. diss., Northwestern University, 1969).

TABLE 7.4. **Rank Order of the Extent of Diffusion in Latin American Nations, 1935–1949; Diplomatic Status, 1940**

Country	Extent of diffusion	Diplomatic status
Costa Rica	1.0	4.5
Brazil	3.0	1.5
Peru	3.0	3.0
Venezuela	3.0	8.0
Argentina	5.0	1.5
El Salvador	6.0	7.0
Guatemala	7.0	4.5
Paraguay	8.0	9.0
Bolivia	9.5	10.0
Ecuador	9.5	11.0
Haiti	11.0	13.0
Panama	12.0	6.0
Nicaragua	13.0	12.0

NOTE: Only countries that experienced coups in this period are included.

diffusion effects occurred in the earlier time interval, the analysis is confined to that period, and only countries which experienced coups are included.

The procedure for calculating the ranks in diffusion is as follows. For a one-year period following the occurrence of each coup in this time period, the number of countries experiencing coups was counted. If a particular country, A, experienced more than one coup, then the number of coups occurring within a one-year period following that coup was divided by the number of coups experienced by A. For example, Argentina experienced two coups in this same period. These were followed by a total of five countries which experienced coups within a one-year period following each of Argentina's coups. Thus, Argentina received a score of 5/2, or 2.50, placing it fifth in rank among Latin American countries. If an observer country experienced a second coup within the one-year period, then the second was not counted since we are concerned only with the number of countries which may have been subject to diffusion effects. In addition, if two coups occurred during the same month, each was counted toward the other's cumulative effect. A Spearman rank correlation coefficient of $r_s = .71$ was calculated. As noted earlier, the use of a test of significance is not strictly applicable, but may be indicated for purposes of comparison. This value of r_s is significant at $p < .01$.[22]

Our second predictor of the degree of diffusion is political competence.

[22] The significance levels for the Spearman rank correlation coefficients are found in Sidney Siegel, *Nonparametric Statistics for the Behavioral Sciences* (New York: McGraw-Hill, 1956), p. 284. The values reported are those for a one-tailed test in accordance with

This concept might be operationally defined by such variables as the extent of democratic rule or political and economic development. However, these are primarily ethnocentric concepts which may be more relevant to political cultures outside Latin America. As a result, we have employed a simpler construct which associates competence with prior history of stability, under the assumption that the more politically stable Latin American nations are perceived as more competent by their neighbors. Competence is defined as the number of years a country was free from the occurrence of coups prior to the occurrence of its first coup in this time period.[23]

Table 7.5 presents the rank order of the extent of diffusion and political competence. A Spearman rank correlation coefficient of $r_s = .67$ was calculated and is significant at $p < .05$.[24]

TABLE 7.5.   **Rank Order of the Extent of Diffusion and Political Competence in Latin American Nations, 1935–1949**

Country	Extent of diffusion	Political competence
Costa Rica	1.0	1.5
Brazil	3.0	4.5
Peru	3.0	1.5
Venezuela	3.0	4.5
Argentina	5.0	8.0
El Salvador	6.0	6.5
Guatemala	7.0	6.5
Paraguay	8.0	11.0
Bolivia	9.5	11.0
Ecuador	9.5	13.0
Haiti	11.0	3.0
Panama	12.0	9.0
Nicaragua	13.0	11.0

the directional hypotheses of the theory, and the correction for tied ranks was used in the calculation of values for this statistic.

The relationship between diplomatic status and diffusion is reported only for the time period 1935–1949. If data on diplomatic status were available for the later time period (the Singer and Small data are published only up to the year 1940), then a Spearman rank correlation coefficient could have been reported for this period as well. Using the data for 1940, a preliminary test yielded an $r_s = -.22$ between diplomatic status and the extent of diffusion for 1950–1964, thus providing a highly tentative substantiation of the inhibitory effect indicated in the mathematical analysis.

[23] In the construction of the measure of competence, the number of years was counted from the first year of this time period, 1935. Another possible measure might be the number of years since a country experienced its last coup, whether this coup occurred prior to 1935 or not.

[24] A Spearman rank correlation coefficient of $r_s = .45$ was calculated for the degree of association between diplomatic status and political competence. This value is nonsignificant, although it does indicate a moderately positive degree of association between the two variables.

With regard to Sub-Saharan Africa, our use of the Poisson and the Poisson with diffusion indicates that only the Poisson is applicable. However, it would be useful to apply the theory of diffusion under the expectation that the results would be nonsignificant. Such an application of the theory would constitute a test of consistency between the results of the mathematical analysis, on the one hand, and the theory of diffusion, on the other. Due to the relatively recent independence of most Sub-Saharan African countries, there is insufficient variation in the political competence measure for it to be used effectively. Hence, we examine only the effect of diplomatic status on the degree of diffusion.

Table 7.6. presents the extent of diffusion and diplomatic status of the Sub-Saharan African countries in the period 1963–1967. The year 1963 was chosen as a lower bound so that countries in the analysis would have been independent long enough for diffusion effects, if any, to take place. The values for the extent of diffusion were calculated in the same fashion as those for Latin America, and the data for diplomatic status are those published by Chadwick F. Alger and Steven J. Brams.[25] The value of the Spearman rank correlation coefficient is $r_s = .23$ and is nonsignificant.[26] It appears that the

TABLE 7.6. **Rank Order of the Extent of Diffusion in Sub-Saharan African Nations, 1963–1967; Diplomatic Status, 1963–1964**

Country	Extent of diffusion	Diplomatic status
Congo (Kinshasa)	1.0	3.0
Central African Republic	2.0	8.0
Nigeria	3.0	2.0
Ghana	4.5	1.0
Uganda	4.5	5.0
Togo	6.5	7.0
Congo (Brazzaville)	6.5	4.0
Sierra Leone	8.0	6.0

NOTE: Only countries that experienced coups through April 1967 are included.

[25] Chadwick F. Alger and Steven J. Brams, "Patterns of Representation in National Capitals and Intergovernmental Organizations," *World Politics*, 19 (July 1967), pp. 646–663; the data are found on p. 652. They differ from the diplomatic data used for Latin America in that they do not include the ranks of diplomats received, giving only the number. In addition, three countries which experienced coups in this time period were not included in the data source: These are Burundi, Dahomey, and Upper Volta. Tanzania was reported as Tanganyika in the data source, and no value was included for Zanzibar. Thus, Tanzania could not be included as a prototype nation. Of course, these four countries were included in the data analysis as observers, since no values for diplomatic status were needed.

[26] This value of r_s is statistically nonsignificant. However, if one country—the Central African Republic—were removed, then the value of r_s would be increased to .67, which is considerably larger than the former value, although still nonsignificant. This serves as an illustration of the strong effect of a single country when the number of cases

results of an application of the theory to the Sub-Saharan African coups is consistent with the mathematical analysis, as is the case with regard to the Latin American coups.

Conclusions and Implications

This approach to the study of Latin American and Sub-Saharan African coups has produced a varied set of conclusions. There are essentially three categories of inference corresponding to the two Latin American time periods and the African coups. For the earlier of the two Latin American periods, the analysis of probability models suggests that the diffusion of instability exists. This inference is substantiated by the correlational analysis of coups occurring in successive time intervals. The alternative hypothesis of heterogeneity can be rejected, in part. A theory of the diffusion of instability is presented, and the use of diplomatic status and political competence as predictors of the extent of diffusion provides further confirmation of the existence of a diffusion effect in this time period. The later of the Latin American time periods exhibits an inhibitory effect, which may be due to a decrease in the prevalence of military intervention in Latin American politics during this period.

The occurrence of Sub-Saharan African coups conforms to the Poisson process, which implies the lack of a diffusion effect. The failure of diplomatic status to serve as a predictor of the extent of diffusion provides further confirmation for this conclusion. An additional inference may be drawn from the derivation of the Poisson itself. Basic to this derivation is the assumption of a constant transition rate in which all elements under consideration have the same likelihood of moving from one state to the next. Countries which have experienced one coup have the same likelihood of another coup as countries which experienced no coups.

Recent evidence indicates that there may indeed be a diffusion effect in Sub-Saharan African instability. However, if the Poisson continues to be applicable in the future (implying that its assumptions may be met), most of the Sub-Saharan African countries eventually may experience at least one

---

is small. In addition, the method used to obtain the rank correlation coefficient does not indicate which *particular* country may have acted as a prototype for an observer country. Nigeria, Ghana, and the Central African Republic all experienced coups within one month of each other, and it may be that countries which experienced later coups might have employed one of the other two countries as a prototype, rather than the Central African Republic. Given a longer time period of analysis, it is possible that future studies may find that the diffusion of instability indeed exists in this region. Nevertheless, it must be observed that two applications of the Spearman rank correlation coefficient, as well as the mathematical analysis, all failed to indicate that significant diffusion effects exist for the occurrence of Sub-Saharan African coups in this time period.

coup.[27] This condition may result from a similarity in the internal conditions of these countries, including a similar tendency toward coups. It should be emphasized, however, that this additional inference is highly tenuous if only because of the limited number of categories (0, 1, and 2 coups) and the short time period of analysis.

Admittedly, this form of analysis does not account for long-range causes of instability. One must differentiate between the *conditions* necessary for the occurrence of coups and *proximate* causes, such as a diffusion effect. An organized military establishment unresponsive to a civilian authority may be a necessary condition for the occurrence of one type of coup; without the presence of such a condition, a theory of diffusion would be unnecessary. The innovation of coups—a concept not treated in this study—might be better dealt with by a comparative case study approach. Nor have we determined which *specific* entity diffuses across national boundaries. One alternative might be the communication of instability by mass media, whereby the knowledge that a coup occurred in one country affects the occurrence of instability in a neighboring country. A second possibility, however, refers to a different process. If one assumes that a relationship exists between economic and political instability, then the successive diffusion of the former throughout the Latin American countries in the period 1935–1949 also could have led to our findings concerning the diffusion of political instability.[28] These alternatives and others could be examined in the future.

Whatever its inherent limitations, however, an analysis of the type presented here has utility in defining the general areas of analysis which may be productive for future research. Certain characteristics of the prototype suggested by a theory of diffusion have been examined and, in the future, characteristics of the observer might be analyzed as well. Concepts such as "reward" to the successful insurgents might be useful in developing the theory, and its utility is enhanced by the similarity of this concept to others suggested in theories of international integration.[29]

[27] Since the time these data were collected, other Sub-Saharan African countries included in this analysis, such as Mali, experienced their first successful coups. Additional analyses by William R. Thompson, *op. cit.*, have indicated that a diffusion effect may now exist in Sub-Saharan Africa, but that it took some time to mature and become evident.

[28] This possibility was suggested in a written communication from Martin C. Needler.

[29] The analogous concept in theories of international integration is the reward to the elements of a pluralistic or amalgamated security-community after integration has taken place. For detailed discussions of the various theories, see Karl W. Deutsch, *The Analysis of International Relations* (Englewood Cliffs, N.J.: Prentice-Hall, 1968), pp. 191–202. Also see Amitai Etzioni, *Political Unification: A Comparative Study of Leaders and Forces* (New York: Holt, Rinehart, 1965), pp. 14–96; and Ernst B. Haas, *Beyond the Nation-State: Functionalism and International Organization* (Stanford: Stanford University Press, 1964), pp. 3–50.

Thus, domestic instability in the case of Latin American countries during the period 1935–1949 may be seen as a partial consequence of events occurring in the regional international system of the nation-states comprising this system. The events occurring within or between certain countries can constitute a source of domestic instability for other countries. Just as elements of the system in the form of alliances and alliance-related uncertainties can lead to war, or a boundary relationship between the state and system (e.g., a status inconsistency) can also lead to international violence, so, too, the systemic environment of a nation-state can affect its internal stability. We turn now to the "other side of the coin" to see the extent to which conditions wholly contained within nation-states can affect international and domestic instability.

VIII

Domestic Sources of War and Instability

Two sets of relationships have now been established. One concerns the effects of internal change which can lead to a status inconsistency if systemic ascribed status is not sufficiently high and, in turn, can result in international warfare. The other refers to the impact of the external environment on the domestic conflict of nations by means of a diffusion effect. In the status inconsistency analysis of Chapter VI, certain boundary relations between the nation-state and international system demonstrated an impact on war. The diffusion of instability from the external environment to the nation-state, treated in Chapter VII, was found to be a significant factor in understanding Latin American coups.

The element common to both analyses is the presence of the systemic environment which became a necessary condition for maximizing the explanation of both types of conflict behavior. Suppose we now remove this element and analyze only the possible domestic sources of international war and internal instability. This was done, in fact, in the analysis of the achievement variables in Chapter VI. However, an entire category of domestic social life has not been treated for its effect on war—that of domestic social structure quite apart from rates of change of economic or economically linked variables. Similarly, the effects of internal variables have not been examined for their possible relationship to domestic instability. This omission becomes particularly important in this case, because of the basic assumption in Chapter VII concerning the relative lack of importance of societal processes in explaining military intervention. The military elite, it was assumed, constituted a small group largely removed from large-scale societal influences and, as a result, could be readily influenced by the behavior of counterparts in neighboring countries. This assumption, therefore, requires testing in the form of some examination of the effects of obvious and theoretically important mass processes such as modernization on the occurrence of military coups. Thus, when we combine our requirements in the analysis of war with that of instability, we have two examinations of the effects of domestic considerations on political violence. In the first one, the effects of domestic social structure are to be assessed with regard to their impact on war, if any; while in the second, internal processes specifically related to modernization are to be examined in relation to domestic instability.

Domestic Social Structure and International Warfare

The purpose of this section is the systematic examination of possible relationships between domestic social structure and international warfare. This question touches on the notion that primitive civilizations, with their generally simplified social structures, tend to have a reputation for being warlike, whereas, by the same token, nations thought to be more developed, or "civilized," are seen as more peaceful. In a similar vein, we can ask about possible relationships between societal sectors and war. When societies are controlled by aristocratic elites, such as a landed gentry, do they tend to be more warlike than when they are controlled by other societal sectors, such as a peasant population? Further questions may be asked about the roles of other groups in society such as a sacred authority or a military establishment. When these groups tend to have more power in the political process, are societies more or less warlike in their relationships with other nations? Thus, a variety of social sectors are examined in relation to war, in addition to the fundamental concept of societal development as a possible antecedent of international warfare.

We seek to examine social structure in relationship to war quite apart from considerations of industrial development (which have been examined elsewhere in this volume and in other studies).[1] There may exist strong relationships between contemporary social structure and industrialization which might confound the relationships that would be derived from the examination of social structure itself.

---

[1] In addition to analyses reported in Chapters V and VI see, for example, Robert C. North and Richard Lagerstrom, *War and Domination: A Theory of Lateral Pressure* (New York: General Learning Press, 1971); and Nazli Choucri and Robert C. North, 'Dynamics of International Conflict: Some Policy Implications of Population, Resources, and Technology," in Raymond Tanter and Richard H. Ullman (eds.), *Theory and Policy in International Relations* (Princeton, N.J.: Princeton University Press, 1972), pp. 80–122.

In order to effect an analysis of this type, we turn to a comprehensive examination of pre-industrial societies which are, at the same time, of some greater complexity than wholly traditional societies. S. N. Eisenstadt has provided a comprehensive description of historical political systems which fall between the "traditional" and "modern" types.[2] He has further provided a detailed characterization for these political systems which, in effect, consist of a large number of coded categories. This large-scale coding of variables pertaining to these historical political systems constitutes our initial data set from which we can derive certain uniformities that then may be related to the characteristics of war.

The overall design is to use data reduction methods, in this case a cluster analysis, validated by an additional factor analysis, in order to collapse the 88 variables initially chosen to a much smaller and, therefore, manageable set. The cluster analysis finds areas of commonality in the many domestic societal characteristics, and these areas of commonality constitute the clusters. Scores for each country are obtained on the several clusters, and these values are then systematically related to several indicators of international warfare using multiple regression techniques. The analysis is inductive to the extent that the areas of common variation in the data are "discovered" and then examined for possible relationships to warlike behavior. On the other hand, it is deductive with regard to hypothesis testing in that the data, even in their initial unreduced form, pertain to the question of central importance in this study; namely, the effects of societal development and specific societal sectors on international warfare.

Methodologically, the purposes here differ from those of Chapter VI. In that chapter, the cluster analysis was used as a data-reducing means of breaking the multicollinearity deadlock. In this analysis, it is simply a method for acquiring a more parsimonious and consequently more manageable description of the data than is found in the original source.[3]

A Cluster Analysis of Societal Characteristics

The basic type of political systems to be analyzed are:[4]

1. primitive political systems
2. patrimonial empires
3. nomad or conquest empires

[2] See S. N. Eisenstadt, *The Political Systems of Empires* (New York: The Free Press, 1963).

[3] The clustering procedure used in the analyses of this chapter is the same BCTRY system employed in Chapter VI. See Robert C. Tryon and Daniel E. Bailey, *Cluster Analysis* (New York: McGraw-Hill, 1970).

[4] *Ibid.*, p. 10.

4. city-states
5. feudal systems
6. centralized historical bureaucratic empires
7. modern societies of various types (until the industrial era)

While there exists a certain degree of subjectivity in this classification and some overlap of categories, this list can be accepted as a working set of differentiations among societies that may lead to further useful distinctions. Comparisons among these societies are based on criteria which involve role and group differentiations, the organization and differentiation of political activities into groups, as well as more formal organizations such as executive, legislative, judicial, and political party organizations, the legitimacy of the system and its rulers, and the goals of the system. The establishment of goals for the polity, in turn, may be classified by their content (e.g., cultural or economic), the extent of identification with any particular group in society; definition of goals in terms of political interests; and the extent of political identification in terms of competition between groups over these goals.

Eisenstadt has identified 65 historical political systems which are compared using these criteria. The entire list is included in Appendix B, while they may be summarized as follows

1. The ancient empires—especially the Egyptian, Babylonian, and Inca
2. The Chinese Empire, from the Han to the Ch'ing
3. The various Persian Empires
4. The Roman and Hellenistic Empires
5. The Byzantine Empire
6. Several ancient Hindu states
7. The Arab Caliphate
8. The West, Central, and East European states
9. The conquest empires—especially the Spanish-American, French, and British colonial empires

The 88 variables used to describe the 65 cases are drawn from the coding of the scope of the political process in these societies, and the social conditions for the institutionalization of the political system. Some of the variables found in these categories are the differentiation of a social structure with regard to economic, political, or legal activity, and the crystallization of legal, military, and religious institutional groups. Other variables are the scope of bureaucratic activity generally, or in specific areas such as the economic, political or legal sectors. The extent of political participation of groups such as the peasantry, gentry, or military also is included.

The steps in this clustering procedure are, first, to establish the relationships of each variable with every other variable in order to determine the most highly correlated pairs. Second, the pairs of variables are clustered according to their highest intercorrelations with others. Finally, the single most representative variable is selected for the resulting cluster, and is known as the *pivot* variable. Additional variables known as key, or *defining*, variables are selected in order to make each cluster as "tight" or collinear as possible, as nearly independent of the others as possible, and able to account for as much variation as possible.

Seven distinct clusters or dimensions result from the analysis ranging from the first dimension, which effectively explains 39% of the initial communality, to the seventh, which explains 3%. A factor analysis, performed as a type of validation, yielded virtually the same set of dimensions as did the cluster analysis. The intercorrelations among the dimensions, given in Table 8.1, indicate a fair degree of independence among them. The seven clusters, therefore, may be understood as reflecting relatively distinct underlying tendencies in the data, which then may be used as independent variables in the explanation of war. Table 8.2 presents the variables selected by the cluster analysis as those with the highest coefficients on each of the dimensions, or as they were termed previously, the dimension definers. The first variable listed for each of the clusters is the pivot variable around which the dimension is constructed. This variable is listed first because of its centrality in structuring the dimension, even though it might not finally have the highest loading after all the variables are chosen by the clustering process. The remaining variables in each cluster are listed in descending order of magnitude of their coefficients.

The coefficients or loadings are listed in parentheses and in successive groupings in the right-hand portion of Table 8.2. In the first row at the bottom of the table is found the proportion communality exhausted by each dimension, while below it is the proportion of the mean square of the correlation

TABLE 8.1. **Intercorrelations Among Cluster Domains**

	1 Develop- ment	2 Gentry	3 Religious	4 Bureau- cratic	5 Legal	6 Military	7 Peasan- try
1. Development	1.00						
2. Gentry	.21	1.00					
3. Religious	.21	.19	1.00				
4. Bureaucratic	.20	−.09	−.24	1.00			
5. Legal	.52	−.11	.14	−.18	1.00		
6. Military	.20	.28	−.13	.42	−.09	1.00	
7. Peasantry	.44	.18	.32	−.05	.29	.14	1.00

TABLE 8.2. A Cluster Analysis of Societal Characteristics

Variable	Dimension						
	1	2	3	4	5	6	7
Differentiation of social structure (sectors-general)	(.95)	.16	.29	.25	.48	.16	.48
Differentiation of social structure (groups-general)	(.96)	.16	.10	.28	.58	.23	.42
Extent of differentiation (general-political)	(.95)	.16	.10	.15	.58	.21	.42
Differentiation of social structure (economic)	(.93)	.16	.19	.24	.45	.15	.39
Development of free-floating power (sectors-general)	(.92)	.35	.23	.12	.39	.23	.46
Extent of differentiation (urban)	(.86)	.22	.06	.13	.46	.16	.25
Development of free-floating power (education-culture)	(.85)	.15	.38	.11	.42	.14	.41
Articulation of political goals (gentry)	.24	(.98)	.18	−.07	−.08	.24	.17
Extent of differentiation (gentry)	.28	(.99)	.19	−.01	−.11	.32	.19
Extent of political organization (gentry)	.11	(.94)	.12	−.09	−.21	.37	.19
Intensity of political participation (gentry)	.19	(.94)	.25	−.16	−.03	.15	.14
Extent of differentiation (religious)	.22	−.01	(.94)	−.14	.10	−.27	.20
Articulation of political goals (religious)	.28	.10	(.95)	−.22	.30	−.14	.39
Intensity of political participation (religious)	.19	.23	(.88)	−.28	.14	.02	.31
Extent of political participation (religious)	.07	.36	(.83)	−.22	−.02	−.07	.26
Scope of bureaucratic activity (sectors-general)	.33	−.03	−.02	(.90)	−.08	.36	.06
Scope of bureaucratic activity (central-political)	.02	−.06	−.36	(.88)	−.24	.25	−.25
Scope of bureaucratic activity (central-legal)	.21	−.16	−.09	(.84)	−.18	.39	.04
Scope of bureaucratic activity (central-economic)	.13	−.04	−.35	(.79)	−.10	.44	−.01
Articulation of political goals (legal)	.40	−.11	.22	−.23	(.97)	−.05	.25
Intensity of political participation (legal)	.44	−.13	−.05	−.10	(.93)	−.15	.17
Extent of political participation (legal)	.43	−.07	.27	−.23	(.92)	−.09	.31
Extent of differentiation (legal)	.67	−.09	.09	−.10	(.86)	−.05	.32
Articulation of political goals (military)	−.33	−.12	−.19	−.04	−.15	(.56)	−.11
Extent of political participation (military)	−.22	.18	−.29	.14	−.36	(.86)	−.03
Extent of professionalization of bureaucratic roles	.48	.39	−.01	.61	.05	(.75)	.22
Autonomy of bureaucratic organization (general)	.62	.33	.14	.46	.20	(.63)	.32
Articulation of political goals (peasantry)	.35	.03	.29	.03	.31	.07	(.85)
Extent of political participation (peasantry)	.41	.28	.27	−.11	.18	.18	(.88)
Proportion of initial communality	.39	.13	.12	.12	.08	.08	.03
Proportion of mean square of correlation matrix	.70	.07	.07	.06	.03	.02	.01
Domain validity	.99	.99	.98	.96	.99	.95	.93
Reliability	.98	.98	.96	.93	.97	.90	.87

NOTE: $N = 65$; $V = 88$.

170

matrix exhausted, as another measure of variance reduction.[5] The domain validities are presented below, and indicate the accuracy of each cluster in terms of the reproducibility of the coefficients with reference to the entire set of defining variables. The reliability coefficient for a dimension, found in the bottom row, is a measure of the correlation between the cluster coefficients for that dimension and those of a collinear comparable set. With the exception of cluster 7, all of the domain validities are at least equal to .95, while the reliabilities are equal to .90 or greater. Thus, the analysis seems to have a satisfactory degree of validity and reliability.

A more intuitive or face validity consideration refers to a variable which is not related in any way to the other 87. This is the coding for the number of rebellions experienced by a country, and given its conceptual distinction from the remaining variables, one would expect it to be rejected from the analysis. This, in fact, occurred with this single variable being the only one not represented in any of the dimensions.

Dimension 1 has the greatest number of variables associated with it (7), with the last dimension having only 2 variables as dimension definers. All of the remaining dimensions are defined by 4 variables each. Thus, from the original 88 variables, 29 were found to be most relevant in describing the historical political systems, and these in turn are reflected by 7 underlying dimensions. Predictably, no variable appears in more than one dimension. All but 4 of the 29 variables have factor coefficients above .80 on their respective dimensions, while none of the remaining 4 is less than .56. The results appear good, since 5 of the 7 dimensions are highly homogeneous, while the remaining 2 (dimensions 1 and 6) are only slightly less so.

Given their use as independent variables in the subsequent analysis of war, each of the dimensions requires some comment and interpretation. Dimension 1 is defined by three interrelated groups of variables. The pivot variable, as well as two others, concern the differentiation of social structure and to this extent may serve as a measure of societal development. Two other variables pertain to the extent of political differentiation. Finally, two additional variables are related to the development of "free-floating" power.

The general definition of the differentiation of social structure employed here is a composite of the separate degrees of differentiation of the economic, political, and social sectors. Differentiation of the economic sector is categorized according to the following indices: activities (agriculture, industry,

---

[5] Because the proportions of initial communality and mean square of the correlation matrix exhausted by the several dimensions provide a description of the empirical cluster analysis as it is being performed, they are included in the table. For those interested in the percentages of common variance exhausted by each of the successive dimensions, they are, respectively, 41.9, 13.0, 12.8, 12.7, 8.1, 8.2, and 3.3, while the percentages of total variance are, respectively, 28.0, 8.7, 8.6, 8.5, 5.4, 5.5, and 2.2.

trade, and finance); roles (craftsmen, traders, and bankers); organizations (manufacturing concerns, guilds, and trading companies); mechanisms (self-regulating markets); values and norms (personal enrichment, economic growth and development, and norms of property transaction); and elites (large traders, bankers, and industrialists).

Differentiation of social structure by groups is similarly defined, and is based on eleven basic indices for the "ecological groups" of peasantry, gentry, aristocracy, and urban groups. Five basic indices are used for the "institutional groups" of the legal, military, religious, and cultural-secular professions. As in the case of differentiation of social structure with regard to societal sectors, the general value is meant to be representative of the entire subcategory.

The extent of political differentiation employs indices similar to those used in the differentiation of social structure, except that political differentiation refers to the scope of the political process, rather than to the social conditions for the institutionalization of the political system. Thus, the criteria are identical to those involved in evaluating the differentiation of social structure. The degree of general political differentiation is a composite value similar to that for social differentiation, whereas the extent of the urban group's political differentiation is a function of eleven indices. These measures include the diversification or differentiation of the group's resources, economic activities, economic organization, participation in a market economy, political organization and leadership, political affiliation of members, religious organization and leadership, religious affiliation of members, status criteria, social subgroups, and individual status.

Development of free-floating power is determined by six criteria. As in the case of the other two categories that form this dimension, the general category is based on the degrees of differentiation of the separate sectors taken together. The six indices are: extent of development of free-floating resources (money and various types of exchangeable commodities); extent of development of free-floating population (free rural population and religiously, politically, and legally non-commited populations); degree of universality of norms and values; extent of flexibility of institutional organizations; degree of mobility in institutional spheres; and extent of development of non-ascriptive and universal status criteria.

Thus, dimension 1 is defined in terms of the various ways and the degrees to which polity and society are differentiated. Because of the strong association between structural differentiation, division of labor, and general societal complexity with development, we may associate this concept with dimension 1. It describes the overall societal state of development and defines the limits within which various groups and institutions operate. It further defines the extent of development for the milieu of the political system itself and in this sense provides a foundation for the examination of other dimensions.

Dimension 2 is defined by four variables, all of which relate to the gentry as a sociopolitical group. The pivot variable is the degree of articulation of the gentry in the political process. According to Eisenstadt, this variable is defined according to the extent to which the political orientation of this group is generalized, in contrast to demands for immediate concrete rewards. The other variables which comprise this dimension are the degree of social differentiation (gentry), the extent to which the gentry are politically organized, and the intensity of participation of the gentry in the political process.

The extent of political organization of the gentry refers to a crystallization process, whereas the intensity of political participation involves the scope of the group's activity in the general political process. In effect, the latter variable consists of the gentry acting as an interest group, while the former indicates the degree to which individual gentry members participate through political organizations. Clearly, both of these types of activities can occur simultaneously. The significance of this dimension lies in the fact that the extent of common variance "explained" here is second only to sociopolitical development delineated in the first dimension. One may conclude that in historical bureaucratic societies, the gentry were well mobilized and participated in the political system in a variety of ways.

The third cluster also concerns the participation of a given social group. All key variables defining this dimension relate to the religious group in society. They also correspond to the same categories as those comprising dimension 2. In this case, the pivot variable is the extent of differentiation of the religious group in the societal process. The other variables are the extent of its political participation in terms of articulation, the intensity of political participation of the sacred authority, and the degree of participation of this sector in political organizations. The criteria on which these values are determined were previously enumerated. As in the case of dimension 2, the extent of participation of the group is distinguished from members of the group acting on their own through political organizations. To some extent this conceptual division is explained by the pivot variable for this dimension— the differentiation of the religious group in the political process. If the differentiation is high, it becomes more likely that an individual can support both his own group, as well as other political channels. But if the differentiation is low, he may tend to rely more on his own group, at least in the societies analyzed here.

Dimension 4 is defined by the scope of bureaucratic activity. All four variables relate to this category. The pivot variable is the general scope of bureaucratic activity, while the remaining three are all focused on the central (geographical) level, as opposed to the local level, and relate to the political bureaucracy, the legal bureaucracy (including diplomacy), and the economic bureaucracy. There are three categories used to determine the scope of bureaucratic activities in general and in regard to the particular functions of the individual bureaucracies. One of these categories is the technical, by which is meant activity referring to the performance of services and maintenance of conditions for the functioning of various groups. A second category used for assessing the scope of bureaucratic activity is the regulative capacity of bureaucracy, or activity focusing on the regulation of major institutional spheres and centers of power in society. Finally, Eisenstadt considers the balance between the technical and regulative to determine the equilibrium between these two policies. All of these categories are used in constructing the four variables which comprise this dimension.

The fifth cluster relates to the legal aspects of society. The pivot variable for this dimension is the extent of political participation of the legal group in terms of articulation of its political goals. The other variables are: the intensity of political participation, the degree of participation of the legal group in political organizations, and the extent of differentiation of the legal group from other societal groups. In essence, this dimension tends to emphasize the participation of this group as a distinct and cohesive entity in the political process, and the intensity and articulation of its goals in the political system.

Dimension 6 is the least homogeneous of the seven dimensions. The two most significant variables relate to the military profession. The pivot variable is the degree of political participation of the military group in terms of the articulation of its goals. This is followed, in terms of significance, by the extent of participation of the military in the political organization of society, the degree of professionalization of bureaucratic roles, and the autonomy of bureaucratic organization in terms of its roles. Thus, the salience of the military in the political system is correlated with extent to which the bureaucracy is autonomous and professionalized. Perhaps as the bureaucracy becomes more institutionalized and routinized, the military becomes more vocal and more active in the political system. Because of their greater prominence in loading on this dimension, the military variables appear to be more important in defining it. In addition, a variable pertaining to military organization, but not a dimension definer, also loads heavily on this cluster.

Finally, dimension 7 concerns the peasantry. This cluster is defined by only two variables. The pivot variable is the extent of political participation of the peasant group in terms of its articulation. The other variable which defines this dimension is the extent of participation of the peasantry in the political organization of society. It is worthwhile noting, that, with the exception of the religious cluster (number 3), each of the dimensions pertaining to specific groups (numbers 2, 5, 6, and 7) has as its pivot variable the articulation of political goals for that group.

Relationships with International Warfare

Scores for each country were obtained on each of the clusters, and these values were then related to war data collected by Sorokin. Each of the scores for a country on a given cluster is a linear composite of the variables loading on that cluster. In this fashion, a country has a score determined by a single cluster, and there were a total of seven values for each country. These independent variables derivative from the cluster analysis then were examined in relation to the three primary characteristics of war which constitute the set of dependent variables in this study—the number of wars, years in war, and battle casualties. Complete data were found in the Sorokin source for a subset of nations corresponding to those found in the prior analysis.[6]

Stepwise multiple regressions were performed with the seven cluster scores as the predictors and the three war variables as the criteria. Five of the seven variables were allowed to enter into each of the equations in order to arrive at a somewhat more parsimonious structure of explanation than that which would be derived from the use of the entire set of independent variables. Furthermore, the extent of explanation afforded by each additional variable after five have been introduced, diminishes rather sharply as a result of the redundancy found in all of these variables.[7]

The regression equations are presented in Table 8.3 with the respective *F* values for the multiple correlation coefficients. Using a strict criterion of statistical significance, for those who would consider this an acceptable procedure for populations of countries, the multiple correlation coefficient for battle casualties is found to be significant at $p < .05$. In addition, a fairly sizable portion of the variance is explained, as is the case for the multiple *R* for the variable years in war. With regard to the effects of the specific predictors, three variables appear to have significant effects on the war indicators. These are the military dimension in the case of years in war, and the religious and bureaucratic dimensions in the case of battle casualties. All beta weights for significant main effects are at least twice the values of their corresponding standard errors.

The interpretations for the findings thus far would appear to be relatively straightforward. The significant effect of the military dimension on war

[6] Pitirim A. Sorokin, *Social and Cultural Dynamics*, vol. 3 (New York: Bedminster, 1962). The societies included in this analysis are indicated by asterisks in Appendix B.

[7] For a discussion of the explanatory power of each successive variable in a multiple regression equation, see Quinn McNemar, *Psychological Statistics*, 3rd ed. (New York: Wiley, 1962), pp. 185–186.

TABLE 8.3.   **Multiple Regression Analyses of Three Characteristics of War**

	Predictor (Beta Weights)								
Criterion	Develop- ment	Gentry	Reli- gious	Bureau- cracy	Legal	Mili- tary	Peasan- try	R	F
Number of wars	−.13	.15	.38	.25			.48	.61	1.44
Years in war			−.26	−.54	.20	.69*	.35	.70	2.30
Battle casualties	.31	−.35	.53*	.64*	.14			.78	3.74*

NOTE: $N = 18$.
* $p < .05$.

duration might be attributable to the desire on the part of the military to continue a war even when it is going badly, perhaps as a result of considerations of lost honor and/or the loss of future political influence. In regard to the significant effect of the religious groups in society on battle casualties, persons adhering to strong belief systems might be willing to suffer larger casualties in order to disseminate or defend their version of revealed truth. The bureaucracy, on the other hand, might be willing to suffer additional casualties in order to further specific political interests, or simply because the bureaucratic machinery is already committed to serving up large numbers of men and, through inertia, it might be willing to continue.

In addition to statistical significance, there are at least two other criteria which may be applied to the evaluation of these results. Given the debatable appropriateness of the concept of significance for populations of countries, another approach is the use of proportions of variance explained, while still another is the consistency of relationships across separate war indicators. The stepwise regression procedure chooses the order of variables to be included according to the greatest variance reduction obtained by a given variable. Thus, if we examine the first two or three variables included in each equation, we will have an additional means of evaluating these findings. In the regression equation for the number of wars, the peasantry dimension is the first introduced into this equation, while the military and the bureaucracy are the first variables included, respectively, in the regressions for years in war and battle casualties. In addition to its primary role in the explanation of number of wars, the peasantry is also one of the first three variables incorporated into the equation for years in war. Thus, the peasantry appears to be important not only from a variance reduction standpoint, but also in regard to consistent appearances across two of the three regressions. The religious and bureaucratic dimensions also were found among the first three variables stepped into the equations in two of the three war criteria.

The importance of the peasantry may reside in the effects of mass movements on the frequency and duration of war. The mass of a population may anger more quickly than their statesmen, given similar provocation, and the desire for victory also may prolong a war begun by mass-oriented political authorities. On the other hand, the fact that the majority of casualties are usually suffered by large groups such as the peasantry might suggest a very weak or small negative effect of this dimension on battle casualties. This, in fact, is indicated in Table 8.3, where this variable is not among the first five incorporated into that equation.

One apparently anomalous feature of the analysis deserves mention. Whereas the bureaucracy variable has a strong, positive, and significant effect on battle casualties, it has a relatively strong and negative, although nonsignificant, effect on duration. This result may be understood in terms of two possible consequences of the large scope of bureaucratic activity. On the one hand, a complex and active bureaucracy might be needed to supply the armies and the front during war—an interpretation which would agree with the small positive effect of development (dimension 1) on battle casualties. The greater the ability of the bureaucracy, and to a much smaller extent, the greater the degree of societal development in the form of complex institutions, the greater the ability to mobilize populations in order to sustain large losses on the battlefield. On the other hand, another function of the bureaucracy would be to maintain domestic services and to insure some internal stability. These goals would be contravened by a war of long duration, and so the bureaucracy might have a simultaneous interest in shortening the war. These potential dual functions of a bureaucratic organization in relation to war deserve additional research.

Perhaps the most surprising and potentially important feature of the analysis, however, is the virtual absence of any important effect of societal development on war. Whether a society is structurally complex and differentiated, therefore, appears to have little bearing on its war experience. The most traditional and/or "primitive" society may have virtually the same probability of experiencing war as the most developed nations. This finding may have important implications for the continuation of war as a vehicle of national policy even as more of the developing countries reach higher stages of societal development.

The cluster analysis of 88 variables and 65 cases, therefore, has yielded a set of underlying uniformities among pre-modern nations, and these, in turn, have given rise to relationships with the characteristics of war for a subset of these nations. The interpretations for certain of the relationships between societal sectors (such as the military, religious, and the peasantry) and war are relatively straightforward. Perhaps of greater interest are relationships concerning the bureaucracy and societal development. If certain of these findings are applied, with appropriate caution, to contemporary modernizing nations, then some illustrations of these relationships may be found.

Two developing countries which have been actively involved in international warfare in the post–World War II period are India and Israel, both of which have rather complex bureaucracies along with extensive bureaucratic activity. Despite the relatively large number of casualties suffered in these wars by post–World War II standards, they were of short duration. What these illustrations imply for the systematic behavior of nation-states in the developing world, however, is a question that can be answered only by further research.

There exist some important implications of the lack of a relationship between societal development and war. Those who would hope for eventual peace through the development of nations appear to have little evidence to support their position, at least within the confines of the present study. On the other hand, there exist societal sectors, such as the military or bureaucracy, which in the contemporary world may have a stake in the continuation of war.

This pessimistic evaluation of the role of the nation-state in future peace-keeping efforts suggests that peace-making through international institutions may have a better chance of success. This implication receives further support from the fairly strong effects on war of certain characteristics of the international system such as alliances, or alliance-related uncertainty, and a status inconsistency. Activity at the level of interactions among nations aimed at preventing war, therefore, may succeed more readily than efforts which find channels internal to the nation-state.

As a result of this analysis, we should perhaps differentiate between characteristics of the international system which lead to the onset of war, on the one hand, and domestic institutions which protract war and lead to a large number of casualties, on the other. Domestic social institutions were least successful in explaining the number of wars or "onset" as a variable. They were more successful in explaining duration and, in particular, battle casualties. Variables such as duration and casualties may be differentiated from frequency in that they pertain to characteristics of the conflict itself. Once under way, the conflict can be governed by processes of escalation, deescalation, attrition, or other policies which may depend more on domestic political considerations and strategic options than on systemic characteristics, such as alliance formation, which may have led to the onset of the conflict. Thus, whereas the origins of war may be more properly found in settings external to the nation-state, the protraction and especially the number of deaths resulting from the war may be better explained by domestic social institutions.

This conclusion finds support from the status inconsistency analysis of Chapter VI. The greatest extent of prediction of the inconsistency over and above the achievement variables themselves was for the frequency of war variables (number of wars and number of wars vs. major), thus indicating the importance of the systemic characteristic, ascribed status. On the other hand, the lowest extent of explanation was for battle deaths—the only significant regression found in this analysis of domestic institutions. A similar pattern holds for the extent of explanation in the dummy variable analysis, with the strongest explanation found for frequency variables and the least, in fact nonsignificant, values for battle deaths. To this extent, the results here are uniformly consistent with those of Chapter VI and, indeed, are complementary to them.

Modernization and Military Coups

Turning now to our second concern, the internal societal effect on coups, we employ a similar time period as that used in the analysis of the diffusion of Latin American instability. This time period is chosen for purposes of comparing the results of the two analyses and then ascertaining the extent to which the assumptions concerning the lack of internal societal influence on the occurrence of military coups is indeed justified. If such a null finding did result from this analysis, it would support the previous result of a diffusion effect wherein domestic instability is, in part, a consequence of external international influences. Another purpose is to assess the effect of modernization on domestic instability[8] to provide an analogue to the previous examination of the effects of development on international warfare.

[8] Although studies directly treating the relationship between modernization and instability are relatively infrequent, those that touch on it, in one form or another, include Seymour M. Lipset, "Some Social Requisites of Democracy: Economic Development and Political Legitimacy," *American Political Science Review*, 53 (March 1959), pp. 69–105; Gabriel A. Almond and James S. Coleman (eds.), *The Politics of the Developing Areas* (Princeton, N.J.: Princeton University Press, 1960); Karl W. Deutsch, "Social Mobilization and Political Development," *American Political Science Review*, 55 (September 1961), pp. 493–514; Phillips Cutright, "National Political Development: Measurement and Analysis," *American Sociological Review*, 28 (April 1963), pp. 253–264; Ivo K. Feierabend and Rosalind L. Feierabend, "Aggressive Behaviors within Polities, 1948–1962: A Cross-National Study," *Journal of Conflict Resolution*, 10 (September 1966), pp. 249–271; Martin C. Needler, "Political Development and Military Intervention in Latin America," *American Political Science Review*, 60 (September 1966), pp. 616–626; Samuel P. Huntington, *Political Order in Changing Societies* (New Haven: Yale Univer-

Aside from the testing of assumptions inherent in the analysis thus far, there are additional reasons for testing a possible relationship between modernization and military intervention. One of these arises from the deep social problems attendant on the modernization process, and the existence of the military in developing countries as one of the few coherent socio-political organizations with the appearance of being able to solve these problems. There exists, for example, the elite–mass gap within developing countries, as well as the distance in modernization between the Western and Third World countries. The problems of corrupt and ineffective, although well-meaning, governments are also factors in the modernization process. Given these problem areas, the military is often more highly organized to meet the challenge of modernization than are civilian political units.

Lucian Pye has argued that, "... in comparison to the efforts that have been expended in developing, say, civil administration and political parties, it still seems that modern armies are somewhat easier to create in transitional societies than most other forms of modern social structures." Furthermore, according to Pye, "the armies created by colonial administration and by the newly emergent countries have been consistently among the most modernized institutions in their societies."[9]

A second reason which makes the military a particularly well-suited agent for resolving political instability lies in the role it plays in the political development process. It is often a prime element in resolving the identity crisis which accompanies the process of nation building. The soldier has a greater sense of psychological security than the average citizen in the transitional society; he frequently is more exposed to modernized societies; he is able to acquire the technical skills necessary for various forms of economic development; and he usually acquires a greater sense of citizenship.

The military is thus in a unique position. The military person is more cognizant of the disparities between his transitional society and the more modernized Western nations. Because he is a member of a highly organized social and political unit, he is more aware of the potentialities and necessities

sity Press, 1968); Betty A. Nesvold, "Scalogram Analysis of Political Violence," *Comparative Political Studies*, 2 (July 1969), pp. 172–194; Alex Inkeles, "Making Men Modern: On the Causes and Consequences of Individual Change in Six Developing Countries," *American Journal of Sociology*, 75 (September 1969), pp. 208–225; Karl de Schweinitz, Jr., "Growth, Development, and Political Modernization," *World Politics*, 22 (July 1970), pp. 518–540; Roger W. Benjamin, Richard N. Blue, with Stephen Coleman, "Modernization and Political Change: A Comparative Aggregate Data Analysis of Indian Political Behavior," *Midwest Journal of Political Science*, 15 (May 1971), pp. 219–261.; and Douglas A. Hibbs, Jr., *Mass Political Violence: A Cross-National Causal Analysis* (New York: Wiley, 1973).

[9] Lucian W. Pye, "Armies in the Process of Political Modernization," *European Journal of Sociology*, 2 (no. 1, 1961), p. 84.

of organization in the modernizing process. His sense of national and personal identity is more pronounced than is his fellow citizen's. His technological skill is usually advanced in relation to others in his society. In short, he is led to adopt an elitist attitude. He perceives the difference between what is being accomplished and what his country is capable of accomplishing, and often feels he has the solution for achieving the latter, based upon his membership in the military. It is perhaps only one short step from this recognition of perceived or actual competence to the seizure of power.

In order to test this hypothesis by means of a wide range of societal processes, 34 indicators of social change involving modernization are subjected to a cluster analysis.[10] The purpose here is to arrive at a simple structure and parsimonious description of domestic social processes in the contemporary period. These indicators are collected for the years 1938, 1949, 1956, and 1963 and constitute the midpoints of the intervals 1935–1941, 1946–1952, 1953–1959, and 1960–1966. The periods are chosen to correspond to those for the dependent variable, military coups, collected by Martin Needler and by Edward Luttwak.[11] The Needler data are used for the earlier period (1935–1941); the data from Luttwak are employed for the rest. This division of the data sources is to insure that the same coup data are used here as those in the period when diffusion was found in the first of the time periods—whereas Luttwak extends his data a bit further in time than does Needler for the remaining periods.

The method of relating the reduced set of independent variables to the dependent military coups is similar to the analysis of domestic social structure and war found in the first part of this chapter. The 34 variables are reduced to the simple structure of maximum collinearity. Factor scores on these clusters can then serve as independent variables in the analysis of military coups. If there exist significant relationships between the clusters of societal characteristics and instability, then the previous assumption regarding the absence of mass societal influences on coups is untenable. Furthermore, the effects of certain types of modernization will have been shown to affect domestic instability. On the other hand, if the relationships are negligibly small, the original assumption is justified. The military coup may then be said to be more a consequence of external systemic characteristics, as assumed in Chapter VII, and internal processes such as modernization would be largely unrelated to domestic instability.

---

[10] These indicators are from Arthur S. Banks and the staff of the Center for Comparative Political Research, State University of New York at Binghamton, *Cross-Polity Time-Series Data* (Cambridge, Mass.: The M.I.T. Press, 1971).

[11] See Needler, *op. cit.*; and Edward Luttwak, *Coup d'Etat: A Practical Handbook* (New York: Knopf, 1969).

The cluster analysis revealed the four basic clusters that are found in Table 8.4. As before, the pivot variable is listed first because of its centrality in structuring the dimension, even though it might not finally have the highest loading after the clustering process is completed. The remaining variables are listed in order of magnitude of their coefficients. The orders of

TABLE 8.4.   **A Cluster Analysis of Societal Indicators in Latin American Countries, 1935–1966**

Variable	Dimension			
	1	2	3	4
Energy production per capita (kilograms)	(.99)	.11	.40	.20
Revenue per capita (U.S. dollars)	(.96)	.48	.58	.55
Exports per capita (U.S. dollars)	(.95)	.30	.43	.39
GDP per capita (U.S. dollars, industrial activity)	(.92)	.42	.78	.64
GNP per capita (U.S. dollars)	(.86)	.37	.46	.69
GDP per capita (U.S. dollars)	(.85)	.53	.70	.70
Total school enrollment per capita	.34	(1.04)	.31	.48
Primary and secondary school enrollment per capita	.33	(.99)	.29	.47
Primary school enrollment per capita	.32	(.94)	.28	.41
All mail per capita	.15	.16	(.82)	.66
Proportion of world trade	.51	.07	(.83)	.37
Population density (cities over 5,000)	.53	.55	.53	(.96)
Population density (cities over 100,000)	.45	.52	.64	(.93)
Telephones per capita	.41	.50	.77	(.92)
Physicians per capita	.38	.37	.80	(.91)
Newspapers per capita	.33	.42	.62	(.90)
Commercial vehicles per capita	.55	.50	.79	(.88)
Passenger cars per capita	.68	.56	.69	(.86)
All highway vehicles per capita	.57	.49	.68	(.81)
Population density	−.16	−.15	−.35	−.28
Expenditure per capita (U.S. dollars)	.53	.41	.33	.37
Defense expenditure/total national expenditure	−.23	−.34	.08	−.07
Railroad mileage per square mile	.02	.19	−.05	.12
Telegraph mileage per square mile	.12	.13	.58	.44
Imports per capita (U.S. dollars)	.76	.50	.36	.55
University enrollment per capita	.44	.60	.67	.82
Percent literate	.31	.72	.54	.80
Rail passengers—kilometers	−.04	.00	.70	.23
Percent GDP—industrial	.68	.34	.79	.58
Energy consumption per capita (kilograms)	.92	.43	.70	.63
Radios per capita	.38	.64	.47	.82
Books per capita	.27	.50	.60	.37
Currency in circulation (U.S. dollars)	.56	.07	.71	.72
Secondary school enrollment per capita	.25	.66	.21	.58
Proportion of initial communality	.42	.22	.23	.13
Proportion of mean square of correlation matrix	.65	.16	.13	.04
Domain validity	1.00	.98	.97	.99
Reliability	.99	.97	.94	.98

magnitude of domain validities and reliabilities found in the last two rows of the table are acceptable.[12]

The first cluster which "explains" the major proportion of the variance may be termed a financial–industrial dimension. Variables which load highly on it are, for example, energy production per capita or revenue per capita. The emergence of such a dimension is not surprising in light of the central importance of variables of this type generally, in domestic societies, and specifically in the modernization process. Other variables loading highly on this factor are those pertaining to national income, such as gross domestic product, or gross national product per capita.

In the second dimension, we see education as a prime factor in societal processes. Variables such as total school enrollment, or primary and secondary school enrollment per capita define this dimension. Again, one would expect variables of this type to be strongly associated with the modernization process.

The third cluster is somewhat anomalous in that only two variables which appear rather distinct from each other load heavily on it. These are all mail per capita, and proportions of world trade. Probably the best interpretation that can be given to this dimension is that of internationality. Mail would tend to be a better indicator of international contact than would telephone or telegraph because of the lesser expense, and this interpretation would accord with the presence of the highest loading variable—proportion of world trade.

Finally, the last cluster is one identified as a density factor with special emphasis on communication and transportation. High loadings of variables such as population density, telephones, and highway vehicles per capita suggest this particular interpretation. Thus, 4 dimensions not only emerge empirically from the cluster analysis of the 34 variables, but also bear conceptual relationships to what we would normally consider aspects of the modernization process.

The dimensions can now serve as independent variables for the possible explanation of military coups. Factor scores were obtained for each of the dimensions and these became the predictors for the explanation of Latin American coups in the period 1935–1966. In a stepwise multiple regression, the following equation was obtained

$$\hat{Y} = .63 - .13X_1 + .11X_2 + .06X_3 - .07X_4$$

where $\hat{Y}$ is the predicted number of coups and the subscripts 1, 2, ..., refer to the respective clusters in Table 8.4. The multiple correlation coefficient for

[12] The percentages of common variance exhausted by the four dimensions are, respectively, 42.3, 21.8, 22.4, and 13.5, while the percentages of total variance are, respectively, 31.9, 16.4, 16.9, and 10.2.

the relation between observed and predicted values is $R = .14, N = 80$, which is hardly significant either statistically or from the perspective of the percentage variance explained.[13] The first variable made the largest single contribution to the variance explained (approximately 1%), but as would be indicated by the multiple R, this amount is inconsequential.

An additional cluster analysis omitting the 1938 data was performed to yield some greater homogeneity in the postwar period. The clusters obtained here were virtually identical to those found for the entire period, and the equation for the reduced data was

$$\hat{Y} = .50 - .20X_1 + .28X_2 - .21X_3 + .13X_4.$$

The value of the multiple correlation coefficient was somewhat higher ($R = .26, N = 80$), but still nonsignificant. Again, the first variable contributed the largest single share, but this percentage variance was of the same order of magnitude found in the analysis of the entire period.

Thus, none of the components of modernization, neither singly nor together, has demonstrated an ability to explain significantly the occurrence of Latin American military coups. The analysis in Chapter VII is supported; namely, the military coup, at least in Latin America, is better explained by diffusion processes originating in the system external to the nation-state. This finding, of course, stands in contrast to those which have established strong relationships between internal societal processes and major revolutions such as the French or Russian.[14] In this fashion, the distinction between coups and revolutions is reinforced both in terms of processes during occurrence, as well as causation.

Complementarities

In addition to the reinforcement of findings in Chapter VII, the results of the two analyses in this chapter complement each other. Although certain aspects of social structure (e.g., religion and the military) were found to be moderately associated with international warfare, the major finding of that analysis was that societal development, as defined by the structural differentiation dimension, did not bear any significant relationship to either the frequency, duration, or number of deaths associated with international warfare. Here, none of the components of modernization bears any relationship

---

[13] There are four time intervals within the entire period examined here and twenty Latin American nations, thus yielding $N = 80$ for the statistical test.

[14] For the development of empirical distinctions between coups and revolutions, see Raymond Tanter and Manus Midlarsky, "A Theory of Revolution," *Journal of Conflict Resolution*, 11 (September 1967), pp. 264–280.

to the most common type of instability, that of military intervention. In both cases, the origins of political violence are to be found in elements of the international system, although the protraction of war and numbers of deaths are due in part to certain domestic considerations. Thus, we would conclude that insofar as we are concerned with the origins or onset of two forms of political violence—war and military intervention in one region—the sources of both are to be found more readily in aspects of the international system than in domestic societal sectors.

CHAPTER

IX

Conclusion

There are several final observations to be made and they fall into three categories: (1) overall conclusions that can be drawn from the related analyses; (2) additional explanations which are derivative of the research; and (3) policy implications and directions for future research.

General Findings

The major substantive conclusions fall into the area of complementarities in the findings. For example, while one set of analyses may be appropriate for the explanation of one type of war, another set might be suitable for the understanding of some different form of violence. The concepts of power loss in alliance systems or power constraints in geographical frontiers provide explanations for the frequency of both large and small wars, mainly as the result of honored commitments and inescapable adjacencies. These limitations on the power of nations, or more formally put, the constraints on the capabilities of nations serve as a type of frustration leading to war.

This mode of violence initiation clearly would not differentiate at the outset between wars that would be of large scope and intensity and those which might "fizzle" after only a few days. The commitment or the adjacency generally would not have an effect on the characteristics of the war after it was begun.

The concept of social disorganization in international systems does, however, explain the onset of the widespread conflict which led to the catastrophic decline of at least two of these systems. Both World Wars I and II were preceded by steady increases in social disorganization as measured by equality of alliance formation. Given the presence of hierarchical organization as a traditional means of social control in the international system, the increased equiprobability of alliance formation by central powers may be understood as a form of such disorganization. With this interlocking set of alliances involving a large number of countries, the presence of widespread and prolonged violence was virtually assured after the first act of assassination or invasion. In this sense, the approach to the attainment of a balance of power by means of equal numbers of alliances among a large number of countries implies a process of disorganization leading to major violence.

In addition to the concepts of power limitations and a social disorganization of the international system, there is another approach which also explains the frequency of war. This is the status inconsistency of nations, which stems theoretically from the concept of constraints on the capabilities of nations and occurs at the boundary between the nation-state and international system. In the several multivariate analyses of the frequency, duration, and intensity of war in the form of battle deaths, the frequency variable was the most strongly predicted by the inconsistency variables and also, in comparison with the other characteristics of war, was best explained by the dummy variable interaction analysis. This stands in contrast with the lower levels of explanation found for duration and intensity. The gap between ascribed and achieved status, the former originating in the system and the latter, a characteristic of nation-states, is therefore found to be strongly related to the onset of war.

In contrast to frequency, when we attempt to explain duration or intensity in the form of battle deaths, domestic processes are more strongly related to war experience. Here, the level of analysis most appropriate for maximizing explanatory power appears to be the nation-state. The national achievement variables themselves have good predictive and explanatory power in regard to duration and intensity, without our having to introduce status inconsistency measures. Thus, internal socioeconomic change is related directly to the temporal and casualty measures of war. Furthermore, in the analysis of the effects of sociopolitical institutions on war, military and bureaucratic institutions—perhaps an analogue of contemporary military–industrial relations—are most strongly related to these variables. In particular, battle casualties are best explained by the entire set of domestic institutions. Conversely, battle deaths was the most poorly explained variable in the status inconsistency dummy variable interaction analysis, and in fact was the only one which did not attain statistical significance in that analysis. Thus, whereas the system or processes occurring at the boundary between the system and state are most important in explaining the onset of war, variables internal to the nation-state are more important in explaining conflict processes such as duration and, in particular, intensity of violence.

Another type of political violence also appears to be dependent on systemic effects in the form of interactions occurring at the boundary between the nation-state and system. The diffusion of military intervention in Latin America is, in part, a consequence of the imitation of one military elite by another. The status and competence of prototype countries increase the likelihood that other countries, lesser in status and perceived competence, will emulate the instability of prototype countries. On the other hand, domestic processes in the form of modernization appear to have no discernible effect on the instability of Latin American nations. Thus, we may be witnessing a rather paradoxical effect. Whereas domestic processes—say, internal economic change associated with achievement—and bureaucratic or military institutions affect international warfare, modernization as almost entirely a domestic process bears virtually no relation to domestic instability.

Certain types of domestic–international linkages may serve as an explanation, in part, of this effect. When events such as military intervention occur primarily among an elite, the awareness by that elite of processes occurring in neighboring countries may in fact account for this domestic sensitivity to international affairs. On the other hand, domestic institutions such as a bureaucracy experiencing inertia may have an effect on attrition or other policies which could determine the war's protraction or an increase of battle casualties found in international war.

Additional Explanations

While we can isolate certain complementarities in the findings, there are, in addition, anomalous features which require further explanation. For example, in the analysis of social disorganization in international systems, represented in Figure 4.1, there is a steady increase in the equiprobability of alliance formation until the five-year interval represented by 1905–1909, but the value for 1910–1914 shows no increase above that found for the earlier period. This stands in contrast to the situation prior to World War II, in which the increase was steady until the outbreak of war. In one case, international warfare resulted in the termination of this process in highest values of systemic equiprobability or uncertainty (World War II), and in the other it did not (World War I).[1] During the ten-year period before World

[1] For systematic treatments of international crises, see the various chapters in Charles F. Hermann (ed.), *International Crises: Insights from Behavioral Research* (New York: The Free Press, 1972); Ole R. Holsti, "The 1914 Case," *American Political Science Review*, 59 (June 1965), pp. 365–378; Charles A. McClelland, "Access to Berlin: The

War I, the same state of affairs with regard to alliances existed in the later interval just prior to the war, as it did in 1905–1909.

A difference between the two wars may be found in the presence of a major crisis in the five-year interval, 1905–1909, whereas no such crisis occurred within a comparable time period prior to World War II. The Bosnian Crisis of 1908 may have served as a termination for the disorganizing tendencies of the previous years, while the only comparison prior to World War II is the Munich Crisis, which took place one year before—too soon prior to the war to detect any unique effects. The separate time period for the Bosnian Crisis enables us to examine its possible role in affecting the onset of war in 1914, just as Munich may have served a similar function in regard to World War II, but because of temporal proximity to the war cannot be detected separately using the methods of Chapter IV.

Initially, in the Bosnian Crisis of 1908, the dispute centered on the disposition of a given territory. This area, Bosnia-Herzegovina, had been administered by Austria-Hungary since the Congress of Berlin in 1878, although still nominally considered Ottoman territory. The Austrians sought to annex it formally and bring it under their full legal control. Toward this end, Aehrenthal, the Austrian foreign minister, met with Izvolsky, his Russian counterpart, to obtain approval for a direct annexation in return for Austrian accession to the passage of Russian warships through the Dardanelles. This resulted in the famous Buchlau agreement.

By early publicizing the Russian agreement to the annexation, Aehrenthal initiated a *fait accompli* without compensation for Russia, and a crisis was now in the making which threatened an Austro-Serb military confrontation as the result of Serbian desires for the territory in dispute.[2] The common Slavic ethnicity among the populations of Serbia and Bosnia-Herzegovina, as well as their common Orthodox faith intensified the Serbian desire for annexation on her own part. A wider regional involvement developed at this time, with the Russians acting in strong support of the Serbs against the

---

Quantity and Variety of Events, 1948–1963," in J. David Singer (ed.), *Quantitative International Politics: Insights and Evidence* (New York: The Free Press, 1968), pp. 159–186; and Dina A. Zinnes, "The Expression and Perception of Hostility in Prewar Crisis: 1914," in J. David Singer (ed.), *Quantitative International Politics*, pp. 85–119.

[2] Among the many treatments of the Bosnian Crisis in relation to the onset of World War I, are Luigi Albertini, *The Origins of the War of 1914*, 3 vols., trans. Isabella M. Massey (London: Oxford University Press, 1952–1957); Sidney B. Fay, *The Origins of the World War*, 2 vols. (New York: Macmillan, 1928); Cyril B. Falls, *The Great War* (New York: Capricorn, 1961); Bernadotte E. Schmitt, *The Annexation of Bosnia, 1908–1909* (Cambridge: Cambridge University Press, 1937); Hugh Seton-Watson, *The Decline of Imperial Russia, 1855–1914* (New York: Praeger, 1952); and Arthur J. May, *The Hapsburg Monarchy, 1867–1914* (Cambridge, Mass.: Harvard University Press, 1951).

Austrians. At a critical juncture in the crisis, the Germans delivered an ultimatum to the Russians, which terminated the crisis with accession of all parties to the *fait accompli* of Austrian annexation.

The Serbian antagonism at having lost any immediate chance at acquiring these territories led to an intensification of pan-Slavic and Serbian nationalist propaganda in the annexed territories. This increase, coupled with the dissatisfaction of the Slavic population in Austria-Hungary itself, resulted in an intense concern in Vienna for the effects of these activities. In the intervening years between 1908 and 1914, the unity of the Austro-Hungarian Empire was perceived to be so weak by Austrian leaders that Serbia and Serbian nationalism were viewed as profound threats to the empire. Factions within Austria had already argued for punitive military action against Serbia[3] toward the end of the Bosnian Crisis. The effect of events during the years between the crisis and the summer of 1914, then, was to increase the Austrian desire for coercive action against Serbia to eliminate this perceived threat to the existence of the Dual Monarchy. When the Archduke Francis Ferdinand was assassinated in 1914, this act was seen as the ultimate expression of the agitation of the previous years, and as an opportunity for settling once and for all the problem of Serbia.[4]

Examination of this process indicates that initially the concern was almost entirely for a given territory, with the element of coercion appearing strongly at the end of the crisis and continuing until the summer of 1914. This process includes elements found in Table 1.1 (Chapter I). There, it will be recalled, the lowest level of warfare was said to be territorial with regional involvement and coercive war following in ascending order. If these be modal types on a relatively continuous scale of the development of intense conflicts, then perhaps we can understand the transition from the earliest stages of the Bosnian Crisis to the final stages of the summer crisis of 1914. At first, the conflict over territory exists and when it remains unresolved, comes to include neighboring actors in the dispute. When active regional policy involvement has occurred, and resolution in some form is still not achieved, coercion may be directed at the internal structure of the target state, or possibly the destruction of its sovereignty, as in the case of Serbia. Finally, when even

---

[3] A treatment of the Austrian and Serbian postures is found in Geoffrey Blainey, *The Causes of War* (New York: The Free Press, 1973), pp. 105–106, 235–236. Also see May, *op. cit.*, pp. 420–421.

[4] The Austrian ultimatum to Serbia on July 23, 1914, emphasized above all the "criminal machinations" of various nationalist societies in Serbia ever since the end of the Bosnian Crisis. For a text of the ultimatum, see Harry Elmer Barnes, *The Genesis of the World War: An Introduction to the Problem of War Guilt* (New York: Knopf, 1926), pp. 192–197. This work is of historical interest in itself since it is one of the then "revisionist" histories of World War I which sought to shift primary responsibility for the war from the Central to the Allied Powers.

this has failed, the conflict may be pitched at the very basis of human organization—the norms or ideological foundations of political discourse.

In the early stages of the summer crisis of 1914, it is clear that the Austro-Hungarian posture was one of coercion toward Serbia. The Austrian view of the crisis in its beginnings was that of localized conflict in Southeastern Europe centering on Serbia. Aside from the documentation of the conflict itself, this understanding of the Austrian position emerges from the orderings of capability perceptions of the Austrian decision makers. In the number of times capabilities were mentioned by these decision makers, Serbia and Bulgaria were ranked ahead of great powers such as France or Russia, which would be major opponents in the event of a widespread conflict.[5] This ordering generally was not true for the other major powers—there being a genuine concern for the dangers of a wider European or even a global conflict. The regional involvement of the Southeastern European nations had occurred in 1908 and again in a different form in the Balkan Wars of 1912–1913, and the coercive policies toward Serbia were a residue of that earlier crisis. Now, in 1914, the initial Austrian concerns were still at the level of regional and coercive involvement (the latter includes the former in this rank ordering—see Table 1.1) which differentiates these decision makers from their counterparts in the remainder of Dual Alliance and Triple Entente countries.

The lack of any substantial difference between the two last points in Figure 4.1 now becomes understandable. With regard to the organization of the system itself, there had occurred no appreciable change of state in this time span of roughly six to ten years. The Balkan Wars which intervened between 1908 and 1914 may have increasingly sensitized the Austrians to the Southeastern European situation, but again did not contribute to the wider or global aspects of the conflict, which is essentially the subject of the increase in alliance-related uncertainty represented in Figure 4.1.

The systemic analysis of equiprobable alliance formation, therefore, is in itself not sufficient for the explanation of the outbreak of World War I. We must add the transitions in process occurring in 1908 and again in 1914 to account for this world war. Whereas the crisis of 1908 began with certain territorial concerns and subsequently passed through regional and coercive policies, the 1914 crisis began where the Bosnian involvement ended—at the coercive level. The rejection of the highly coercive Austrian ultimatum by

[5] For a listing of these capability orderings and other perceptions related to the onset of World War I, see Dina A. Zinnes, Robert C. North, and Howard E. Koch, Jr., "Capability, Threat, and the Outbreak of War," in James N. Rosenau (ed.), *International Politics and Foreign Policy: A Reader in Research and Theory* (New York: The Free Press, 1961), pp. 469–482.

the Serbs made it far more likely that the conflict would continue to escalate in intensity.

With the entry of Germany into the war and the subsequent invasion of Belgium, two strong normative components were introduced into the system. First, the principle of neutrality, which had been a cornerstone of European diplomacy for almost a century, especially with regard to Belgium (the London Treaties of 1831 and 1839), was violated. Second, ideological conflict between democracy and authoritarianism developed in the ensuing confrontation between Great Britain and Germany. The first violation was perhaps more serious at the outset since it was directed at the foundations of European diplomacy and hence at the normative order of the international system in that period. But the second was perhaps to become equally important because, from the Allied perspective, only an authoritarian–tyrannical form of government such as that found in the Kaiser's Germany could commit the treacherous act of invading a neutral country. Thus, any compromise to shorten the war was rendered more difficult. To understand fully the onset of war in 1914, therefore, it may be necessary to introduce a conflict process beginning with territorial concerns in 1908 and ending in a normative war at the end of the summer crisis.

The normative elements of World War I may have continued into the Versailles Conference (Wilsonian democracy, self-determination, rights of sovereignty, or neutrality). Indeed, the Treaty of Versailles became the embodiment of norms championed by the victorious Allies, particularly those which insured a continued Allied domination of the international system. To the extent that the Axis Powers in World War II challenged the norms of Versailles and their extensions, for example, in the Naval Conferences of 1922 and 1930, this second war may have been a direct extension of the first. This normative extension would account for the very rapid involvement of European countries in World War II. However, a conflict process similar to that outlined above for World War I did appear with regard to original Nazi demands for territories in Czechoslovakia and Poland, followed by the regional involvement at Munich, and then direct coercive action against Czechoslovakia and later against Poland. It may be said that the conflict process prior to World War II was acted out at two levels—first, the process of transition beginning with territorial concerns, and second, concern with norms of the international system rendered explicit at the end of World War I. The two processes may have coalesced with the outbreak of war in September 1939.

This conflict process originating in territorial disputes may, in fact, have been a necessary condition for the outbreak of war. The disorganization process as measured by alliances may have lasted until 1938, when territorial concerns first were openly manifested by Germany. In the time between Munich and the outbreak of the war, these issues may have escalated to coercion against Czechoslovakia and later against Poland with all the attendant normative implications of the violation of agreements and the loss of self-determination and sovereignty.

The existence of territorial disputes at some point in the history of a conflict may be a necessary condition for the later outbreak of war. Indeed, the finding of uncertainties associated with common borders as verging on a necessary condition for war (see Chapter III) may be related to this analysis. Territories and boundaries have in common the property of specific geographic location. The twin concepts of security and sufficient territory to insure security may contain within them the seeds of major international warfare.

Just as it is possible for a conflict to escalate through the various modal phases indicated in Table 1.1, so it may deescalate through a similar process. It is possible that the Korean War was deescalated in this fashion. The normative position against aggression articulated by the United Nations slowly was deemphasized after the attempted coercion of North Korea by the United States and United Nations, a regional involvement by the Chinese, and finally, individualized battles for control of particular territories. The Arab-Israeli conflicts, although still bloody and intense, nevertheless seem now to be oriented more to the seizure or return of specific territories than to the earlier highly coercive policy of destroying one of the participants in the conflict, or expunging Zionist "imperialism" as a normative goal. Whether these modes of escalation or deescalation apply in a variety of situations, however, requires detailed and systematic evidence that should be the object of future research.

Policy Implications and the Future

Aside from the possibilities for researching the processes by which conflicts intensify, there are policy implications that can be derived from the several analyses. In regard to alliance formation, Figure 3.1 indicates that beyond the first five or six allies, the extent of uncertainty added to the environment of the central power is considerably less than that added in the beginning portion of the curve. Thus, a policy of alliance formation, once adopted, will likely result in the greatest increase in the danger of war at the outset, with those alliances formed beyond the first five or six supplying a disproportionately smaller amount of uncertainty in regard to the probability of war.

Similar arguments may be extended to policies concerning international polarity. The same logarithmic relationship applies here to the increase in the probability of war as new polar actors are added. Opposition to the emergence of a new actor in the system would be needless, if the increase in the probability of war would be very small, especially if there already exist five or six such actors. This small increase in the probability of war might be more than offset by the decrease in the probability of large-scale and deadly wars which are more likely to occur in bipolar or tripolar systems.[6]

As an historical comment, seldom have there been more than five polar actors, and so any increase in the range from one to five might have added a sizable increment to the probability of war, in comparison with the smaller increases at the numerically higher levels of polarity. The greatest increase in the danger of war would emerge with the transition from unipolar to bipolar systems, as in fact has been suggested previously in international relations research.[7] From the perspective of insuring peace, then, unipolar or hierarchical systems are most desirable, although from the perspective of justice or equality this obviously would not be the case. The greater the equity of distribution of international power via an increased number of international poles, the greater the probability of war (see Figure 3.4 in Chapter III). In this sense, equity with regard to power, and the insuring of peace are opposed to one another. On the other hand, although this increased multipolarity would lead to a greater frequency of war, the total number of persons killed might be smaller than in bipolar conflicts.

The existence of boundary effects, such as a status inconsistency on war or a boundary permeability exhibited by nation-states with regard to domestic instability, suggests that a genuine autonomy of nation-states in relation to violence does not exist. This set of findings is reinforced additionally by international boundaries acting as constraints on great powers which can lead to war. Other findings such as the effect of foreign investment and trade on domestic violence[8] are outside the scope of this analysis, but are consistent

[6] See Michael Haas, "International Subsystems: Stability and Polarity," *American Political Science Review*, 64 (March 1970), pp. 98–123. This study includes an empirical confirmation of the relationship between polarity and the frequency of war suggested by Richard N. Rosecrance in his "Bipolarity, Multipolarity, and the Future," *Journal of Conflict Resolution*, 10 (September 1966), pp. 314–327.

[7] Morton Kaplan speaks of the inherent stability of hierarchical or unipolar systems in his *System and Process in International Politics* (New York: Wiley, 1957), pp. 49–50. The emergence of a challenger to the dominant nation in a stratification system is treated throughout in A. F. K. Organski, *World Politics*, 2nd ed. (New York: Knopf, 1968).

[8] See, for example, Manus Midlarsky and Raymond Tanter, "Toward a Theory of Political Instability in Latin America," *Journal of Peace Research*, 4 (no. 3, 1967), pp. 209–227.

with the concept of boundary permeability used here.[9] Coupled with this existence of permeable boundaries between the system and state is the existence of periodic social disorganizations of the system, and the lack of a permanently organized effective peace-keeping force at the systemic level.

These conditions of permeability and social disorganization, combined with quasi-effective international peace-keeping institutions such as the United Nations, suggest the image of the international system not simply as a "developing" system, but as a "perpetually developing" system. Prior research has indicated a similarity between certain characteristics of the system and developing countries, particularly with regard to semi-autonomous tribal entities which can come into conflict with one another and central governments which only partly maintain domestic order.[10] The implication, if not the argument itself, has been that just as these nations may one day reach higher levels of societal development, so will the international system via its organizational components reach higher stages of development and peace.

The evidence in this analysis suggests that instead of this process of development, there occur periodic forms of organization such as equiprobable alliance formation which essentially disorganize the system in regard to hierarchical control and result in war. International organizations such as the League of Nations or the United Nations, which were formed essentially to preserve a specific peace, also may fall into this category of institutions contributing to the social disorganization of the system. If the norms of a given treaty such as Versailles or San Francisco are oriented toward the maintenance of a continued dominance of a specific group of nations, then the net effect at a later point in time might be to increase the probability of war as a challenge to the norms included in the treaty.

In any event, the pattern appears to be: the introduction and later dissolution of an element of organization into the system. This pattern may in fact be traced back to the period of the Roman Empire and the subsequent attempts at religious supremacy by a supranational church (and ancillary institutions such as the Holy Roman Empire), followed by the Concert system, and the present alliance-uncertainty analysis. The repeated pattern of dissolution of these institutions, followed by their reintroduction at a later point in time in a

[9] Some of these concepts are related to James N. Rosenau's theory of linkage politics. For a recent statement of the theory in relation to empirical findings, see Rosenau's "Theorizing Across Systems: Linkage Politics Revisited," in Jonathan Wilkenfeld (ed.), *Conflict Behavior and Linkage Politics* (New York: David McKay, 1973), pp. 25–56.

[10] See, for example, Chadwick F. Alger, "Comparison of Intranational and International Politics," *American Political Science Review*, 57 (June 1963), pp. 406–419. Roger D. Masters compares some characteristics of both international and predeveloping systems in "World Politics as a Primitive System," *World Politics*, 16 (July 1964), pp. 595–619.

somewhat different form, is suggestive of the state of perpetual development of the international system.

The problem of this system apparently always in a state of "becoming" has certain implications for its future structuring. Until now, some new organization with overarching powers across nation-states has come into existence, and efforts have been made to strengthen its level of institutional development. However, these institutions are almost always only partly successful, and the present analysis implies that partial success may be worse than no success at all. That is, given the tendency of these institutions to increase boundary permeability of the nation-state (by definition of purpose, in trying to maintain peace) they may actually increase the probability of violence by some status inconsistency or other boundary effect. This is especially dangerous when an organization such as the United Nations accords status via representation and certain other policy orientations, which then can have an effect obviously counter to the intentions of the founders. Only in the case of complete success, where the permeability is thorough, and the nation-state wholly responsive to the legitimate demands of the central institution, would such institutions serve their essential purpose.[11]

The other alternative is to consider not the international institution as a focus of activity, but the boundaries between the system and the individual nation-states. Failing the establishment of near complete dependence of the nation-state upon the central international institutions or a "successful" permeability of the nation-state by the institutions with regard to peace, then another possible alternative is to strengthen the boundary between the state and system to the extent that its permeability would no longer seriously affect the probability of war. The two models of system development, on the one hand, and autonomy or decreased permeability, on the other, are shown in Figure 9.1.

In Figure 9.1a we have the previously outlined condition of a boundary permeability with regard to the system; in Figure 9.1b there exists an increased boundary maintenance between the nation-state and its environment, which includes organizational components as well as other nation-states.

Examples of societies which follow Figure 9.1b can be found in island peoples such as Polynesian societies which generally avoided war historically by means of a successful boundary maintenance. Adjacencies or other systemic boundary effects are removed, and to this extent, this may be a relatively

---

[11] This treatment of the effectiveness of international centralization relies on arguments similar to those concerning the need for a near total response to aggression from virtually all nation-states in order to make a collective security system workable. These arguments are found in Inis L. Claude, *Power and International Relations* (New York: Random House, 1962).

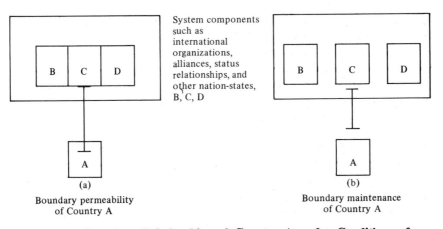

Figure 9.1 **Boundary Relationships of Country A under Conditions of Boundary Permeability and Maintenance**

uninteresting example as the result of geographical fixedness. A more policy-relevant example may be Sweden, which as the result of consistent policy decisions since the Congress of Vienna, has not entered into a single alliance nor an international war and has regulated its involvement in international organizations—decreasing or increasing it based almost entirely on perceptions of national need. Switzerland also has been highly successful in this boundary maintenance effort, but has had a considerable topographic advantage in maintaining this policy. Somewhat less successful at these efforts has been Belgium since the fourth decade of the nineteenth century, as well as Denmark and the Netherlands. All of these latter countries had their neutrality violated only under rare and generalized conditions of international violence.

It might be possible to institutionalize this process of boundary maintenance or autonomy. A widespread process of this type, however, has little international precedent. The only historical process of some precedence that might interest us occurs at the level of domestic societies with regard to the minority group experience. The traditional boundary maintenance process for many minorities has been a process of segregation or encapsulation in which certain procedures are clearly set down with regard to dwelling place, business activity, or other forms of interaction with the majority. Sometimes this can be an involuntary process, as in the case of segregation of blacks in the United States, or largely voluntary, as in the experience of many Chinese communities in Southeast Asia. It can also be some mix of voluntarism and external coercion, as was the case for the majority of Jews in Eastern Europe during the early nineteenth century.

In many respects the Jews are the classical prototype of this process of encapsulation and isolation in the East European village (shtetl) or the ghetto in the city. The Jewish ghetto in the towns or the village in the countryside became relatively isolated places where religious, cultural, and intellectual activity could continue and in some cases, as in Vilna in Lithuania, even experience a considerable development under conditions of an agreed upon boundary maintenance with the majority. It was only with the partial integration and assimilation of the late nineteenth and early twentieth centuries that an increased contact may have resulted in exacerbated hostilities ending in the holocaust of World War II. In this sense, Israel may be understood as an attempt to recreate the successful autonomy and boundary maintenance of nineteenth-century Eastern European Jewish life, but in the somewhat more feasible twentieth-century mode of national sovereignty.

The experience of the Ibos in Nigeria in passing from autonomous tribal existence into vigorous contact with other tribes in the colonial British civil service may have set the stage for the hostile reaction of certain tribes, particularly the Hausa, and an attempt by the Ibo to recreate boundary maintenance in the form of the independent state of Biafra.

After emerging somewhat from their relative isolation, the Chinese in Southeast Asia, particularly in Indonesia, opted for a somewhat different response to the problem of boundary maintenance with perhaps equally savage results.

Partial integration or assimilation in domestic social life may be worse than none at all, for once the boundaries are breached between social groups, then the differences, latent hostilities, and threat values can become activated with repeated contact, and violence leading to processes of extermination may result, at least in the three cases offered here. These instances of partial integration domestically may, in fact, be comparable to the boundary effects on war detailed in this volume, with perhaps similar implications for the desirability of either complete integration for groups and nation-states within one sociopolitical rubric, or effective boundary maintenance for groups and nation-states. The intermediary stages of partial integration or partial development of international institutions, particularly in a state of "perpetual development," appear to be considerably worse than the other two alternatives.

A multipolar world with strong boundary maintenance, therefore, may be recommended for the foreseeable future, if nuclear war is deemphasized. The greater frequency of war in multipolar systems would be offset by the reduced casualties and duration of war in comparison with bipolar systems. The strengthening of boundaries would even lessen the frequency of war and possibly limit great power involvement, which has been a serious problem in processes of intervention. In contrast, the "bi–multipolar" world recommended by Rosecrance[12] would have the disadvantage of perpetuating a system structure of partial great power leadership with the concomitant increased permeability of boundaries of smaller nations in relation to larger ones, and the limited degree of integration that this structure provides. However, in the case of widespread nuclear weapons diffusion, even a small increased probability of war in a purely multipolar world obviously would be undesirable and another alternative preferable.

Finally, we consider the implications of this analysis for policies of "peace through national development." In the analysis of the effects of domestic institutions on international warfare, there was no relationship of any size or significance between national development, in the form of structural differentiation or complexity, and the war experience of nations. The clear implication of this analysis was that the most primitive or underdeveloped country may have the same probability of experiencing war as the most developed nation. Peace through national development, hence, may be an ephemeral goal, with efforts at boundary maintenance and eventual complete systemic development probably being more profitable loci for peace-making efforts.

At the same time, the pitfall of perpetual development of the system, with all its implications for continued international violence, should be avoided. Relatively swift conquest has historically been the way that intermediary processes have been avoided and an "instantaneous development" imposed (e.g., Rome). This alternative, however, is undesirable ethically for obvious reasons, and instrumentally because the historical evidence suggests that serious backsliding occurs when the empire fails.

How the process of a rapid and relatively painless development may be instituted is a problem for future research. Until that time, it seems that efforts at boundary maintenance should continue with the attendant implications that injustice and inequity in the international system and within other nation-states might have to be allowed. Planetary survival may demand the temporary continuance of inequity, or even, in the final analysis, the toleration of evil.

Perhaps it has been the quixotic effort to eliminate actual violence and at the same time to attempt to rectify perceived inequalities or injustices which has been a cause of this state of perpetual development with its ever-threatening violence. In any event, it is clear that a set of priorities for survival must be constructed in which peace is a foremost item. Problems of inequity may have to be resolved in ways that do not significantly increase the probability of war. Despite the extreme difficulty of this task, it may constitute a major challenge for future theoreticians and practitioners of international relations.

[12] Rosecrance, "Bipolarity, Multipolarity."

APPENDIX A Derivations of Maximum Uncertainty in the Continuous Case

Two derivations are included here to demonstrate the equality of maximum uncertainty when calculated in a straightforward maximization process, and upon the transformation of coordinates.[1] In order to obtain directly a value for uncertainty in the case of a maximum value M, we establish the constraint that

$$\int_0^M F(x)\, dx = 1 \tag{1}$$

where $F(x)$ is a continuous function defined only for non-negative values of x. This restriction on x arises from the positive values of variables discussed in Chapter III. When $U(x)$ is subject to the constraint imposed on $F(x)$, we establish the function

$$G(x) = U_0(x) + \lambda F(x) \tag{2}$$

where λ is a Lagrangian multiplier and

$$U_0(x) = -F(x) \log_e F(x).$$

Now in order to maximise $G(x)$, we set

$$\frac{\partial G(x)}{\partial F(x)} = 0 \tag{3}$$

and

$$\frac{\partial}{\partial F(x)}\left[-F(x) \log_e F(x) + \lambda F(x)\right] = 0, \tag{4}$$

or

$$-\log_e F(x) - 1 + \lambda = 0.$$

[1] The previous derivations are based on the presentations in Claude E. Shannon and Warren Weaver, *The Mathematical Theory of Communication* (Urbana, Ill.: University of Illinois Press, 1964), pp. 90–91; and John B. Thomas, *An Introduction to Statistical Communication Theory* (New York: Wiley, 1969), pp. 558–559, 562–563.

Thus

$$F(x) = e^{\lambda - 1}. \tag{5}$$

Since λ and e are both constants, we can set $e^{\lambda - 1} = k$ and

$$\int_0^M F(x)\, dx = \int_0^M k\, dx = kM = 1. \tag{6}$$

The value for maximum uncertainty, therefore, is

$$U(x) = -\int_0^M \frac{1}{M} \log \frac{1}{M}\, dx = \log M \tag{7}$$

for non-negative values of x.

The second calculation proceeds by means of a transformation of coordinates in order to illustrate the meaning of a maximum uncertainty in the continuous case. Let us consider first the uncertainty associated with the joint distributions

$$F(X) = F(x_1, x_2, \ldots, x_n)$$

and

$$F(Y) = F(y_1, y_2, \ldots, y_n).$$

The uncertainties of these distributions are, respectively,

$$U(X) = -\int_{-\infty}^{+\infty} \cdots \int_{-\infty}^{+\infty} F(X) \log F(X)\, dX \tag{8}$$

and

$$U(Y) = -\int_{-\infty}^{+\infty} \cdots \int_{-\infty}^{+\infty} F(Y) \log F(Y)\, dY \tag{9}$$

where

$$dX = dx_1 dx_2 \cdots dx_n$$

and

$$dY = dy_1 dy_2 \cdots dy_n.$$

In order to transform from the X to the Y coordinate system, we require that a relationship exist between the two distributions $F(X)$ and $F(Y)$. This relationship is given by

$$F(Y) = F(X)|J(X/Y)| \tag{10}$$

where $J(X/Y)$ is the Jacobian, and

$$J(X/Y) = \begin{vmatrix} \dfrac{\partial x_1}{\partial y_1} & \dfrac{\partial x_1}{\partial y_2} & \cdots & \dfrac{\partial x_1}{\partial y_n} \\[2mm] \dfrac{\partial x_2}{\partial y_1} & \dfrac{\partial x_2}{\partial y_2} & \cdots & \dfrac{\partial x_2}{\partial y_n} \\[2mm] \vdots & \vdots & & \vdots \\[2mm] \dfrac{\partial x_n}{\partial y_1} & \dfrac{\partial x_n}{\partial y_2} & \cdots & \dfrac{\partial x_n}{\partial y_n} \end{vmatrix}.$$

The reader is referred to the cited references for derivations of equation (10). Now

$$U(Y) = -\int_{-\infty}^{+\infty} \cdots \int_{-\infty}^{+\infty} F(X)|J(X/Y)| \log [F(X)|J(X/Y)|]J(Y/X) dX \quad (12)$$

where the expression

$$dY = J(Y/X) dX \tag{13}$$

has been substituted for the differential dY.

Since

$$|J(X/Y)|J(Y/X)| = \pm 1 \tag{14}$$

and we can expand the logarithm, equation (12) can be written
$U(Y) =$

$$-\int_{-\infty}^{+\infty} \cdots \int_{-\infty}^{+\infty} F(X) \log F(X) dX - \int_{-\infty}^{+\infty} \cdots \int_{-\infty}^{+\infty} F(X) \log |J(X/Y)| dX. \quad (15)$$

It will be recognized that the first term in equation (15) is an uncertainty measure and the second is the expected value or average with regard to X of the logarithm of the magnitude of the Jacobian.
Thus

$$U(Y) = U(X) - E_x (\log |J(X/Y)|). \tag{16}$$

For a linear transformation from X to Y coordinates, we have

$$y_1 = a_{11}x_1 + a_{12}x_2 + \cdots + a_{1n}x_n$$
$$y_2 = a_{21}x_1 + a_{22}x_2 + \cdots + a_{2n}x_n$$
$$\vdots \qquad \vdots \qquad \vdots \qquad \qquad \vdots$$
$$y_n = a_{n1}x_1 + a_{n2}x_2 + \cdots + a_{nn}x_n$$

and the magnitude of the Jacobian is given by

$$|J(Y/X)| = \begin{Vmatrix} a_{11} & a_{12} & \cdots & a_{1n} \\ a_{21} & a_{22} & \cdots & a_{2n} \\ \vdots & \vdots & & \vdots \\ a_{n1} & a_{n2} & \cdots & a_{nn} \end{Vmatrix} = \|a_{ij}\| \tag{17}$$

and

$$U(Y) = U(X) + \log \|a_{ij}\|. \tag{18}$$

For the one-dimensional transformation where $y = ax$,

$$U(Y) = U(X) + \log |a| \tag{19}$$

or

$$U(Y) - U(X) = \log |a|. \tag{20}$$

It can be seen, then, that in the continuous case the uncertainty changes when the coordinate system is transformed. Whether the uncertainty increases or decreases upon such a transformation, however, depends on the value of $|a|$. For values of $|a|$ greater than unity, the logarithm of $|a|$ is positive, and the uncertainty increases when the coordinate frame is transformed from X to Y coordinates. By equation (20), the value of the increase in uncertainty is equal to $\log |a|$ or

$$\Delta U(X:Y) = \log |a|. \tag{21}$$

In this one-dimensional case, values of $|a|$ greater than unity can be understood as expansions of the continuous x axis. For example, transformations of $|a|$ equal to 2 or 3 would imply a doubling or trebling of the coordinate frame, in this case a single line. No point in this expansion space is more probable than any other, and a maximum uncertainty now exists to the extent of the transformation, $\log |a|$. If we set $|a|$ equal to M, a positive number, then we have a result equal to equation (7).

Maximum uncertainty, therefore, can be seen as a spatial uncertainty resulting from a transformation of coordinates in behavior space, with the value of the increase in uncertainty equal to the extent of the transformation. An equivalent argument holds for a decrease in uncertainty for values of $|a|$ lying between 0 and 1.

APPENDIX B The Historical Political Systems

Name (Time Period)[1]

Greece (fifth century B.C.—Periclean and post-Periclean Athens)
Mongols (beginning of thirteenth century—period of Genghis Khan)
Feudal Europe (tenth to thirteenth centuries, specifically with reference to France)
Ahmenids (sixth to fourth centuries B.C.)
Carolingian Empire (770–814—era of Charlemagne)
Inca Empire (1500–1525—eve of the Spanish conquest)
Ancient Egypt (2778–2065 B.C.—Ancient Empire until First Intermediary Period)
Ancient Egypt (2065–1785 B.C.—Middle Empire)
Ancient Egypt (1785–1580 B.C.—Second Intermediary Period)
Sassanid Persia (226–310)
Sassanid Persia (310–488—from Shapur II until reign of Kovadh; period of decline of centralized power)
Sassanid Persia (488–579—reign of Kovadh and Chosroes)
Sassanid Persia (579–650—period of decline)
Ptolemies (300–30 B.C.—approximately from the end of the Diadochian Wars to the Roman Conquest)
Seleucids (300–100 B.C.—approximately from the end of the Diadochian Wars to the Roman Conquest)
T'ang Dynasty (618–755—represents the peak of centralized power, the decline of which set in with the rebellion of An-Lu-shan in 755)
T'ang Dynasty (755–874—Huang Ch'ao's rebellion, which began in 874, marks the beginning of the disintegration of the T'ang regime)
T'ang Dynasty (875–907—this final phase saw the rise of more or less independent military satrapies)
Sung Dynasty (960–1127)
Sung Dynasty (1127–1250)

[1] The time periods and order of presentation are given as in the data source: S. N. Eisenstadt, *The Political Systems of Empires* (New York: The Free Press, 1963), pp. 442–447.

Sung Dynasty (1250–1279)

Yuan Dynasty (1279–1368)

Ming Dynasty (1368–1644)

Ch'ing Dynasty (1644–1912)

Maurya (327–274 B.C.—Chandra-Gupta to ascendancy of Asoka; period of organization of bureaucracy)

Maurya (273–236 B.C.—Asoka's reign; high point of bureaucratic development)

Gupta (320–495—from ascendancy of Chandra-Gupta to the death of Budha-Gupta; principal reference: period between Samudra-Gupta and Chandra-Gupta, which is the period of highest development)

Mogul Empire (1526–1554—Baber and Humayun; founding of empire; beginning of bureaucratic organization)

Mogul Empire (1556–1657—Akbar, Jahangia, and Shah Jehan; highest development of empire)

Mogul Empire (1657–1705—Aurangib; decline of empire)

Byzantine Empire (330–610—from founding of Constantinople to Heraclius I)

Byzantine Empire (610–1025—period of maximum development)

Byzantine Empire (1025–1453—period of increasing aristocratization until decline and fall)

Abbassids (750–847—from rise of dynasty until after al-Wathik; height of centralized bureaucracy)

Abbassids (847–940—from al-Mutawakkil until the rise of the Buyuwids and disintegration of the empire)

Saffawids (1502–1587—from Ismail until the rise of Abbas I; rule based on allegiance of tribal elements)

Saffawids (1587–1736—from Abbas I to the Afghan occupation; height of centralized bureaucracy)

Ottomans (1451–1520—Mehmed II to Selim I; pre-bureaucratic regime; period of military expansion)

Ottomans (1520–1566—Suleiman I; period of maximal centralization of bureaucracy)

Ottomans (1566–1789—Selim II to Selim III)

Moslem Spain (750–912—from the rise of the Marwanid Ummayads until Abd-ar-Rahman III; the polity based mainly on aristocratic–tribal elements)

Moslem Spain (912–1000—from Abd-ar-Rahman III, when Caliphate of Cordoba was at its height, to period of progressive disintegration)

*Rome (27 B.C.–A.D. 96—Julio Claudius and Flavius)[2]

*Rome (96–193—enlightened emperors)

*Rome (193–350—from the military autocracy until the approximate end of the importance of the Western Empire)

*Spanish-American Empire (1520–1580—from the conquests to the middle of Philip II's reign)

Spanish-American Empire (1580–1759—Philip II to Ferdinand VI)

[2] Societies identified by asterisks are discussed in Chapter VIII.

Spanish-American Empire (1759–1820—Charles III to independence)
*Austria (1740–1790—Maria Theresa to Joseph II)
*Spain (1520–1621—height of absolutism)
*Spain (1621–1701—decline of absolutism until the War of the Succession)
Sweden (1523–1720—height of absolutism)
Sweden (1720–1770—"Age of Freedom")
Sweden (1770–1809—enlightened absolutism)
*Russia (1682–1725—Peter the Great)
*Russia (1725–1761—decline of absolutism and instability)
*Russia (1761–1796—Catherine the Great; enlighted absolutism)
*Prussia (1640–1740)—from Great Elector to Frederick Wilhelm I)
*Prussia (1740–1792)—Frederick II; enlightened absolutism)
*France (1589–1660—Henry IV to the personal rule of Louis XIV)
*France (1660–1715—Louis XIV)
*France (1715–1789—Louis XV to the Revolution)
*England (1509–1640—absolutist rule of Tudors and early Stuarts)
*England (1660–1688—Restoration of the Stuarts)
*England (1689–1783—the "Glorious Revolution"; the Hanoverians, to the reforms resulting from the loss of the American colonies)

Index

Name Index

Aehrenthal, Austrian Foreign Minister, 189
Albertini, Luigi, 189n
Albrecht-Carrié, René, 90n
Alger, Chadwick F., 7n, 117n, 161, 161n, 195n
Alker, Hayward R., Jr., 144n
Almond, Gabriel A., 179n
Andrews, Neil R., 80n
Apter, David E., 98n
Ardrey, Robert, 43, 43n
Arendt, Hannah, 10, 10n, 16, 17n, 40n
Aron, Raymond, 92n
Artz, Frederick B., 90n
Ash, Ronald, 55n

Bailey, Daniel E., 138n, 167n
Bandura, Albert, 32, 32n, 44, 44n, 156n
Banks, Arthur S., 181n
Barnes, Harry E., 190n
Bartlett, John, 1n
Bendix, Reinhard, 113n
Benjamin, Roger W., 180n
Berkowitz, Leonard, 29, 30n, 31n
Bismarck, Otto von, 91, 106
Blackstock, Paul, 107n
Bladen, Christopher, 49n
Blainey, Geoffrey, 190n
Blake, Robert R., 157n
Blalock, Hubert M., Jr., 67n, 99n, 128n, 134n
Blue, Richard N., 180n
Boulding, Kenneth E., 9n

Bowen, Don R., 30n
Bowlby, J., 78n
Box, Steven, 142n
Brams, Steven J., 15n, 19, 19n, 117n, 161, 161n
Brewer, Marilynn B., 136n
Brillouin, Leon, 55n
Brinton, Crane, 146n
Brody, Richard A., 7n
Broom, Leonard, 100, 100n, 133, 133n, 137, 137n
Burke, Peter J., 98, 98n, 134n, 137, 137n
Burnstein, Eugene, 157n
Bwy, Douglas P., 29, 30n, 35n

Campbell, Donald T., 136n
Cartwright, Dorwin, 15n, 17, 17n, 20, 20n, 21
Chambliss, William J., 99n
Choucri, Nazli, 101, 101n, 166n
Chouproff, Al. A., 155n
Christina of Denmark, 105
Churchill, Winston, 105
Claude, Inis L., 196n
Clausewitz, Karl von, 1, 1n, 15
Coleman, James S., Political Scientist, 179n
Coleman, James S., Sociologist, 149n, 150n
Coleman, Stephen, 180n
Coplin, William D., 7n
Corning, Peter A., 43, 43n
Coser, Lewis, 113, 113n

Subject Index

Absolute uncertainty: decrease in period 1845–1864, 88–92; defined, 81; in historical systems, 82–88; increase in period 1815–1844, 88; increase in period 1865–1914, 84–93; increase in period 1915–1939, 84–93; tabs., 82, 83; figs., 84, 86. *See also* Uncertainty

Achieved status, 93, 179, 187; as centralization and capability, 113–118; common variance in, 138–139; and communication, 113–116; and economic development, 113–115; and education, 124, 137; in experimentation, 142, 142n; and income, 124, 137; measures of, 115–127; and occupation, 124, 137; and population, 113–115; prediction to war, 131–132; relationship with ascribed, 131; and transportation, 113–115; and urbanization, 115–116; and war, 113–118; tabs., 115, 131, 132, 140; fig., 108. *See also* Status inconsistency

Achievement. *See* Achieved status

Additional explanations, 188–193

Afghanistan, tabs., 53, 63

Africa, instability in, 147–164

Aggression: evolutionary adaptive, 43; and frustration, 28–43; instinctual, 43; and social learning, 43–44; and uncertainty reduction, 28–43; figs., 41, 44. *See also* Political violence

Aggressive attitudes: and helping behavior, 142, 142n; and status inconsistency, 142

Albania, 52; tabs., 53, 63

Alliances, 48–68; defensive, 49n, 62; as enmeshing process, 87–88; entente, 49n; equiprobability of, 187, 191; as interlocking set, 187; neutrality pact, 49n; number, 63–64, tabs., 65, 82, fig., 66; number defensive, 63–64, tab., 65; as power loss, 5–6, 48–51, 58–68; saturation, 87, 87n; and social disorganization, 187, 192; and uncertainty in, 48–51, 58–68, 164; years, 63–64; tabs., 63, 64, 65, 67; figs., 8, 44

Allies, and Versailles, 192

Alsace-Lorraine, and Franco-Prussian War, 13

American Telephone and Telegraph Company, 115n

Andorra, 51

Animal societies, social disorganization in, 78n

Arab Caliphate, empire of, 168

Argentina, 150n; and severity of war, 112; tabs., 46, 53, 63, 111, 125, 159, 160

Aristocracy, 172

Armies. *See* Military

Ascribed status, 93, 113–115, 179, 187; and diplomats received, 116–118; ethnicity, 124, 137; in experimentation, 142, 142n; measures of, 116–127; race, 137; relationship with achieved, 131; and religion, 137; and war, 97–109; tab., 140; fig., 108. *See also* Status inconsistency